T0290537

Money in the Metaverse

Series editor: Professor Diane Coyle

Why You Dread Work: What's Going Wrong in Your Workplace and How to Fix It — Helen Holmes

Digital Transformation at Scale: Why the Strategy Is Delivery (Second Edition) — Andrew Greenway, Ben Terrett, Mike Bracken and Tom Loosemore

The Service Organization: How to Deliver and Lead Successful Services, Sustainably — Kate Tarling

Money in the Metaverse: Digital Assets, Online Identities, Spatial Computing and Why Virtual Worlds Mean Real Business — David Birch and Victoria Richardson

Money in the Metaverse

Digital Assets, Online Identities,
Spatial Computing and Why
Virtual Worlds Mean Real Business

David Birch
Victoria Richardson

With illustrations by Helen Holmes

LONDON PUBLISHING PARTNERSHIP

Published by London Publishing Partnership
www.londonpublishingpartnership.co.uk

Published in association with
Enlightenment Economics
www.enlightenmenteconomics.com

ISBN: 978-1-916749-05-4 (hbk)
ISBN: 978-1-916749-06-1 (iPDF)
ISBN: 978-1-916749-07-8 (epub)

A catalogue record for this book is
available from the British Library

This book has been composed in Candara

Copy-edited and typeset by
T&T Productions Ltd, London
www.tandtproductions.com

Cover eye image: Adobe Stock

Contents

Foreword by Eva Pascoe

'Imagination is the air of mind.' — Philip James Bailey

If you, like me, are a frustrated Metaverse explorer, then you will find it hard to put this book down. I read it on a flight from London to San Francisco and I was so engrossed in it that on touchdown I thought that the flight had been unusually short!

David and Victoria deliver a dazzling glimpse of what could be possible in the Metaverse. They paint an image of secure digital identities that can not only be attached to individuals like you and me, but also to companies or groups. They explore the feasibility of person-to-person transactions and the swapping of tokens, as well as looking at the role that banks and financial institutions might play in providing customer-centric guardrails for security and trust.

Virtual worlds conjured in electronic space have always been something of a secret passion for me. Hidden in the matrix, filling the cracks between escapism and play – those mystical worlds opened-up via online games, concert watch parties and virtual gallery shows. Back in the mid 1990s, when I co-founded the Cyberia Internet Café in London, we often organized virtual parties using CuSeeMe (early videoconferencing software), connecting clubs in London, New York and San Francisco. We co-created environments that were low on bandwidth but high on imagination, enabling us to mingle in electronic space with David Bowie, to beam up Gary Barlow or to organize a fan meet-up with Kylie Minogue – all early pioneers of music in virtual worlds.

The spirit of those early, pioneering virtual reality efforts was captured beautifully by a project called Virtual Nightclub (VNC), developed by Phillips in 1994. The glamorous digital music world created by Team Phillips mirrored those emerging spaces, conjured out of existing clubs, but creating something virtual and entirely new. But what it did not do was commerce. There was no possibility of buying a signed digital poster or e-swag from the music events that we were hosting. Imagine if we had had a digital t-shirt with David Bowie's signature on it from the online Bowie. net and Cyberia event, or an electronic poster with Kylie's digital dedication. The current value of those items would be enormous!

Online commerce became my life. A few years later I co-founded Topshop Online, the first online fashion store, where young fashionistas could buy physical fashion designed by Kate Moss and Maharishi. Most of our investors were dubious about whether people would change their behaviour and buy fashion online, but we proved them wrong: our Topshop e-store was a huge success, and in time it overtook Topshop's biggest physical store in Oxford Street, London, in terms of sales. Last year I put some ideas about the future of online commerce to the test in a virtual Cyberia cybercafe, built in 3D and available via a headset or an app from a mobile phone. Along with colleagues I also organized a live virtual reality (VR) event: a launch for a sci-fi book anthology. As many of the stories in the book explored metaverses, it made sense to launch it in one: not in an off-the-shelf commercial space but in our own, gritty-but-vibrant, London-by-night kind of place.

I invited 3D artists to recreate the actual Cyberia cybercafe from mid-1990s London (see figure 4 in chapter 2), right down to the computers running Windows 3.2 that were used for internet surfing, the wobbly bar stools and our famous clocks showing all of the times zones in which we had our cybercafes: from the Philippines to Tokyo and Bangkok, from Paris to London. Kylie Minogue digital posters were added to the wall because she was our most revered guest and fan.

To allow people to buy the book, we built a huge 3D version of it in the courtyard, to take advantage of the fact that the Metaverse has no ceiling, and we showed a large QR code on it. Once out of the VR space, people could grab the QR code using their mobile phones and then follow the link to Amazon to buy the book. This all worked, but as David and Victoria write here, it was cumbersome. We need better ways to transact in an era of spatial computing.

The Metaverse is essentially a secure internet: a connected network of e-worlds that provide secure trading environments. Big Tech is racing to provide secure payments guardrails, but at the cost of locking visitors into their proprietary identity walled gardens. Our Cyberia VR visitors are not going to be happy with a repeat of locked-down app stores extrapolated into the Metaverse, so imagine my delight when I first read David and Victoria's new ideas about bringing web3 and digital identity together in a framework for safe and open ways of trading in the Metaverse (i.e. not within a walled garden).

The book tackles the challenges and limitations of current shopping and trading in the Metaverse head-on, and it does so with imagination, innovation and a pragmatic mindset. David and Victoria discuss the reasons why virtual objects, weapons, prizes and so on can only be bought and sold within the constraints of a single VR world. They explain why these limitations hold back economic growth. You cannot take your earned digital sword or a skin from Fortnite to Call of Duty – just as you cannot take a digitally signed book from the Cyberia cybercafe VR book launch to your home library in Roblox. They take us through a spectrum of options that are available to world-builders, with financial organizations doing their bit.

Rarely does a business-oriented book bring as much imagination to underpin its arguments as this one does. It gives us a peek into a future where the Metaverse will not be a place, but a process: a structure with building blocks but also a chance to join others, to share music, stories and art experiences with friends and family, and – in fact – with anyone anywhere. It will be a place to trade ideas and concepts as well as goods and services, such as learning courses and skills training.

It will be a world in which the only limit will be our imagination. My favourite poet, Philip James Bailey, would be pleased.

Preface

Financial innovation has, historically, had a geographic focus centred on markets. Look at how the great mediaeval Champagne fairs – which were instigated to exchange the resources of the Baltic and the North Sea with the luxuries of the Mediterranean – were gradually replaced by financial fairs in which no actual trade took place except in money: the first stage in a process of dematerialization that runs from the Medicis to the metaverse.

In his wonderful book *Money Tales*, Alessandro Giraudo explains that even after the main continental trade routes had shifted away from the north–south axis that had depended on those fairs to a more decentralized set of trading routes between growing cities, the fairs themselves continued to function as an international clearing house for paper debts and

credits (Giraudo 2007). This was down to the fact that they had built up a system of commercial law, regulated by private judges and quite separate from the feudal social order.*

Our good friend Daniel Gusev, a thorough scholar of the times, notes the period of Renaissance fintech innovations in Florence (Gusev 2022). In essence, there was a major expansion of cashless transactions at that time that was enabled by replacing specie or bullion transfers with credit transactions verified by audit, backed by sound accounting methods across numerous industries – and secured by personal trust and reputation. Gusev goes on to say that the social changes underpinned by the propagation of these tools supported Florence's premier position on the European trade market: the first 'embedded fintechs' can be seen in the activities of the trade houses of Italian merchants.

The volume of trade was so big that even a theoretical fallback settlement in coin was not possible: there simply wasn't enough coin to cover the volumes. From that came another benefit to international trade: bills of exchange. These further lowered both the costs and the risks associated with cross-border payments (and therefore reduced the interest rates charged). In this new world of paper money and ledgers, order was maintained without a police force because of the absolute necessity to maintain a good name, prior to the later third-party enforcement of legal codes by the nation-state.†

Despite such innovation in the world of finance, it must still have been quite a shock when Marco Polo arrived home after his travels in the East with wild tales of a place where there was no gold and silver in circulation, and where paper money

---

* If a decentralized privately regulated system with its own payment instruments rings any bells... Well, we'll come back to that later.

† New instruments but no new institutions; new technology beyond traditional law enforcement and a private reputation-based scheme that grew up to facilitate commerce where previously gold and silver had been the oil that greased the wagon wheels. It's almost as if identity had become the new ... No, let's not get distracted.

was used by the people and not only by the bankers. That new financial system and the idea of money made out of paper astonished the traditional Italian bankers, much as non-fungible tokens astonish the bankers of today, but they all had to adapt to the new reality in order to avoid being swept aside by this technological revolution.

Giraudo tells us how, over time, the power of the Genoese bankers rose, and he recounts how they shifted the fairs from France down to Piacenza, near Milan. The Genoese had established the function of the banker as a money merchant, and they had separated this function from that of the 'merchant banker' with holdings. Now there were trusted intermediaries that dealt only in paper money. Imagine how the idea of paper replacing gold and jewels and spices must have seemed to the institutions of the time. Fairs in which no goods were exchanged but money was!

In time, all business came to be done this way. Those Piacenza money market fairs became the largest in Europe from the end of the sixteenth century and into the seventeenth, with bankers from Flanders, Germany, England, France and the Iberian peninsula converging four times a year to meet with the Genoese, Milanese and Florentine clearing houses. The latter put down a significant deposit in order to participate in the fairs and in return they fixed the exchange and interest rates on the third day of the fair.* As well as the bankers, there were money changers, who also had to put down a (smaller) deposit to present letters of exchange, and representatives of firms and brokers who participated in the trading were floating around as well.

During such fairs, the participants tried to clear all of the transactions in such a way as to limit the exchange of specie: that is, it was a net settlement system. Any outstanding amounts were either settled in gold at the end of the fair or carried forward to the next one with interest. This was the first structured clearing

---

* This was when interest rate fixing wasn't the thing it is today.

system in international finance and it lasted until 1627, when the Spanish Empire went bankrupt (again), causing serious losses to the Genoese bankers who were its principal financiers (and who, sadly for them, had no access to a taxpayer-funded bailout).

As a result of that Spanish default, the financial centre of Europe shifted to Amsterdam, where the Bank of Amsterdam had been set up in 1609. It was owned by the city and fully backed by gold and silver. It was a highly trusted institution. Indeed, as Adam Smith himself wrote of it: 'No point of faith is better established than that for every guilder, circulated as bank money, there is a correspondent guilder in gold or silver to be found in the treasure of the bank.' The Bank of Amsterdam's paper stablecoin was a great success, contributing significantly to the Dutch Golden Age, because it meant that Amsterdam had a very efficient system for inter-merchant transfers (i.e. account-to-account transfers with gross settlement). New and innovative financial instruments, including futures and options, were soon under development by the Bank of Amsterdam.

Later still, Europe's money markets moved on first to London (but that's another story) and then, after further technological developments in communications, to New York, which became the centre of world finance, with the dollar as the reserve currency. But the point is made: Giraudo observed that while geography and politics had a strong influence on the location of financial centres, the deciding element has always been the capacity to invent and use new financial techniques, and above all to create a dynamic sense of innovation.

The locus will in time shift again. But what if that capacity to invent new financial techniques is in the future better exploited in Kenya, say, or in the Far East – or, perhaps, in the online world? What if financial innovation slips its mundane anchors and begins to float free on the tides of cyberspace? As the examples of Genoa and Amsterdam teach us, we need a digital money infrastructure that is quite separate from the infrastructure for digital assets that might be used for speculation, we need a digital identity infrastructure that is capable of managing the reputations needed to support the ownership and trading of assets, and we need a place where these trades can take place in an efficient (i.e. safe, trusted and cost-effective) manner.

Where is this place? If it's not New York or London or Amsterdam (or Hong Kong or Sao Paolo or ...), where will trading go and financial innovation follow?

Louis Rosenberg is the CEO of Unanimous AI. His doctoral work at Stanford University resulted in an immersive augmented-reality system being built for the US Air Force in 1992. Rosenberg recently predicted that by 2035 people will laugh at images from today that show people walking down the street staring down at a phone. He thinks that we will see metaverses (built on virtual worlds) and augmented metaverses (with layers of rich virtual content overlaid on the real world), and he goes on to predict that they will replace mobile phones as the primary gateway to digital worlds, with the transition from mobile phones beginning in the middle of the 2020s and being complete by 2035, or 'possibly sooner'.

If that sounds hyperbolic, in the light of current technology, bear in mind that 'Gen Z' already spends far more time in the proto-metaverses than they do in the web world that is familiar to you (see figure 1).

To put it simply: the metaverses are coming. A new place for international commerce – and therefore a new place for innovation in financial services – is on the way.

This book explores the future of those financial services in the emerging metaverses and the always-on immersive future Internet. It came about because of the response to a paper that we wrote about payments in the metaverse. The paper set out a simple but useful model of what metaverses are and how transactions might work (Birch & Richardson 2023), and this book explores that model to look at the business strategies that financial services players might adopt to exploit the new possibilities.

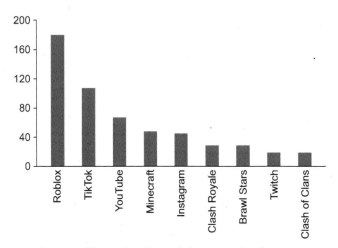

Figure 1. Where Gen Z spend their attention (average minutes per day). (*Source*: GEEIQ, September 2023.)

We both spend a lot of time in rooms (both virtual ones and real ones) with people from banks, payment schemes, retailers, telcos, governments and identity network operators. We participate in many discussions regarding the inherent challenges of bringing the separate but complementary networks of payment and identity together. We are also actively engaged in conversations regarding the tokenization of real-world assets, and we support the view that tokenization will fundamentally change existing commercial models for financial services. And, like many people who are active in this area, we have a very positive view about the ideal end state being more efficient and safer, and delivering a better customer experience.

Our hope in writing this book is that it sets out a pathway to achieving that positive end state and that it will provide useful input to a range of organizations building strategies for the Metaverse.

This is not a manual for programmers writing smart contracts or for service providers who want to use the European Digital Identity wallet. Rather, this book aims to bridge the gap between the creators of metaverses and financial services strategists looking to create value from virtual worlds, digital assets and digital identity. Our goal is to facilitate more efficient interactions between the stakeholders and more effective development of new products and services.

We think that a clear view of virtual worlds, a practical taxonomy for digital assets, and a tried-and-tested model of digital identity will lead to a better understanding of the available opportunities in the many metaverses in which we will work, rest and play in the near future. Developing a strategy to support real business in virtual worlds is imperative, and we hope that you will agree that we have delivered a practical and accessible handbook to achieve this.

CHAPTER 1

Introduction

In Neal Stephenson's seminal 1992 novel *Snow Crash*, the concept of the metaverse – a virtual reality-based successor to the internet – is a central theme. Early in the novel, Stephenson uses the seemingly mundane task of pizza delivery as a way to introduce readers to this new world in which his story is set.

The book's central character, one Hiro Protagonist, starts as a delivery driver for a Mafia-owned pizza franchise. In Stephenson's view of the future, timely delivery is taken extremely seriously, to the point where failing to deliver within thirty minutes of an order being placed can have dire consequences for the

driver. These high stakes set the tone for the novel, conveying that technology and commerce have evolved in unexpected ways in this world, and that the implications of the digital realm can have very real, physical consequences. By juxtaposing the high-tech, virtual world of the metaverse with the physical task of pizza delivery, Stephenson cleverly intertwines the digital and physical worlds in a plausible future. Interestingly, in terms of financial services innovation, reading about payments in *Snow Crash* today seems oddly anachronistic. The payment experience served up by Apple, Square and Stripe has already far outstripped the magnetic stripe card reader on the back of the pizza delivery motorbike that Stephenson describes.

Three decades on from the publication of Stephenson's landmark work, the management consultants McKinsey produced a report in 2022 that said that 'the metaverse' has the potential to generate up to $5 trillion in value by 2030 and that it is simply too big for companies to ignore (Elmasry *et al.* 2022). In a similar vein, Bloomberg Intelligence has said that the metaverse is the next big technology platform, attracting online game makers, social networks and other technology leaders to capture a slice of what they claim is already an $800 billion market opportunity (Kanterman & Naidu 2021). They call the metaverse the next evolution of the internet and social networks.

Deloitte has said that, 'in the simplest terms, the metaverse is the internet, but in 3D', but we do not think this explains why the metaverse is so important or why it will change the world of financial services (Deloitte 2022). If the metaverse is just going to be something like Fortnite but with people selling each other insurance instead of shooting each other, it doesn't sound like a lot of fun. There has to be something more going on.[*]

---

[*] By new convention we will henceforth capitalize the Metaverse to mean the superset of metaverses that will serve many different global communities.

Making metaverses

Metaverses are founded in spatial computing (Hackl 2023): 'An evolving form of computing that blends our physical world and virtual experiences using a wide range of technologies, thus enabling humans to interact and communicate in new ways with each other and with machines.' The term is not new. It dates back to 2003, when researcher Simon Greenwold, then at the MIT Media Lab, defined it as 'human interaction with a machine in which the machine retains and manipulates referents to real objects and spaces'.

As Cathy Hackl notes in the *Harvard Business Review* article cited above, one could argue that mobile phones are already primitive spatial devices. The example that most of us are likely familiar with is Google Maps on our phones; geolocation is the referent data that powers our search for 'good coffee near me' or 'closest fuel station now'. The emerging generation of spatial computing is far more sophisticated, enabled by a much richer set of referents. And it is the manipulation of this richer data set – generated by cameras, scanners, microphones and other sensors – that people working in augmented reality (AR), virtual reality (VR), extended reality (XR), mixed reality (MR) and artificial intelligence (AI) have been exploring for years.

Spatial computing means that people can interact and communicate in new ways with other people, content and machines. It also means that people can create new content, products and experiences, vastly expanding the boundaries of everything you can see, touch and know.*

Back in 2022 the Pew Research Center published a report looking at where the Metaverse might be by 2040 (Anderson & Raine 2022). The report was based on a survey of hundreds of

---

* It also means interacting with AIs, which means, as we will see, that the idea of non-human economic agents interacting in metaverses is central to the future of transactions.

experts in a variety of fields, and it identified two main themes, as follows.

- AR, XR and MR will dominate VR applications (and they will all be enabled by AI) and people will find those applications particularly appealing when they expand on real-world experiences and improve users' daily lives by making reality more 'understandable and interesting'. VR will have enthusiastic but smaller user bases, especially in 'select business, medical, education and training settings'.

- Advances in Metaverse technologies will magnify the problems now associated with the current web2 environment, and the immersive properties of the Metaverse could raise significant threats to human agency and human rights as 'surveillance capitalism' expands and authoritarian governments take advantage of these new technologies.

We take both of these starting points very seriously, and in this book we will explore both how AR, XR, MR and VR will be used for business and, just as importantly, how the new infrastructure can deliver both security and privacy, which are lacking in our current online interactions. While current, more detailed definitions of a Metaverse may vary – and vary pretty wildly: from the most nebulous notions of online interaction to some more specific, functional uses of spatial computing – we feel that what is lacking is an overarching shared narrative that can help inform strategies (and some short-term tactics) for new products and services that will be the basis of new business in this new environment.

Trust

So how should we go about formulating that narrative? Central to any useful narrative about the new virtual space for business to move into is the issue of trust. As has often been said about the internet, the lack of a security and privacy infrastructure, and the consequent lack of what we might think of as the identity and value layers, has led to no end of imperfect (and, in many ways, dangerous) patches being applied without fixing the underlying problem: the internet is not safe.[*]

Where there is sufficient trust to enable transactions to take place, by and large it is provided by platforms and not by the infrastructure itself. What is more, trust in the platforms themselves is eroding. Defining digital trust as 'the confidence people have that a platform will protect their information and provide a safe environment for them to create and engage with content', a recent annual benchmarking report found that trust had 'declined substantially in key areas including privacy [and] safety' (Williamson 2022). With metaverses of various kinds on the horizon, encompassing higher-risk interactions such as medical consultations, it is time to develop a narrative to explain why everyone should be developing a Metaverse strategy that focuses more on secure and resilient infrastructure and less on the interface. As Ram Rao Balla, the chief architect at Tata Consultancy Services, neatly summarizes the imperative (Balla 2023): 'An application going down in a bank or an office may lead to financial loss, but in healthcare, it can mean life and death.' This means that 'requirements such as security, privacy, performance, usability, scalability, and so on are vital'.

A simple place to begin is to reflect on that earlier comment by focusing less on the three-dimensional aspect of it and more on the trusted infrastructure, stating that: 'In the simplest terms, the Metaverse is the internet, but with trust.'

---

[*] And we don't just mean it's untrustworthy in that you get emails about penis extension and links to ransomware masquerading as information from the 'Microsoft Support Department'. We mean untrusted as in no one knows what is real any more, with AI-fuelled coordinated inauthentic behaviour about to overrun our sensors while the internet has toasters, automobiles and remote oil pipeline monitoring applications on it and they are all getting hacked.

It's more than that, of course. In his book *Virtual Society*, Herman Narula talks about how, in practical terms, a Metaverse is going to be a set of complex real-time simulations mediated by what he refers to as 'an economic and social layer'. This layer must incorporate mechanisms for the storage and transfer of value: the basis of a functioning market. The building blocks of a Metaverse are the core of the narrative in this book.

The burning platforms

The Metaverse is not a greenfield site. As a simple framing exercise to identify opportunities for improving trust, we want to start by unpacking some of the successes and failures of early proto-metaverses. Roblox provides a helpful example here, not only because it has already been around for eighteen years, but also because during this time it has experienced significant highs and lows. In terms of daily active users it is a standout success, but in terms of making a positive contribution to society, or delivering sustainable profits, the picture is less clear. It is not hard to argue that claims of child abuse (Court Record 2022) and gambling by minors (Weitz & Luxenberg Attorneys 2023), or concerns raised about children engaging in an unprotected gig economy (Parkin 2022), do not align well with the safer internet we are looking for.

Many of the serious claims being made against Roblox could have been avoided if the type of building blocks that we will go on to describe had been in place when the game became massively popular during Covid. At the heart of Roblox's challenges there are some common themes of digital identity, the ownership of digital assets, and a reliance on 'web2' payments infrastructure and monetization models. Commentary about the game often focuses on its poor community moderation. Criticism includes claims that the operating company was aware of the harms to minors, perpetrated by known paedophiles, but chose to prioritize profit and engagement over safety. While we have no intention of defending any apparent lack of action by Roblox, it is fair to say that in order to have had accurate information about users, the platform would have needed to have some sort of identity verification, and it didn't have any. And while the game now has mandatory age verification for its 17+ content, it is still possible to create an account with a freshly minted email address and start talking to minors in one of the free-to-access games in a matter of minutes. Like many discussions focused on age verification, the onus has been placed on keeping minors out of adult spaces, whereas keeping adults out of children's games seems equally important. It's unsurprising that this is still the case because, as yet, there is no easy-to-implement, widely adopted solution.

Meta has also faced claims of prioritizing engagement over safety. In a bid to grow platform stickiness, Meta introduced the 'People You May Know' feature, which suggests people to 'friend'. A case has been made that based on their own internal research, Meta employees were aware that this feature 'contributed up to 75% of adult/minor grooming that occurs on Meta's social media products' (IATA 2022). When people on these platforms have a range of easy-to-verify attributes, linking them with other people, or even with other AI avatars, it will be simpler and significantly harder to abuse.

Not knowing who is on the platform has probably also contributed to charges of money laundering – charges that Roblox disputes. Nonetheless, a recent court filing describes the behaviour of around 300 Roblox players who 'appear to be using the Roblox platform to send money to one another by purchasing fake items, a highly inefficient and costly means of transferring money which suggests they may be engaged in money laundering or other "improper behaviour"' (Farivar 2023). Interestingly, this case surfaced because of a separate case brought against Roblox that was all about ownership. The case alleges that: 'Roblox acts irresponsibly when the corporation arbitrarily deletes such items – various accessories, hats, or other items of virtual clothing – after they have been sold from one player to another because the company suddenly decides the item violates the company's own policies.' It seems reasonable for Roblox to remove fake items; it is undoubtedly next to impossible to get this right when the concept of ownership of these items is in its current early stages.

The moderation of assets is a lively topic on the Roblox developer forums, and as brands become more involved in these virtual spaces there is the potential for more unpopular moderation. A quick search on YouTube delivers very clear tutorials on how to create a pair of Converse Classics for your avatar's feet, using standardized creator templates. It is not clear why anyone would purchase a branded pair of shoes if you can take the design from a regular e-commerce site and build your own.

One of the most interesting takeaways from the history of Roblox is the challenge of delivering sustained revenue alongside user growth – and you can see why when you consider that growth in certain jurisdictions does not equal increased revenue. A model based on 'free-to-play' with paid artefacts does not deliver revenue in countries where there is limited disposable income. Roblox operates its own cloud infrastructure and servers, which means relatively high fixed operating costs. This presents a balance sheet challenge when there is insufficient revenue from goods sold. Where Roblox has successfully monetized content – with the sale of accessories and pay-to-play games – the major challenge is the commission fees charged by the app stores. Roblox's primary variable cost is third-party payment processing, with up to 30% of the transaction value passing to the app stores. This is not a sustainable model.

The app store challenge is not something that Roblox faces alone. Epic Games (the producers of Fortnite) decided to use the power of their user base (more than 400 million registered players) to take on the app stores, offering players discounts if they used Epic's payment system instead of using Apple or Google. In response, Apple and Google removed Fortnite from their app stores, which led to a rather unsatisfying recognition of the power of these platforms in court. The judges acknowledged that 'there is a lively and important debate about the role played in our economy and democracy by online transaction platforms with market power', but they stopped short of taking action and gave a somewhat fatalistic sign off (Browning 2023): 'Our job as a federal Court of Appeals, however, is not to resolve that debate – nor could we even attempt to do so.'

The promise of the Metaverse is that these platforms will be effectively challenged, with market forces – rather than regulation – paving the way for a more equitable share. This is because the platforms currently provide two invaluable features: interoperability and reach. They connect the buyers and the sellers, the creators and the gamers. With more mature, decentralized protocols and more convenient ways for people to manage their money and identity (i.e. their keys), it seems likely that the balance of power will shift.

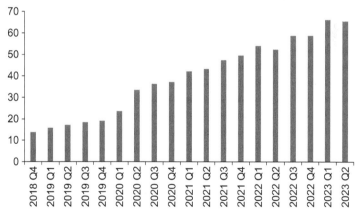

Figure 2. Roblox daily active users (millions). (*Source*: Statista, 10/23.)

Level the playing field
How, then, should we think about platforms and data in the Metaverse? In a fascinating paper on the data economy for the UK's National Institute of Economic and Social Research,

Diane Coyle and Wendy Li talk about the growing data gap between global big tech and potential competitors, disruptors and innovators (Coyle & Li 2021).

Coyle and Li argue, convincingly, that this data gap is a barrier to entry that affects not only businesses but also aggregate innovation, investment and trade. As they point out, as data-intensive companies, online platforms can scale up their business operations quickly, not only domestically but also internationally, without facing traditional physical operational constraints: they are subject only to cross-border legal constraints on data transfer. In a safe and secure Metaverse, we would expect to see the drivers amplified.

Large data holdings, rich in volume and variety, thus give large online platforms a significant competitive advantage, powered by network effects and the virtuous cycle between data and the AI algorithms improving the services and increasing revenues.

How big is the problem? While the data economy is clearly large, a robust measurement has yet to be developed (Siegle 2020). Coyle and Li propose a new and consistent impact-based approach to estimate the size of the overall data market in a sector by comparing the values of data with and without the entry of an online platform. They use the impact of AirBnB on the hospitality sector as an example, and they calculate that the market size for data in the global hospitality sector was US$43 billion in 2018, and that it grows by around a third each year on average. But as their calculations show, the benefits of this growing market are not distributed evenly.*

Many countries are revising their data policies and localization rules in a thrust for 'digital sovereignty'. This is a useful

---

* This methodological analysis gets even more interesting when applied at the aggregate level as it shows that there is a developed country that is a net importer of data and a net exporter of digital goods: yes, as you would guess, it is the United States. America's online platforms collect data from around the world to feed centralized digital production in the US. China is also a net data importer and digital goods exporter, but more of its digital consumers are domestic.

catch-all description of the many ways in which governments are trying to assert more control over their digital infrastructure. It has long been a concern in supply chains, affecting the kinds of hardware and software available in a given market. Now, of course, this form of resurgent nationalism is fragmenting the cloud and damaging data trade (Rawding *et al.* 2020). Governments around the world are passing measures that require companies to host infrastructure and store certain kinds of data in local servers.*

These policies are not currently based on economic calculation, which is why the measurement of data markets should help policymakers understand the dynamics and should contribute to sane policies for at least some metaverses, if not all of them!

One final point on this: as Coyle and Li note in their paper, the General Data Protection Regulation, or GDPR, restricts firms from repurposing data beyond its original intended use without reobtaining consent from individuals (to safeguard privacy), and this limits data sharing among firms. Yet blocking data flows benefits no one.

Fortunately, as we explore in this book, digital identity technologies provide a new approach that the Metaverse can build on. We (society) do not want data to be locked away, but nor do we want personal data flowing through every nook and cranny of the internet. What we need is to develop new data holding and sharing structures that can provide the facts about data that are needed to make decisions without disclosing the data itself. How can we do this while protecting privacy? This is the difference between providing a date of birth and providing proof that you are over 18 or 21 to get into a bar, or the difference between providing proof that a company's assets exceed its liabilities and having to actually disclose what any of those assets or liabilities actually are. It is also the

---

* China, for example, has long required that cloud infrastructure be hosted in China by local companies. In fact, China's Cybersecurity Law mandates that certain data be stored on local servers or undergo a security assessment before being exported.

difference between a single enterprise building up terabytes of data to work out which product to promote to a customer segment and an individual customer giving time-bound and purpose-specific access to all their data to a single entity to get the most relevant recommendation.

We therefore think that it is not only banks that should provide open application programming interfaces (APIs) for access to customer data with the customer's permission: it is everyone. This is along the lines of what is being implemented in Australia, where open banking is part of a wider approach to consumer data rights and there will indeed be a form of symmetry imposed by rules that prevent organizations from taking banking data without sharing their own data. Banks as well as many other entities want this method of opening up to be extended beyond what are known as the 'designated' sectors – currently banking and utilities – so that if a social media company (for example) wants access to Australia's banking data, it must become an 'accredited data recipient', which means in turn that it must make its data available to others. This approach would not stop Facebook and Google and so on from storing my data, but it would stop them from hoarding it to the exclusion of their competitors.

It seems to us that regulators might adopt the open banking, API-based approach across developed and developing economies to kill two birds with one stone: requiring both big banking and big tech to provide API access to customers' data would both open up their data hoards and stimulate competition. This would energize the economies of the metaverses and make them a focus for competition and innovation.

Addressing data-driven inequity is also at the heart of the European Data Spaces initiative, which is part of the broader European Strategy for Data. By focusing on data governance, interoperability, access and roles, the strategy aims to put people rather than businesses first, recognizing that while open data models can become a new industry standard (if the value of open innovation, early involvement of customers, and strategic alliances are well understood), there must be trusted data networks (that is, data exchange mechanisms and contracts) provided under well-defined data sovereignty principles (Scerri *et al.* 2022).

Data is not the new oil

The idea that with these trusted networks in place data economies can grow in the Metaverse is central to the attraction of it as a place to build new businesses. But this means careful handling and it is not without risks, because personal data comes with risks.

To explain why we say this, cast your mind back to the 'data is the new oil' aphorism, commonly attributed to Clive Humby (co-creator of the then-revolutionary Tesco Clubcard loyalty scheme many years ago), who said back in 2006 that 'it's valuable, but if unrefined it cannot really be used'. Humby thought that just as oil has to be refined – to create gas, plastic, chemicals and so on, to create the actual resources needed to power the economy – so must data be broken down and refined (i.e. analysed) to create value.

It is a potentially useful analogy, but as James Bridle (author of *The New Dark Age*) points out, attention has focused solely on the first part of Humby's insight. The important qualification that 'unrefined' data has no value has been ignored. Increased processing power and cheaper cloud storage has led to the speculative over-collection of data. As Bridle (2018b) puts it: 'In the process of simplification, the analogy's historical ramifications – as well as its present dangers and its long-term repercussions – have been forgotten.'

So if data isn't the new oil – or the new water, or the new black – then what exactly is it? Bridle put forward a much better metaphor, saying that data 'more closely resembles atomic power than oil – an effectively unlimited resource that still contains immense destructive power and that's even more explicitly connected to histories of violence'. From this perspective data isn't the new oil, it's the new plutonium – and it's when you put it in an AI-powered fast breeder reactor that the fun really starts.

This was also the perspective of Bernard Marr when he wrote about Shell (an actual oil company) becoming a data-driven organization (Marr 2020). As he put it, data is an asset but it is also a potential liability, which is why we are so curious about the next generation of business models built around credentials rather than attributes, proofs instead of facts, information about data rather than data itself. That is a practical narrative for the future and should be central to corporate strategies.

It's the economy, stupid

Deutsche Bank's October 2022 report 'Metaverse – the next e-commerce revolution' talked about 'multiple metaverse ecosystems that allow interoperability through standard solutions for digital identity and asset ownership'. We agree with their view that the Metaverse could indeed usher in the next e-commerce revolution as it gains traction and that 'financial services firms have a significant role' in this evolution to a post-post-industrial economy.

This e-commerce revolution will come about because those standard solutions of the trading of assets between digital identities will form the trusted value exchange layer that is missing from the internet today, because security and privacy will be integral parts of the Metaverse.

The specifics of whether it's web3 or web5, verifiable credentials or soulbound tokens that provide trust will be discussed in more detail later in this book, but the heart of the narrative is that the Metaverse will have trust baked in. It won't require security and privacy to be assured by platform providers, and as a result it will support different business models, with cheaper transactions and the potential for more equitable participation by a great many new stakeholders.

This is not an ideological issue – it's simply that safe transactions are cheaper, and financial services will inevitably follow those transactions (Feyen *et al.* 2021). The research in this field is clear: there is a positive link between trust and better economic outcomes. The implications of reduced economic frictions, the ability to reconfigure the value chain, new opportunities for entry, and shifting economies of scale and scope are that different financial services organizations will face different pressures and will need to formulate strategic responses.

The opportunities go far beyond simply offering conventional services in a new space. The trade in new kinds of digital assets that we will explore later is already expanding, with virtual commodities, especially in the art and fashion sectors, seeing strong investment, and the transactions underlying these purchases will potentially benefit from the involvement of players in the financial industry.

If the Metaverse is indeed an environment with trust built in – one that is capable of supporting mechanisms to exchange assets, and to establish the ownership of those assets, which we might crudely categorize as a digital value platform and a digital identity platform – then it is not an unreasonable prediction that individuals and organizations will steadily migrate their transactions from the dangerous badlands of web1 and the restrictive walled gardens of web2 in order to take advantage of that fundamental property: safety.

A metabubble?

While there is a strong trend here, because of the safety (and therefore transaction cost) drivers, it is important to address scepticism about the Metaverse. Jeffrey Funk, Lee Vinsel and Patrick McConnell have written in some detail about what they call the Metaverse 'bubble', and they have examined the economic effects of bubbles by comparing this technology bubble to past ones (Funk *et al.* 2022). Their view is that the biggest difference is that some goods did emerge from the dot-com bubble but 'probably not much will result from the current bubble'. We are unconvinced, because the 'goods' are not the Metaverse itself but those that will be delivered because it becomes a nexus for safe interaction and improved customer experience, and a locus for better financial services.

We think we can already see a digital value layer – with mechanisms for the exchange of assets without clearing and settlement – coming into existence via the technologies of tokens and decentralized finance. But for these services to scale, we need identity, Know Your Customer (KYC), risk and liability management, and it is perhaps less clear how this layer will come together – although we are optimistic that the relevant technologies will soon be deployed in institutional settings that will accelerate the shift of business into the new space.[*]

By bringing together new virtual worlds with digital objects that can be owned, we can create that spectrum of metaverses with specific and desirable properties. These worlds will connect people just as the internet did, but this time they will do so safely. In summary, the Metaverse is a big deal and the financial services world should be formulating strategies to exploit the new opportunities. We get it. So let's nail it down.

What *exactly* is the Metaverse?

We like the basic definition, as originally set out in the *Financial Times*, that the Metaverse is a collection of shared virtual worlds that are interoperable in the sense that people can navigate them while taking with them their digital identity and their digital objects (Moore 2021). This is a very straightforward

---

[*] We say institutional because we are unconvinced that the majority of consumers will want to manage their digital identities themselves, preferring regulated institutions to do this for them. This is why we think that, to choose just one example, JP Morgan's digital wallet, which will enable people to select which credentials they share with counterparts, could be so important.

and practical description and it resonates perfectly with the discussions above. But what does it mean for business? While many people have an idea about what virtual worlds are, they are often less clear on what digital objects are and how digital identity might work. The time is right to bring these basic technologies together to see what they mean for business in the real world, so to speak,

We begin with Narula's perspective on 'socially constructed realities', which he regards as forms of 'proto-metaverse' that have been present in every society throughout recorded history. Helpfully, he breaks down these socially constructed realities into some key components:

> A society or grouping of humans; another world or reality involving events, identity, rules, and things that are deemed to be in some way real; and an ongoing transfer of value between the two, which grows individual and group fulfilment, wealth and meaning.

The Metaverse is, therefore, a collection of socially constructed realities able to support transactions between what Jaron Lanier (in his 2013 book *Who Owns the Future*) usefully labelled economic avatars: that is, digital identities that are able to buy and sell digital objects.

The promise of the Metaverse is that it will be built up from more immersive and experiential components than previous forms of socially constructed realities. Our economic avatars can already try on clothing and cosmetics, check out with Apple-Pay and have their purchases shipped through the usual e-commerce route. While this may seem trivial, digital commerce and tools to support a seamless customer experience are big business. The report 'Gartner magic quadrant for digital commerce' in 2022 predicted that 'by 2025, organisations offering a unified commerce experience by frictionlessly moving customers through journeys will see at least a 20% uplift in total revenue'.

It's not hard to imagine that a differentiating factor for providers of B2B tools in the Metaverse will be their ability to deliver better customization and increased satisfaction. The growing sophistication of 3D-printed apparel may also dramatically shorten, if not entirely remove, the lengthy marketing cycle and costly advertising for some brands. For example, it's already possible to manufacture shoes on demand based on 3D scans of your feet, taken at home (Schwear 2023). An avatar in Roblox will be able to 3D print the skate shoes it created inspired by Vans World, with Robux flowing directly to Vans in a safe and fulfilling transaction.

This is a simple example that shows that there are direct business benefits to be gained. Many online retailers offer free returns and encourage customers to buy different sizes and different colours in one shipment to give them freedom to select at home. The cost of supporting this inevitably ends up in higher goods costs. Removing the uncertainty is likely to lead to reduced returns and lower operating costs.

Rapid advances in AI diagnostics, alongside VR, mean that beauty brands are at the forefront of this. The CEO of Glosswire, a leading marketplace for beauty brands, confirms the benefits, citing increased consumer confidence and 'better conversions and repeat customers' resulting from the use of VR and AI (Carney 2023).

There is more to it than 3D shopping, of course. The mention of experiential building blocks suggests that, as Leo Lewis observed in the *Financial Times*, the Metaverse creates an environment in which certain socially constructed realities are defined by experience rather than physicality (Lewis 2022). An obvious example is fans coming together to enjoy a concert that they could never attend in real life. We already see this sort of thing going on in proto-metaverses such as Fortnite, where VR functions as a place for friends to come together and communicate. Would the average consumer put on a headset to leave their home in the cyburbs and jet pack over to a bank branch to apply for a loan? Probably not. Would they put on a headset so that they could sit next to some good friends at a concert featuring a favourite pop star? Probably.

A digital object that is a ticket for a concert – whether that's in a real or virtual space – would be a digital asset worth paying for, as we will see.

Why now for business?

Over the last few years, the Metaverse has been making the transition from future fiction trope to consumer and business trials. Now that Apple has entered the VR and AR field with its Vision Pro headset, we can begin to see how many and varied metaverses are going to permeate everyday life as we all gradually become more comfortable with spatial computing. Apple's launch of the Vision Pro – rather than Meta's acquisition of Oculus – will in time be seen as the cusp for the next generation of computing, and therefore of financial services (just as the iPhone was at the end of the PC era and the beginning of the smartphone era). This is because Apple's entry acts as a resounding endorsement, which in turn brings healthy competition. And this competition will come in the form of lower prices as well as compelling functionality. We can already see this with Meta's rapid evolution: while the first-generation headset initially targeted gaming, the Meta Quest 2 supports virtual travel, fitness and web browsing, all of which present real opportunities for commerce and will appeal to a broader community than gamers.

We should also look beyond the US and these two giants vying for headlines. At the 2024 Consumer Electronics Show, Chinese start-up XREAL was taking preorders for the Air 2 Ultra, which now retails for under US$1,000 and is positioned as a competitor to Apple's Vision Pro. The headset, which looks more like a pair of classic Ray-Ban sunglasses than a headset, needs to be paired with a computing device to work, and immersive spatial computing features are only available with specific Samsung devices – the experience with iPhones and with other Android devices is restricted to screen mirroring. Nonetheless, the Air 2 Ultra is viewed as a viable competitor to the offerings from Apple and Meta, and, interestingly, in terms of broader value chain disruption, XREAL is working on a custom computing unit, promising an even richer experience.

XREAL's Air 2 Ultra is reminiscent of Google Glass, famously banned from some public places before it was officially launched. Ten years on from that ban, it will be interesting to see how consumers and proprietors of public spaces react this time round. In response to the public beta of Google Glass, UK-based group Stop the Cyborgs campaigned for better guardrails, wanting to actively set social and physical bounds around the use of technologies. At the time of writing, you can still buy 'Google Glass is banned on these premises' stickers and T-shirts, but it seems we have collectively moved on, if the videos of people trying out their headsets in cafes and at work are anything to go by. Perhaps there is safety in numbers this time.

While many observers were taken aback by the $3,499 launch price of the Vision Pro, especially when set against the $500 price of Meta's Quest, it was not really that expensive in a historical context. It was less expensive in real terms than either the IBM PC or Apple's own Macintosh when they were launched. Many of you will remember going out to buy one of those early PCs without really knowing what you were going to use it for (except to play games – quite a novelty back then). For a great many people, if not most, the real transformation in their daily lives came not through the computing power that the new device delivered but through the communications power. The addition of a modem allowed people to take their first steps into cyberspace, with bulletin boards and Compuserve. We hardly need to point out just where those steps have taken us. Whether Steve Jobs's reported comment that the devices should have been called personal communicators rather than personal computers is apocryphal or not, that is what they ended up being used for.

Apple's device in particular is going to change the way that people look at – or, more accurately, through – computers. It is therefore reasonable to be optimistic about it: an early report said that it could follow the trajectory of AirPods, whose shipments roughly doubled in size each year between 2017 – their first full year on the market – and 2020 (Ma & Weinberg 2023). Perhaps it is best to think about the Vision Pro as being more like that first Macintosh: it cost more than $7,000 at today's prices when it launched, and most people didn't know why they needed one – but they certainly wanted one (Evans 2023). One early reviewer said that his demo of the Vision Pro was 'the most mind-blowing moment of my 14-year career covering the technology scene' (Viticci 2023), which is a good description of how some of us felt when the Macintosh came out. Remember the first time you used MacPaint?

Perhaps the Vision Pro heralds the dawn of the post-graphical, immersive era – the era of the spatial computer. And this brings us to AR, VR and the metaverses of our shared future.

- Augmented reality is about changing the user's perception of their environment (remember Google Glass notifications?), which Apple does by placing 2D displays into environments so that they appear to be there in your current environment. Imagine this being built into CarPlay so people can drive with a personal Head-Up Display (HUD) while wearing the headset!
- Virtual reality is about immersing the user in a virtual environment. The way that Apple have implemented the mundane world as one mode among many that the user can switch between in a proto-teleportation system is, by all accounts, a revelation.

If there is a role for AR/VR, then, it is as applications that run on a spatial computer (Gans & Nagaraj 2023), and the best use cases will be in contexts where the shared social space is key, giving value to VR, or in complex environments (e.g. brain surgery) where the value that digital overlays bring via AR is high.

It would be reasonable to ask if customers are yet demanding financial services in this emerging environment – to which the answer would, of course, be that they are not. But Palm Pilot users were not calling for a Blackberry, and Blackberry users were not dreaming about an iPhone (Lucas 2023). Metaverses may be unformed now, but that is not a bad thing as companies begin exploring what they can do in them now as well as beginning to think about their longer-term strategies in the field. And, importantly, as we saw from the Roblox example, early proto-metaverses are in dire need of safer transactions, enabled by KYC and risk management, which directly lend themselves to regulated entities, such as financial institutions.

New business, new financial services

Where do financial services come into these strategies? We will return to this theme later in the book, but for now we will simply say that financial institutions could certainly begin by developing new payment experiences for metaverses, such as consumer-focused wallets similar to those used for e-commerce, but with decentralized technologies at their core – something we will explore later. As well as making peer-to-peer payments easier, this approach would enable smoother consumer transactions, all the while maintaining the security and lower transaction costs that will make the metaverses more appealing transaction spaces for innovation. With Amazon Anywhere already out of the gate, with its high transaction costs and traditional payment fraud, the race is on.

In addition to digital money, of course, metaverses need digital identity to move beyond being mere virtual worlds, and here, as futurist Tracey Follows has noted, the Vision Pro uses iris biometrics (an obvious step up from FaceID) in such a way as to cement the relationship between the user, the platform and their identity (and, in time, those wallets) (Follows 2023). These kinds of changes will mean that the ability to present credentials bound to the user will become a natural and inherent part of interactions in metaverses accessed through the Apple device: pop on the headset and pop in to Whisky a Go Go Go (or whatever the virtual version of cool music discovery will be called), and the system will automatically check for and authenticate an IS-OVER-18 credential, the limited release music non-fungible token (NFT) required for entry, and accept the necessary payments in tokens with no need to dip out into the banking system.

The Vision Pro is a 'statement of intent rather than an end in itself' (Waters 2023). It might be a few years before quantum computer contact lenses or biocomputer brain implants replace the headsets, cables and batteries, but by that time developer ecosystems will have already created the applications that none of us knew we wanted. All of us will naturally switch between the universe and the metaverses multiple times every day without even thinking about it.

Our approach to strategy

The Metaverse is important to financial services not because we will all be selling each other insurance in Call of Duty but because it will be a more trusted infrastructure (more trusted than either the current internet or the mundane world) for commerce and will therefore be more attractive to both businesses and consumers. Given that an increasing number of interactions will migrate into metaverses of many kinds, so will transactions. And where transactions go, financial services will follow.

It is a challenge to envisage this new environment and the new and better (as we will show) financial services sector that it will shape. This is because of current regulatory, technological and commercial uncertainty; the uncertainty means that there are several *possible* futures. To help organizations navigate this uncertainty, we've broken the problem – and, by extension, the opportunity – into four parts, which form the structure of this book. At each stage we use models that are easy to understand and that are designed to enable strong correlation between business and technology strategies.

In part I of the book we look at the key **technologies** and at how they are evolving, and we take an informed view of the ways in which they might interact with each other.

In part II we look at how those key technologies come together to create the **building blocks** of metaverses – components that are very different from those of the virtual worlds of yesterday. These are the building blocks that transform those virtual worlds in places where people can work, rest and play in safety.

In part III we look at the new **services** that these building blocks will enable, and we explore how they create a very different kind of market and, in turn, new demand for financial services of all kinds, including payments.

Finally, in part IV, we explore what those markets will look like and we make the prediction that the digital **wallet** will become the key consumer channel across both the universe and the Metaverse. We look at what this new way of doing business will mean for organizations ranging from financial institutions to fintechs to governments to gaming companies, and we discuss how those organizations and others should begin to formulate practical strategies.

Here is a bold promise, but one that we expect to keep: if you work in financial services, then at the end of this book not only will you have changed your perception of what the Metaverse is, you will also be able to formulate strategies for exploiting it and its building blocks for your business.

Case study: Axie Infinity

Axie Infinity was created by Vietnamese studio Sky Mavis based on the vision of a player-owned economy. The story goes that, spurred on by the success of online gaming, cryptocurrency, Pokémon, World of Warcraft and NFTs, the Sky Mavis founders Trung Thanh Nguyen, Aleksander Leonard Larsen and Jeffrey Zirlin set out to combine the crypto universe with online gaming in December 2017. Axie Infinity's popularity, like many digital success stories of this era, was spurred by Covid. With job losses and stay-at-home orders and people having more time on their hands, communities across the world were able to make reasonable returns from playing games.

Axie Infinity's gameplay revolves around collecting and battling Axies. These creatures, much like Pokémon, belong to different classes, each with unique attributes. The Axies are represented as NFTs and they each possess distinct genes, enabling players to breed them for offspring with varying abilities. At launch, the game supported the following four main 'play-to-earn' activities for gamers.

- *Battling Axies*. Players assemble a team of Axies and engage in player-versus-player battles or player-versus-environment adventure modes. Winning battles rewards players with Smooth Love Potion tokens, which can be sold on crypto exchanges.
- *Breeding Axies*. Axies can be bred to create new ones. Players can earn by selling these newly bred Axies on the marketplace, with the price depending on their quality and attributes.
- *Scholarships*. Some players lend their Axies to others through Axie Scholarship programmes, earning a share of their scholars' earnings.
- *Lunacia land plots*. Lunacia is the Axie homeland, divided into tokenized plots of land. Players can customize land plots in

the game, host shops and battle monsters. These plots can be rented or sold, providing income.

For its part, Sky Mavis generated revenue through the following means.

- *Marketplace fees.* Sky Mavis earns a fee from Axie Infinity's marketplace transactions when players buy, sell or trade Axies and in-game items.
- *AXS token sales.* Sales of Axie Infinity Shard, the game's governance token.
- *Smooth Love Potion token sales.* Sales of Smooth Love Potion tokens, which are used for breeding and can be traded.
- *Lunacia land sales.* Profits from land sales within the game's ecosystem.
- *Staking fees.* Sky Mavis offers staking options for its tokens and earns fees from stakers.

Initially built on Ethereum, Axie Infinity later migrated to Ronin, a permissioned Ethereum-compatible sidechain developed by Sky Mavis. This migration aimed to enhance scalability and reduce transaction costs. Hindsight's perfect vision now claims this migration as a fatal error, because in March 2022 Axie Infinity faced a major hack, which resulted in the theft of more than $600 million, making it the poster child of crypto hacks rather than the face of player-owned economies that it set out to headline. There are two things that stand out as interesting about this hack: the root cause of it, which is basically about identity; and the bail out.

The compromise was down to social engineering and a fake job offer by a fake company who approached a senior Sky Mavis engineer through LinkedIn. The fake offer was delivered in the form of a PDF that the engineer downloaded, allowing spyware to infiltrate Ronin's systems. As Sky Mavis is reported to have commented in a post mortem, 'employees are under constant advanced spear-phishing attacks on various social channels and one employee was compromised' (Weeks 2023). It's almost as if Microsoft had this very incident front of mind when they launched Verifiable Credentials for LinkedIn (sadly about a year too late for that Sky Mavis engineer): 'In the digital world, when you meet professional contacts for the first time online, you need additional trust signals to increase your confidence that they are who they say they are.'

The final step in the compromise acts as a cautionary tale about decentralized autonomous organizations (DAOs) and the requirement for robust security architecture. To establish control of the Ronin network, hackers needed to access five out of nine validators, and they were able to reach four through the duped engineer. They used the DAO to gain access to the fifth. Sky Mavis had set up a DAO to provide support to the wider gaming community, and, facing a heavy transaction load in November 20201, they had asked the DAO for help. As the SkyMavis post mortem revealed: 'The Axie DAO allowlisted Sky Mavis to sign various transactions on its behalf. This was discontinued in December 2021, but the allowlist access was not revoked... Once the attacker got access to Sky Mavis systems they were able to get the signature from the Axie DAO validator.'

The bail out stands out because Sky Mavis pledged to compensate user losses and secured investments from the venture capital community to do so. In the absence of insurance, given the experimental and uninsurable nature of the digital assets, the venture capital community stepped in to shore up their losses and provide funding to compensate victims.

In the evolved Metaverse that we envisage, the unlucky Sky Mavis engineer wouldn't fall foul of such a simple attack – because it will take thirty seconds or less to verify the credentials of any company. And the venture capital community won't have to bail out the owners of the compromised digital assets, because thanks to better security and protocols that can be audited, the assets will be insurable and the insurers will pay up.

PART I

THE TECHNOLOGIES

As mentioned in the book's introduction, the basic technologies of the metaverses are the virtual worlds where entities come to transact, the assets that they exchange and the entities themselves. We bring these together to form a basic but very useful framework, as shown in figure 3 over the page.

We will explore each of these technologies in more detail in the rest of this part. If you are more interested in what these technologies will do than in how they work, feel free to skip this section and move on to part II right away!

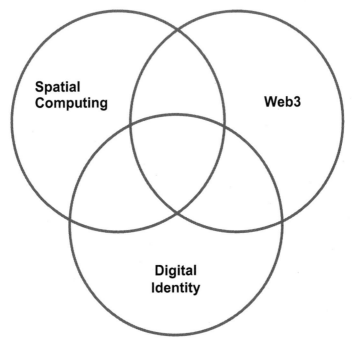

Figure 3. The three building blocks of the metaverses.

CHAPTER 2

Virtual worlds and markets

The obvious place to start when discussing the metaverse is virtual worlds. They make a good case study because, again in the words of Narula, 'virtual worlds are not and have never been just about games, and activity within them is not just an entertainment activity' (Narula 2022). They are in fact already a very, very big business, and there are already big businesses inside them.

Consider the decision by EVE Online – the long-running sci-fi massively multiplayer online game known for its enormous and long-running space battles – to add Microsoft Excel support

(Webster 2022). This illustrates the intersection of imaginary spaces and business rather well, and it builds on observations back in 2021 by the venture capitalist firm Andreessen Horowitz that consumers were already spending more than $50 billion on livestock in FarmVille, skins in Fortnite and extra lives in Candy Crush. These virtual worlds, immersive experiences and in-game purchases have been around for many years, and financial services organizations have been experimenting with them for a generation (remember those virtual bank branches in Second Life?). It is therefore reasonable to ask what it is that will now transform these virtual worlds into a metaverse where useful transactions can take place?

Virtual worlds – the socially constructed realities at the heart of all metaverses – are not simply created using virtual reality headsets. After all, you can use a headset right now to play 3D World of Warcraft, say, and it would be a lot of fun, but it would still not be a virtual world. Similarly, moving Grand Theft Auto from a games console to a spatial computer does not turn it into a metaverse. Reflecting on our earlier comments, the things that makes metaverses different are the interconnection between different virtual worlds and the compelling ability to trade digital objects in virtual environments safely.

It is useful to think about the Metaverse as a new version of the internet. The interface (2D, HTML, whatever) is not as important as the infrastructure.

Digital gone natives

It must be recognized that there is an emerging overlap between virtual worlds, AI and (as we will see) the idea of non-human economic agents interacting in metaverses.

The idea of virtual worlds that go beyond games or shopping to embrace human interaction and relationships may seem a staple of science fiction, remote from daily life, but it has to be said that we have already passed the point of no return here. The reality of emotional relationships with bots is that, not only are such relationships common, for many people they are in fact preferred. Rather than encouraging solitude, these emotional interactions often prime people for real-world interactions, with one example being a woman who, after finding a bot companion, signed up for dance classes and started to hike, 'since I had him to share it with' (Singh-Kurtz 2023). The woman in question also bought a VR headset to enhance her experience and said that the only downside of having a bot companion was being 'reminded of what I am lacking in my real life'.

Safer spaces

Douglas Rushkoff writes eloquently about the rich moving out of the city to comfortable mansions in the country to avoid the pandemic (Rushkoff 2020). He talks about the rich building their 'escape pods' and (with frightening prescience) about how the journey from video doorbells to autonomous robot sentries is constrained by money rather than ethics. Inept government responses to Covid accelerated interest in full cyberliving. Indeed, as Rushkoff also says, he 'can't help but wonder if the threat of infection is less the reason for this newfound embrace of virtual insulation than it is the excuse'.

We normal people might never be able to afford that country house with an electric gate, high walls and live-in help, but we can afford a nice chair for the study, a comfortable set of patio furniture and super-high-speed broadband. And that's all we need to retreat from a dangerous, unpleasant and confusing physical world into a controlled, organized and – above all – safe virtual world. Many people will be more than happy to commute through cyberspace instead of on crowded, unpleasant and disease-ridden trains.

There must be a lot of people thinking this way right now, judging by the deserted shops and offices seen in many big cities. And this is interesting to us because we agree with Sam Lessin's observation that if a result of the pandemic is more online working, online commerce, online education, online government and so on, then digital identity becomes a crucial pivot (Lessin 2020). His point that 'if the jobs people need are in digital rather than physical space, the internet's side of the fight will gain a lot of power' is accurate, and the consequences of that win are more significant and more far-reaching than might initially be obvious.

The key takeaway is that the digital identity that we use to traverse the highways and byways of the online world will be vastly more important to us than the physical identities that we occasionally need at an airport. Never mind a flight to the suburbs, we predict a flight to the cyburbs.

A crucial difference, however, between these gated communities in cyberspace and their real-world equivalents in the Hamptons is that digital identity will form a more effective boundary in the virtual world than the barbed wire and armed guards of the gated communities that the rich will retreat to in the real world. In *Snow Crash*, Stephenson's depiction of privacy in the exclusive Black Sun club in the Metaverse gives a useful glimpse of what is possible. Within Black Sun, data security and privacy are paramount: conversations cannot be overheard unless you are specifically invited into them, and the facial expressions of avatars are protected data.

The people living in the cyburbs will be happy to pay 'taxes' for better broadband, efficient home delivery and neighbourhood security, but it is going to be pretty difficult to persuade them to pay tax to support public transport in the nearby city that they never visit, police they never see or services for (as they see it) the unchecked angry youth roaming the urban streets.

When the residents decide on a new ordinance, they can enforce it instantly and effectively by excluding transgressors by removing access to their virtual selves. Life will be ordered and managed. It will be safe.

Out in the cyburbs, code is law

If society divides across the online/offline fault line, then the emerging Metaverse will look much more appealing than the old physical world to a great many people. Lessin's observation that 'a world where people come to earn money mostly online and disconnected from the physical world is a world of internet ascendancy' reinforces the view that we are going back to the future – in other words, mobile phones, the Internet and social media allow us to escape the urban anonymity of the industrial revolution and organize ourselves by communities (see *Identity Is the New Money* for more discussion around this (Birch 2014)).

In the neolithic world, of course, people lived in one community, and its boundaries were geographic. Our brains are wired for optimal interaction in a clan of around 150 people – the 'Dunbar number' that is well known to social scientists. In the online world, each of us will belong to multiple overlapping clans that are defined by *what* people are rather than *who* they are, and the boundaries will be soft, defined by credentials not identity.

The make-up of these clans will range from friends and family to work and play, and, we suspect, they will map to metaverses. We are already familiar with this dynamic in games, but it extends across age groups and applications. The way that Meta's Quest headset is used by older people who want to exercise together with peers but who do not want to go to a gym or be seen while exercising is illustrative. Doing sit-ups in the physical world while enjoying encouragement and interaction in the virtual world turns out to be a great combination!

Cyburbia might sound like a virtual Disney village – a bland echo chamber existence – but it isn't hard to see why people will prefer to live this way. If someone breaks the rules, they are (cryptographically) shunned and no longer a threat to the community.

Shopping in Cyburbia

Eva Pascoe (who kindly wrote this book's foreword) was one of the founders of Cyberia, Britain's first internet cafe, way back in 1994 (Brace 1994). With investors including Mick Jagger and Maurice Saatchi it soon became a hub for London's burgeoning web scene. It was located at 39 Whitfield Street in the West End, and it included a basement area where Webmedia, one of the UK's first web design companies, was a tenant of gamer space Subcyberia: a 24/7 space frequented by the game developer Richard Bartle (who will reappear later in this book) and many others pioneers of the virtual.

In 2022 Eva helped to create a virtual world replica of the original cybercafe to host a variety of events and interactions, including the launch of the book 22 *Ideas About the Future*. This was a collection of near-future speculative fiction from new authors along with non-fiction commentaries from leading experts (including one David G. W. Birch) to explore the impact of technology on society.

At the book launch, the question of payment naturally arose. How could someone in a virtual world pay for a physical good to be delivered in the mundane world? For this experiment they chose to use a QR code that could be scanned using a mobile phone when looking into the 3D environment through a 2D web browser, as shown in the image above. While this was expedient, it was not ideal, and it set us thinking about how payments should work – leading to our paper on the topic (Birch & Richardson 2023).

Unsurprisingly, platform incumbents are already creating a more seamless experience. Launched in August 2023, Amazon Anywhere integrates Amazon Prime into games, mobile apps and virtual experiences, but this comes with the usual platform clip, naturally. And while the percentage cut that Amazon takes varies based on a number of different inputs, it's reported to be in the region of 50% in most categories (Juozas 2023). This is not exactly the democratized web that proponents of the next evolution of the internet have been touting. A more equitable model might see peer-to-peer transfer of value and relevant attributes (e.g. a delivery address) directly between the buyer and seller inside the virtual world.

Figure 4. Eva Pascoe in the virtual Cyberia, looking at a model of Cyberia.

Here is an example. One of the virtual worlds that has attracted a lot of attention is called Decentraland, and players can connect a cryptocurrency wallet to their account. This of course means that people can pay using forms of digital assets, which points us towards the world of 'web3' that we will discuss in chapter 4.

World building

Where are the virtual worlds that will form the transaction spaces of the Metaverse going to come from in practice? Most commentary begins with games, and games are certainly a good place to start (and are fun to explore), but they are of course only one category of future metaverses. In fact, both the private and public sectors are already taking baby steps into metaverses. South Korea provides us with a couple of useful examples in both areas.

- Seoul is the first city in the world to have its own metaverse platform, with a 3D virtual space providing next-gen public services for both administrative and cultural needs. Spaces include a fintech incubator, a virtual mayor's office and the Metaverse 120 Center, where avatars help citizens file complaints and solve problems.

- In the private sector, Kookmin Bank is leading the way with the development of its KB Metaverse VR Branch. The metaverse platform enables customers to access banking services through VR devices, from one-to-one consultations with employee avatars and personalized financial advice to financial literacy courses for young people.

These and other early examples demonstrate the spectrum of virtual worlds that lies ahead of us. This idea of building 'digital twins' in the Metaverse is well established but there are people looking to build the other way around! The Spectra project is exploring the idea of building a VR 'digital sibling' city in order to experiment with urban planning and community practices before implementing them in physical cities. It also plans to host VR entertainment and gaming to foster interconnection between cyber inhabitants (Rzepecki *et al.* 2023).

Branching out

Banks already use VR, although mostly for internal purposes. Bank of America and TD Bank Group have been using it for employee onboarding for a couple of years and have seen good results. New employees can meet their co-workers and senior-level executives in one place, and the banks have found that VR has generated significant enthusiasm among their new hires (Cross 2023).

When it comes to the future of financial services, though, early visions seem to focus on virtual bank branches, which seems a limited and somewhat unimaginative view of the future. The J.P. Morgan virtual bank branch of 2022 looked much the same as the ABN Amro virtual bank branch of 2007 (although the former did have a tiger in it – for no obvious reason) and much the same as an actual branch. But, as Umberto Eco (the polymath semiotics professor, better known to the general public as the author of *The Name of the Rose*) wrote in *Travels in Hyperreality*, his prescient 1986 collection of essays, we are heading for hyperreality (reality as it should be) rather than virtual reality (a simulation of reality). In hyperreality, there is no such thing as a bank branch because no one wants to go to a bank branch when they could be enjoying other, better, more rewarding experiences. Technology is already taking us in that direction. We are already in the world of embedded banking and open finance, a world in which financial services are pumped to wherever they might be consumed.

The scepticism about virtual bank branches may be well founded (after all, neither of us ever goes to a bank branch in real life), but maybe there is another use for a virtual bank branch. Until late 2022 Bank of America branch staff would learn how to handle a potential armed robbery through books and videos. Today, however, they are immersed in a 3D VR environment in which a gunman aims a weapon at them or hands them a threatening note or whatever (LaCapra 2023). The software measures people's reactions and provides analytics for instructors to use in targeted coaching about remaining calm and making the right choices – for the safety of both the employees themselves and for others. Similarly, we have a friend in Canada who used to work in the far north there, and her 'bear attack' training was all done in VR.*

Industry

The Metaverse is not simply about retail commerce and immersive consumer space. Even as we are trying to envision what the Metaverse will bring for businesses and consumers, the industrial metaverse is already transforming how people design, manufacture and interact with physical entities across industries (*MIT Technology Review* 2022).

This industrial metaverse is evolving in a way that will revolutionize the way sustainable manufacturing practices are implemented. It is integrating the virtual and physical worlds, using digital representations of products, processes and systems to enhance efficiency and sustainability in manufacturing (Santos 2023). By harnessing technologies including VR, AR and the internet of things (IoT), the industrial metaverse should help manufacturers to optimize operations, reduce waste and minimize environmental impact.

Overall, this presents a substantial business opportunity. The management consulting firm Arthur D. Little estimates that, at the time of writing, the industrial metaverse is a $100–$150 billion market (smaller than comparable estimates for 'industry 4.0' markets, as you would expect, given that it excludes technologies such as robotics and 3D printing as shown in figure 5), but its conservative estimate for the end of the decade is that the

---

* For the avoidance of doubt they are trained to defend themselves from bears, not to attack them.

sector will have grown to be worth around $400 billion – and its upper limit estimate is more than $1 trillion.

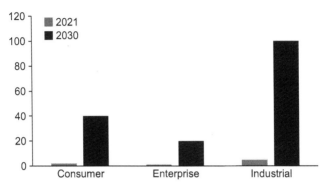

Figure 5. Metaverse sector revenues ($ billions).

And we believe that with the 'building block' technologies shown in table 1 developing rapidly – with multiple implementations of AR, VR and mixed reality (now gathered together under the banner of 'spatial computing'), with AI advancements, and so on, transforming both consumer and business applications – this might even be an underestimate.

Table 1. Building blocks of the industrial metaverse.
(*Source*: Arthur D. Little, July 2023.)

Building blocks	Industry 4.0 (previous decade)	Industrial metaverse (coming decade)
Digital twins	***	***
IoT	***	***
AI	**	***
Simulation	**	***
Visualization	*	***
Web3	*	**
Edge computing	**	***

The more asterisks, the greater the importance.

The implementation of such an industrial metaverse is not without its challenges. One of the main obstacles is related to data security and privacy. Because the industrial metaverse relies heavily on interconnected devices, there is a vast attack surface and, therefore, an increased risk when it comes to the confidentiality, integrity and availability of data. Consequently, stakeholders will demand robust cybersecurity measures to protect their data and ensure the integrity of their operations. As we will see, though, if metaverses are built on the sound and secure digital identity and digital asset structures set out in later chapters, these risks can be made manageable.

Case study: Digital Singapore

Digital Twin Singapore is a dynamic, 3D digital model of the city-state. It is designed to simulate, visualize and analyse real-world scenarios in a virtual environment. The idea of developing a 'digital twin' of Singapore was driven by the country's ambitions to become a 'Smart Nation', where digital technologies are harnessed to improve citizens' lives, create economic opportunities and build stronger communities.

To help make better use of Singapore's limited land and to figure out which areas are most at risk from flooding, the Singapore Land Authority started creating a 3D map of the country in 2012. This map later developed into Virtual Singapore, adding data from laser-scanning aircraft and vehicles to combine all relevant data sets, allowing citizens to view and verify information to help inform urban planning. Completed in 2023, it is the first digital twin of an entire country – a highly detailed 3D representation used across government agencies to support decision-making (Walker 2023). The Singapore Land Authority is now working on the next stage of the project: a national subsurface digital twin of Singapore.

The digital twin's wide variety of uses include the following.

- *Urban planning.* With the digital twin, urban planners can simulate the impact of new infrastructure projects, from skyscrapers to public parks, and make more informed decisions.
- *Disaster management.* The platform can be used to simulate scenarios such as flooding, allowing for better preparedness and response.
- *Environmental monitoring.* The digital model helps with monitoring and managing resources like water, electricity and transportation more effectively. Factors like temperature, humidity and pollution can be tracked, helping in the design of policies for a better living environment.
- *Public services.* By integrating data from various sources, the digital twin can help optimize public services like waste collection, public transport, etc.
- *Research and innovation.* The platform can be used by researchers, businesses and innovators to test new ideas and solutions in a virtual environment before implementing them in the real world.

Digital Twin Singapore is an ambitious project, representing a significant step forward in the realm of smart cities. It demonstrates how virtual worlds can be harnessed to help decision-makers visualize the potential impact of their choices, making governance more data-driven and allowing a variety of stakeholders to collaborate more effectively using a shared digital platform.

The digital twin is a virtual world, not a metaverse, but it demonstrates how real and virtual collaboration can work to create spaces that could then evolve into metaverses when they gain transactional infrastructure.

CHAPTER 3

Owners and digital identities

Without digital identity we cannot have the Metaverse with an economy in it, because an economy needs both objects and owners of those objects to make markets. We need digital identity to make our metaverses work, and that has been missing from the internet from the very beginning.

Professor Bill Buchanan OBE from the School of Computing at Edinburgh Napier University points out that we joined together a set of internet protocols with very little trust built into them and then patched them up with 'simple methods'. He

says that our digital future must be pointed towards an infrastructure that properly integrates trust into the digital world
(Buchanan 2022). We agree. Digital identity plus web3 gives us
the trust infrastructure that we need.

But what exactly is digital identity? It's time to drill down into
the concept.

We have all read countless articles, sat through countless
conference presentations and seen countless blog posts and
tweets that highlight the key role of digital identity in the new
economy. Commentators may not be entirely clear on what a
digital identity actually is, but they share the common suspicion
that unless we have some form of digital identity infrastructure
in place, the potential growth and attendant benefits of the
transition to a new online economy cannot be fully realized. We
more than share this suspicion. In fact, we would go further:
unless an appropriate infrastructure can be put in place, we
have no chance of moving forwards.

Digital identity is – not to put too fine a point on it – critical infrastructure. But how will it work (with the ever-changing
technologies of identification, authentication and authorization), how will it be governed and what important use cases
does it open up?

Digital, not digitized

We think that the problems caused by our ineffective and out-
moded 'digitized' identity infrastructure in an interconnected,
always-on, networked society are many and serious. We will
therefore set out a framework for thinking about the kind of
digital identity infrastructure that we need to tackle those problems, and then, later in the book, we will explore in some detail
how digital identity technologies might be deployed to form a
reputation economy in the Metaverse – to the significant benefit of individuals, organizations and governments.

Digitized identity and digital identity

When originally thinking about how to explain the difference between bureaucratic digitized analogue identity and post-modern digital identity, we decided to use the decision of the Australian state of New South Wales to provide citizens with 'digital driver's licences, stored on a user's smartphone, allow-ing them to ditch their physical ID card' as a starting point. That language illustrates a key point very well. These are not *digital* driver's licences, or anything like them. They are *digitized* driver's licences – nothing more than virtual shadows of their mundane progenitors. They have no functionality beyond their heritage in industrial age bureaucracy and provide absolutely nothing new for the new economy.

This is the start of the narrative that we want to build around the topic in order to facilitate constructive co-creation of the new infrastructure that society needs. To see what digital iden-tity, as opposed to digitized identity, might look like, it is helpful to return to McLuhan's (pre-internet) concept of identity as being dependent on the interactions between entities, creating what Ian Grigg called 'edge' identity (Grigg 2017). If this is indeed the correct vision for post-industrial online identity (and since he was right about most other things, we are certainly not going to call McLuhan out on this one), then what would it mean for the driving licence? How exactly would a digital driving licence differ from a digitized one?

Well, a good way to see a digital driving licence is as a creden-tial: the embodiment of a relationship between the citizen and the state, comprising some form of unique identifier together with attributes that have been attested to by trusted third par-ties that can be used in a bunch of claims. We (and others) have long argued that shifting to an infrastructure where transactions are between virtual identities and are enabled by credentials is the way forward. It seems to us that the diffuse identities that

McLuhan talks about, the edge identities that Grigg talks about, and the relationship identities that we talk about all fit very well inside the concept of claims as the basis for transactions.

That seems like a reasonable working definition, so let's move forward with that. We note that the attributes that are needed to enable transactions might be very varied, but let's assume for the sake of discussion that in the case of the driving licence there are three claims that should be supported.

1. A law enforcement officer might need to know who you are.
2. A car rental company might need to know you are allowed to drive.
3. A bar might need to know that you are over 21.

Now, the digitized driving licence doesn't know who is asking, what they are asking for or whether they are allowed to ask for it – but a digital driver's licence could know all of these things. When the law enforcement officer asks your digital driving licence who you are, your digital driving licence can check the digital signature of the request and the authorizations that come with it. The digital driving licence knows that the bar can ask if you are over 21 but can't ask who you are (it's none of their business – although the licence may give a service provider a specific meaningless but unique number that can be used for loyalty and barring), and so on.

Note that these are not new ideas, and while they are well suited to the Metaverse, they predate it by decades. Let's look back to 2007, and the book that Dave edited on *Digital Identity Management*:

> Because computers, biometrics and digital signatures can work together to disclose facts about someone without disclosing their full identity ... your ID card could, for example, send a message to a machine confirming that you are

over 18 without disclosing who you are or what your citizen number is.*

All very nice in theory. But what about deployment? How will you connect up all of the bars and car rental counters and police cars and so on? What would the person in the bar use to interrogate your digital driving licence? Well, their digital driving licence of course!

It is surely one of the defining characteristics of the digital-age driving licence that it is software rather than a piece of paper, which means it is now a node in the great network of things and *it can talk to other driving licences.* There is a beautiful symmetry to this: no digital driving licence is different from any other digital driving licence, nor privileged above any other digital driving licence. There is no need for custom equipment. Everyone has the same digital driving licence – you, the policeman, the barman – but these licences are loaded with different claims. Or, to put it another way, they are all the same kind of passport but they contain very different visas.

Table 2. Digitized versus digital identity.

Digitized identity	Digital identity
Nodes	Edges
Static	Dynamic
Single	Multiple
Hierarchy	Network
Asymmetric	Symmetric
Stand-alone	Connected
Dumb	Smart

---

* This seems trivial and obvious, but a problem then, as now, was that the people in charge of identity cards – and driving licences, and passports, and all of the other identity infrastructure – still saw those documents only as dumb emulations of paper documents.

Identity in action

To set a baseline, let us look at a practical example of using identity in the physical world. In his book *Defining Digital Identity*, Phil Windley sets out just such a practical use case perfectly, so we will use his example here (Windley 2023).

- When a customer (the subject or entity) wants to buy beer (perform an action on a resource) they are required to submit proof that they are of legal drinking age. In America this is generally achieved by presenting a driver's licence. A driver's licence is a *credential* that contains claims asserting that the subject has certain attributes and traits and permissions that authorize the holder to drive a car (perform an action).

- The barman (the policy enforcement point, or PEP) examines the licence to see if it looks real (determines the authenticity and validity of the credential) and uses the picture (embedded biometric authentication factor) to see if the person presenting the licence is the same person who owns it (authenticates the licence).

- Once certain that the licence is authentic and is being presented by the person to whom it was issued, the barman reads the date of birth (an attribute) from the licence and determines whether the person is over 21 (consults a security policy determined by the state and makes a policy decision about permissions associated with the identity for a particular resource).

This process happens millions of times every day around the world, but it is an imperfect solution to the mundane problem of age verification for the obvious reason that the licence may be forged, the barman may fail to authenticate the holder, there is no record of the check, and so on and so forth.

Digital identity's different approach

If we use a digitized identity – that is, a copy of the licence on a phone – nothing changes. The customer shows the barman a phone screen with a picture of a driving licence on it instead of showing the physical licence.

But compare this with how Windley's example of digital identity could work in practice: I want to get a drink so the barman sets his digital driving licence (a smartphone app) to request a claim for IS_OVER_18 and then, via NFC (near field communication), Bluetooth or QR code, interrogate my digital driving licence (a smartphone app). My smartphone app sees that his request is signed by a valid licensing authority and has not expired and then checks what credentials it has to hand. It discovers two virtual identities containing the relevant IS_OVER_18 attribute: one from the Driving License Authority and one from my car insurance company. It selects the first one and sends it to the barman's app.[*]

The barman's app checks the signature and sees that it is valid. Since the barman is using his smart driving licence app, it either stores or has access to the public keys of the driving licence authorities, the car insurance companies, the car rental companies and so on. My smart travel app would have similar information for airlines and car rental companies, hotel companies and so on. The barman's driving licence sends back a message encrypted using the public key. My app can decode this, because it has the corresponding private key (this is all down to the miracle of asymmetric cryptography), so it asks for me to authenticate myself. I use my fingerprint or PIN or whatever and the app decodes the message. It then replies to the barman's app. The barman's app now knows that I have the corresponding

---

[*] The virtual identity contains an identifier, a cryptographic key, a number of attributes and a digital signature. At this point it's irrelevant how it all works, but if you do want to understand the mechanisms involved, we can assure you that they are covered later in the book.

private key and it can therefore accept that IS_OVER_18 applies to me.

We stress that it's important not to get hung up on the technical details here as we are going to look at these in appropriate detail later in the book. For now, what's important is to take hold of the basic concept of a claim as a process, as shown in table 3.

Table 3. A claim: digital ID in action.

Alice the bartender	Bob the patron
Are you over 18?	Yes
I want to see a persona that includes this attribute: IS_OVER_18	Here is such a persona: Persona P has attribute IS_OVER_18
It is acceptable	Thanks
OK, that is signed by a bank, and I trust them	
Not so fast, prove it is you	OK.
Decode this message encrypted for the Persona P	Here you go, I decoded your message
Thanks, I'm happy to provide you with service	Cool.
Persona P is now in my customer database!	

This process can be implemented to deliver both security and privacy, and it shows that we use digital identity to create an infrastructure that goes far beyond emulating our broken physical industrial age identity system to provide something so much better.

What does this give us? Well, in the real world we use documents such as passports to recognize who people are, and we look at visas stamped into their passport to see where they are allowed to travel. The same should be true in the digital world: when a delivery robot comes up to a house's border control, it should have to present a passport – just like a delivery driver who wanted access to my shed would. These passports are not paper and pictures, of course – they are built from cryptographic keys held in tamper-resistant memory and pointers to transaction data on quantum-resistant shared ledgers. But you get the point. They may not tell anyone who you are, because they want to provide privacy as well as security, but they will tell people what you are: that you're an employee of a given company (WORKS_FOR_DHL), that you're old enough to drink (IS_OVER_18), or that you're in possession of a permit to drive (HAS_VALID_LICENCE).

Persona

When Alice talks to her brother Adam on Facebook, it is her online persona sending messages to his online persona. Since each of them controls their online persona (using passwords, in this case), it's all good. If you think about extending and generalizing this principle, you will soon realize that this one-to-one mapping is a special case: special because Alice has only one Facebook persona, special because only she can make it send messages, and special because the online persona and Alice are synonymous.

In the more general case, however, none of these things is true. There may be several persons who have the password to control a persona (this is true for a company's online persona, to give an obvious example), there may be several ways for those persons to authenticate their control over the persona, and there may be several personae that are under the control of those persons.

If you try to map 'people' to 'persona' you get a headache. That's because one of the basic problems with this way of thinking is that economic avatars do not map one-to-one with real identities. A single virtual identity may be linked to a number of different real identities: several people in a 'shop' may share an eBay identity and crucially – as we discuss later in the book – the associated reputation used for selling (just as two family members may share an eBay identity used for purchasing).

The way to get rid of this headache is to get rid of the direct link between person and persona and to introduce the concept of digital identity as the bridge between the two (Birch & McEvoy 2007). Using this concept of digital identity, we can cope with the absence of a one-to-one link between a person/thing/bot and a persona. One can envisage people having a number of different digital identities (just as they have a number of different credit cards), and one can further envision a digital identity being shared between a number of people (e.g. corporate officers). One could certainly imagine niche identity issuers springing up across both horizontal and vertical sectors (the government, from this perspective, becomes a special case of a niche identity issuer) where economics or other pressures dictate.

Therefore, in the general case, an economic avatar in the Metaverse does not map one-to-one with a mundane identity, and any transaction structure built for the Metaverse must recognize this fact.

Identification, authentication and authorization

We know what we want from digital identity that spans the mundane and the Metaverse, so how do we go about implementing it? In this book we use the Three Domain Identity (3DID) model as a framework for an effective discussion of the identification, authentication and authorization process – a framework that we find to be generally useful across sectors: a narrative, again, to facilitate communication between regulators, technologies and businesses.

This model actually has a long history, going back to the genesis of that *Digital Identity Management* book we mentioned earlier. When Dave began to conceptualize digital identity, he did so less as an abstract concept and more specifically as a connection between mundane and virtual identities. This basic insight was developed over the years, as Dave and Victoria (along with colleagues at Consult Hyperion) expanded and enhanced the model to ensure both that it remained congruent with emerging global standards and that it grew in its capacity to facilitate effective communication between different groups of stakeholders. The objective was to enable the development of identity strategies for the world that is evolving rather than the world we are leaving behind (this is why, for example, we repeatedly draw a distinction between the implementation of digital identity and the digitization of analogue identity).

With these factors in mind, then, let us begin to lay out a suitable version of the model so that we can explore its implications later in the book. This model frames digital identity as the bridge between the mundane and virtual worlds, and it sets out a clear framework for thinking about the dynamics of the bindings between them, which in turn frames the technological discussions in a useful and productive manner. The model rests on the core concept that the 'real' identity of something (which may be a person, an object, a bot or whatever) is not used in electronic transactions because such transactions are interactions between virtual identities with associated credentials. To illustrate the difference we can point to the simple example of people interacting online, where the need to distinguish between the person and the persona brings clarity to many otherwise-opaque discussions about social media, electronic commerce and online interactions of all kinds.

With this thinking, we transform 'digital identity' from a general concept, generic description and nebulous notion into a very specific (and very useful) concept.

The 3DID model

The 3DID model, as shown in figure 6, frames digital identity as the bridge between the mundane and virtual worlds, between the universe and the Metaverse, between persons and personae, and it sets out a clear framework for thinking about the dynamics of the bindings between them. At a high level, it's sufficient to know only that these bindings are highly asymmetric: it is time-consuming, complicated and expensive to bind a digital identity to something in the real world, but it is inexpensive and quick to bind the digital identity to something in the virtual world. It's all about encryption and keys and how you manage them.

Figure 6. The 3DID model.

There are a number of reasons for thinking that while there are a wide variety of organizations that could instantiate these bindings – and indeed a number of different institutional arrangements that could come into existence around them – it is a plausible hypothesis that it should be banks who are in the vanguard as the providers of digital identity. It is clear to us that prime candidates to create and manage these bindings are regulated financial institutions in general and retail banks in particular.

This view was reinforced recently when a friend had some problems with his Facebook account being taken over by fraudsters. He was extremely frustrated by his efforts to contact Facebook and have something done about it. As one of us pointed out to him, there was no reason why he should have expected anything different. Facebook has no statutory obligation to remedy such problems. Banks, on the other hand, are regulated financial institutions, so if they were to provide identity services, they would be compelled to act. If your bank account is taken over by thieves, then you might reasonably expect the bank to do something about it after being notified of the problem, and to have some procedures in place to establish quite who the rightful owner of the bank account is, to restore control of the bank account to that person, and to provide appropriate compensation if it has behaved negligently in some way.

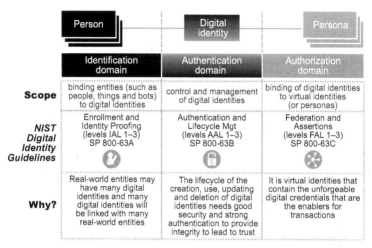

Person		Digital identity		Persona	
	Identification domain		Authentication domain		Authorization domain
Scope	binding entities (such as people, things and bots) to digital identities		control and management of digital identities		binding of digital identities to virtual identities (or personas)
NIST Digital Identity Guidelines	Enrollment and Identity Proofing (levels IAL 1–3) SP 800-63A		Authentication and Lifecycle Mgt (levels AAL 1–3) SP 800-63B		Federation and Assertions (levels FAL 1–3) SP 800-63C
Why?	Real-world entities may have many digital identities and many digital identities will be linked with many real-world entities		The lifecycle of the creation, use, updating and deletion of digital identities needs good security and strong authentication to provide integrity to lead to trust		It is virtual identities that contain the unforgeable digital credentials that are the enablers for transactions

Figure 7. Standards and 3DID.

The model is suitable for both public sector and multiple private sector uses. Figure 8 shows an example in which the model supports the relevant Financial Action Task Force guidelines on digital identity in the financial services world.

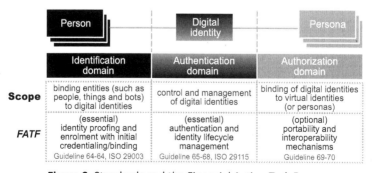

Person		Digital identity		Persona	
	Identification domain		Authentication domain		Authorization domain
Scope	binding entities (such as people, things and bots) to digital identities		control and management of digital identities		binding of digital identities to virtual identities (or personas)
FATF	(essential) identity proofing and enrolment with initial credentialing/binding Guideline 64-64, ISO 29003		(essential) authentication and identity lifecycle management Guideline 65-68, ISO 29115		(optional) portability and interoperability mechanisms Guideline 69-70

Figure 8. Standards and the Financial Action Task Force.

Identity in action

Let us imagine a non-financial use case to illustrate how identification (IdN), authentication (AuthN) and authorization (AuthZ) work together. Internet dating sites provide a rich and practical environment for exploring different notions of identity, so let's go back to that use case for an example to explore. Suppose that when Alice went to a dating site to create an account, as part of that process the dating site asked her to log in via her bank account. At this point, the dating site bounced her to her bank, where she did the appropriate two-factor authentication to establish her identity to the bank's satisfaction. The bank then returned a cryptographic token to the dating site to confirm that Alice is over 18, resident in Australia and has funds available for the dating company to bill against.

In this example, Alice's real identity remains safely locked up back in the bank vault, but it is now bound to a virtual identity that she can use for online interactions. The internet dating persona contains no personally identifiable information (PII), therefore, but if someone uses that persona to get up to no good, the dating sites can then provide the token to the police, the police can then see that the token comes from the bank, and the bank will then tell them which account is behind the persona. This seems a very appropriate distribution of responsibilities. When the dating site gets hacked, as they inevitably do, all the criminals will obtain is a meaningless token: they have no idea who it belongs to and the bank won't tell them.

One of the key attractions of this core identity architecture for the Metaverse is that it delivers an expectation of redress in the event of failure, which inevitably happens sometimes. Things always go wrong. What's important is the structures, mechanisms and processes that are in place for dealing with those failures. If some fraudsters take over a bank account and use the identity associated with it to create a fake profile on a dating site, then it is reasonable to expect the bank to have mechanisms in place to revoke the tokens and inform both the dating site and its customers that such revocation has taken place without disclosing any PII. This is important because PII is, in essence, a kind of toxic waste that no companies really want to deal with unless they absolutely have to. Under the provisions of the GDPR, the potential fines for disclosing PII without the consent of the data subject are astronomical. The complete cycle therefore needs to be thought through because it will be crazy to have an infrastructure that protects my personal data when the system is operating normally but gives it up when the system fails, or when we attempt recovery from failure.

The 3DID model presented here provides a structured and practical way to think about digital identity as well as providing a way to think about using new identification, authentication and authorization technologies to solve practical problems. It does not, however, solve the problem of how to deliver digital identi-fiers into the mass market – a subject we will return to in part II.

Identity and inclusion

We feel very strongly that the Metaverse should play a role in advancing financial inclusion. Providing a safe space for con-sumers to interact with financial service providers as a bulwark against the seemingly relentless advance of fraud, scams and general malfeasance would be a good thing.

While there are a variety of different ways we could imagine the infrastructure being delivered to meet the needs of inclusion as well as economic efficiency, it certainly seems to us that align-ing the goals of banks and society here is a sensible first step.

A bank business?

Banks ought to obtain significant advantage as infrastructure providers here, because the collaborative economy stakehold-ers do not want to have to create their own identification, authentication and authorization infrastructures. The Metaverse should therefore present a great opportunity for them to deliver non-payment value-added services into the new environment.

This is not a purely technological perspective. Across the world there are multiple examples of banks stepping into this space. There are also multiple examples of countries where banks have not stepped in; British banks, for example, have long believed that they have a future role as repositories of digital identities, but as yet they have not had much success (Davies 2014). Increasingly, there is no inevitability about this bank-centric vision. While banks appear to be well placed due to the nature of their heavily regulated business, which requires adherence to stringent KYC processes, the time for them to monetize this regulated position of being trusted entities may be running out. It is entirely possible to construct an alternative view that is based not on banks and bindings and regulated financial institutions but on regulated big data, artificial intelligence and a more inclusive view of the world.[*]

Let's again return to that internet dating example, because it's easy to explore. Alice goes to the internet dating site and creates an identity. During this process, the internet dating site asks her to validate her identity. She presents a credential issued by Microsoft that says she is over 18, based on her LinkedIn profile, which contains verifiable college qualifications and the year of award. There are a few reasons why we think this is more likely than a bank-asserted credential in this instance.

---

[*] Note that the current experiences of open banking tend to support the view that the role of banks was reinforced by mandatory data sharing. Far from the 'challengers' replacing incumbents, open banking has meant that customers retain their primary bank relationship and use connected third-party specialists such as Wise for multi-currency accounts. The same dynamic might apply in data, where the position of a regulated platform with mandatory data sharing becomes reinforced.

- Firstly, in the years that we've been working in this space, banks have consistently side-stepped this much-needed use case. Despite the fact that a reported one-in-five partnered adults under the age of 30 in the United States say they met their current spouse or partner on a dating site or app (Vogels & McClain 2023) and – possibly even more compellingly – the fact that the FBI's Internet Crime Report for 2022 notes that romance scam losses more than doubled in the previous year, enabling trusted dating is something the banks are squeamish about.

- Secondly, executive matching services already use LinkedIn profiles to discover potential partners for their clients. A friend of ours was approached out of the blue by US East Coast-based Lunch Dates[*] solely on the merits of his LinkedIn profile. He was thoroughly screened during a zoom call by a Lunch Dates agent acting on behalf of one of its clients, before being provided with details of the confirmed date.

- Finally, in terms of technology enablement, we are pretty much there. Microsoft Entra Verified ID, recently launched by LinkedIn, promises that 'in just minutes, organisations can use Verified ID to create customised digital employee IDs that reflect their brand and business needs' (Chik 2023).

Alternatively, Alice could present a credential issued by Amazon that says she is over 18, that she is resident in the continental United States and, crucially, that Amazon will accept liability (to a maximum amount) if either of these credentials turns out to be incorrect. Amazon can be pretty sure about these facts because, apart from anything else, the company has access to her bank account because of open finance initiatives (as Apple does in the United Kingdom). Amazon also knows almost everything Alice

---

[*] https://www.lunchdates.com.

buys, where she is and when her salary gets paid into her bank account. It can give the dating site a pretty accurate picture of her without disclosing any PII, and it can allow the dating site to bill against the token if necessary.

The fact is that – as the World Economic Forum suggested in its blueprint for digital identity – the banks do not have the *right* to exploit digital identity (McWaters 2016). But if banks do not offer digital identity services that are relevant to the post-industrial revolution, they won't simply miss out on the opportunity to offset some of their costs with some revenue-generating (and generally useful) new services: they will instead cut themselves off from the sources of data that they need to feed their artificial intelligence engines of the future. They will not be able to do risk analysis or information management of any value absent the vast quantities of information, relationship and reputation data that are needed to feed the voracious appetites of the machine learning behemoths that will be at the heart of the banks of the next generation.

Digital identity should be central to bank strategy in the Metaverse just as it should be central to bank strategy everywhere else.

Case study: Sweden's BankID

In conversations about successful digital ID, the Nordics are inevitably raised as a powerful example of bank-led collaboration. And it is easy to see why. Twenty years on from launch, Sweden's BankID is a key component of the country's digital infrastructure, showcasing cooperation between regulators, banks and other stakeholders. It is the leading digital identity scheme in Sweden, used by four-fifths of the population (and almost all working-age adults) for a wide range of both public and private services, although the overwhelming majority of use cases are private. Statistics show that more than 99% of all Swedish adults between 18 and 65 have a BankID and that those BankIDs are used nearly 7 billion times a year.

Transaction volumes are set to grow further following a 2023 update that also lets people verify their ID in face-to-face settings. Instead of producing their physical passport or driving licence, Swedes who have registered for the new service in the BankID mobile app can present their 'ID-kort' – a virtual card comprising a QR code – to be scanned by (for example) a bar tender for verified proof of age. The instructions to set this up on the company's website are enviably simple: 'You activate the digital ID card by allowing your phone's NFC reader to read the chip embedded in your physical ID document.'*

As with all national ID schemes, some of the dominant factors that contribute to BankID's success are specific to Sweden and cannot be replicated easily elsewhere. For example, many countries have a government-issued digital ID whereas Sweden does not (yet). The lack of a viable alternative undoubtedly worked in BankID's favour and drove uptake for public sector use cases. Conversely, jurisdictions such as the UK and Australia that do not have any form of mandatory government-issued identifier may also struggle to replicate the Swedish scheme's success. This is because the 'personnummer' – a personal identity number issued by the Swedish Tax Agency – is a prerequisite for getting a BankID. Nonetheless, there are two interesting lessons for financial services providers that are considering their role in the future of money and trusted digital infrastructure.

First, trust in banks was foundational to BankID's success. In 2001 Sweden held the presidency of the EU Council and there was a drive to make digital signatures legally binding. Banks were seen as the natural choice to lead the scheme both

---

* As a side note, while this may seem somewhat futuristic compared with current practices in many jurisdictions, it is worth bearing in mind that the Nokia 6131 NFC flip phone could achieve this simple user experience back in 2006.

because they enjoyed a high level of public trust and because, in terms of an existing user base, there were already 2.7 million internet banking customers. The following year, Finansiell ID-Teknik BID AB was formed by a consortium of banks with the aim of owning, operating and developing digital identity infrastructure. The first BankID was issued in 2003, and later that year the country's tax and benefits agencies accepted it for account log-in. Two years later the banks themselves began using it for internet banking authentication, and banks became the largest users of the service following the launch of the mobile app in 2009.

The next significant milestone came in 2012 when Sweden's banks launched the Swish P2P payments service using BankID for authentication. Swish is now used by 7 million people (out of a population of 10 million) and there are around five transactions per customer per month, with an average transaction size slightly above €50. In the words of Sveriges Riksbank (Sweden's central bank), 'Swish is replacing cash' (Sveriges Riksbank 2022c). In order to set up a Swish account, customers must first have a BankID, and it is this link to payments and the important role that digital ID plays in the future of money that presents the second major lesson from Sweden.

In October 2023 the central bank responded to a multi-year government-led Payments Inquiry (Sveriges Riksbank 2023). The inquiry's mandate was to consider the role of government in the payments system, including 'taking a position on the significance and need for certain means of payment to be legal tender' and also on whether there was a need for a central bank digital currency. The trigger for this was the rapidly growing concern that 'the digitalisation of payment may lead to cash not being generally accepted in the future' and that this, 'in turn, may lead to the general public no longer having access to central bank money, which can affect the function and efficiency of the entire payment system'. Avoiding this somewhat bleak future scenario was at the heart of the inquiry and its recommendations. The resulting report, published mid 2023, highlights the critical role that digital ID plays in securing the digital economy, and it called unequivocally for a 'national e-id … with the highest levels of security as soon as possible'.

Sweden's central bank agreed wholeheartedly with the inquiry's finding that there was a need for a government-issued digital ID. Commenting directly about the downside of BankID's dominance, the Riksbank highlights the delicate balance of both power and interests between public and private sector entities: 'The state cannot rely solely on private sector actors for electronic identification, especially in the current situation where one actor dominates a large number of payments and other socially important areas such as identification at the Swedish Social Insurance Agency and the Swedish Tax Agency.' Reading between the lines of the report, which also deals directly with competition in the payments system, you are left with the distinct impression that the e-id that is so urgently needed is also seen as a cornerstone of competition in payments more broadly. This echoes a much more direct statement made by the central bank a year earlier, in its 2022 Payments Report, which also called for a government-issued digital ID: 'Such ID would promote competition in the payments market.'

CHAPTER 4

Web3 and digital assets

So what exactly are the digital assets that can be traded and exchanged in the Metaverse, and how will they be bought and sold? We can begin to explore the possibilities here by going back to the comments of Mark Zuckerberg, who once said that he wants to make sending digital money over the internet as easy as sending pictures of cats.

But it isn't. When you send a picture of a cat you are not really sending the picture itself: you are sending a copy of it. Someone gets a picture of your cat, but you still have the picture of your cat. That's great for sending cat pictures but not very good for sending money. This is because the process of sending money

works on the basis of transfer of ownership, whether it's physical cash moving from Alice's leather wallet to Bob's leather wallet or the digital transfer of funds between their digital wallets.

If bitcoin worked like sending pictures of cats, it would have got off to a very slow start – but it doesn't. The bitcoin blockchain transfers digital assets (i.e. bitcoins and other data such as 'ordinals') from place to place without 'double spending'. If you send a bitcoin from your wallet to a friend's wallet, you are not sending a copy, you are transferring ownership. The blockchain now records it as theirs, not yours, and in this sense the inability to clone objects* means that the blockchain makes virtual reality more like, well, reality.

Ownership and the uniqueness of digital assets has been a focus for operators of virtual worlds since their inception. But as the value of digital items has increased, protection of rights and ownership hasn't kept pace, meaning that the burden of protection has fallen on the operators of the proprietary platforms (Hoppe 2021). What works for siloed platforms, however, will not work in a cross-platform Metaverse, which is where 'tokens' come in. A token is a unique digital representation of an asset – either virtual, such as bitcoin or a unit of certified offset carbon, or physical, such as gold – tied to a record of ownership by economic avatars (that is, identities that can buy and sell such assets).

Tokens are special, because unlike other types of data, *tokens cannot be copied*: they can only be transferred from one owner to another.

Tokens

Taking on board Narula's view that what he calls 'cryptocurrencies and blockchain-style technologies' will be integral to any efforts to build and maintain a bridge for the transfer of value within a metaverse, we need to explore what these technologies will actually be. We agree with his view that they will be

---

* Until such time as the Star Trek replicator shows up in Walmart.

the guarantors of self-interest that will serve to populate the Metaverse with lasting meaning: he is right to say that we are going to have to rely on stakeholders to create meaning within the metaverse, and these parties are going to want to make money in exchange for their work.

He says that, for this to happen, a 'transparent financial instrument, will have to be part of the core Metaverse infrastructure. In our view this instrument is the token. To explain why, let us begin by introducing a simple taxonomy and layered architecture designed to facilitate communication between technologists, businesses and regulators in the financial services world, and then we will explain why the various forms of shared and distributed ledger technologies (including blockchains) might be attractive to financial services organizations. We will base this on the Birch, Brown and Parulava model (Birch *et al.* 2016), updated with the language of the Bank for International Settlements DeFi Stack Reference Model to form our basic framework, as shown in figure 9.

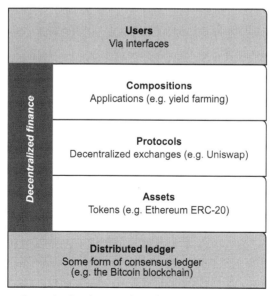

Figure 9. The decentralized finance (DeFi) stack.

What we are interested in here is the use of the shared ledger platform: to support tokens, we need decentralized exchanges and applications that together are labelled decentralized finance. This is the collection of technologies required to turn virtual world assets into Metaverse digital assets.

Tokens took off with the development of the ERC-20 standard back in 2015 because ERC-20 defined a way to create a standard form of token using 'smart contracts' on the Ethereum block-chain. ERC-20 tokens are a kind of data exchanged between these persistent scripts: a practical implementation of digital bearer claims on assets with no clearing or settlement involved in their exchange (and hence a more efficient marketplace for their trading). Decentralized exchanges use protocols based on smart contracts to exchange these tokens between owners.[*]

We must caution here that smart contracts are not really contracts at all, because there is no possibility of uncertainty in their execution and thus no compliance issues. Strictly speaking they are just automaticity created by the consensus-forming process. Vitalik Buterin, the inventor of Ethereum, says as much (see DuPont & Maurer 2015): 'I now regret calling the objects in Ethereum "contracts" as you're meant to think of them as arbitrary programs and not smart contracts specifically.' He later said that 'persistent scripts' might be a better name, and we agree, although neither of us is a marketing maven. As it happens, they are not smart either, because they are of course immutable (as is in the nature of things on blockchains) and therefore cannot learn.

Nonetheless, persistent scripts are useful. For example, if I want to licence some Microsoft software for $100, I tell my smart contract to send tokens for this value to a Microsoft smart contract and the smart contract then creates a permission for me to use the software. Using these tokens it is possible to implement

---

[*] Throughout this book we distinguish between crypto assets, tokens that have no reality beyond the consensus protocols of the ledgers, and digital assets, which are tokens that derive their value by linking to assets in the 'real world'.

the programmable money of the future ('this money cannot be used before 1 January 2029', and so on): the long-envisaged programmable value that people have been thinking about for two decades.

Programmability
Programmability in token exchanges is a fascinating topic. While it is outside the scope of this book, it is nonetheless integral to future transactions strategies. We will take as our reference here a broad version of the MIT Digital Currency Initiative's four-part definition of programmability (George *et al.* 2023) as comprising

1. a well-defined format for the digital storage of value and data;
2. a well-defined, expressive set of programmable instructions for writing programs that access that data and specify the conditions for the movement of that value;
3. an environment in which those programs are executed and enforced that provides some 'coherence guarantee' that the instructions will execute as specified (i.e. the environment must be trusted by the participants); and
4. rules specifying who can create, call and verify the execution of programs.

Taken together it is easy to imagine how, in a metaverse for commodity traders, for example, complicated trades involving multiple tokens (designed to manage risk and reward in complex networks) might be executed efficiently.

These layers of programmability will play an important role in shaping the 'narrow waist' required to enable interoperability and widespread adoption. The narrow waist or 'hourglass' model was popularized by computer scientist David D. Clark, who played a significant role in the design of the internet (Clark 2017). His conceptualization of the hourglass model emphasized the importance of having a narrow waist in network architecture, specifically the Internet Protocol layer, which allows for a wide range of technologies above and below this layer to interoperate efficiently. This model has been critical in enabling the scalability and success of the internet, demonstrating how a simple, standardized layer can support a vast and diverse ecosystem of applications and network technologies – and we think it will be equally important in driving scalability in the more decentralized environment of web3.

Token cusp

We are writing this book in the shadow of the so-called crypto winter: a period of depressed cryptocurrency and cryptoasset trading activity following the well-documented collapses of major crypto players such as Three Arrows Capital and Sam Bankman-Fried's FTX. The impact those collapses had on retail cryptocurrency holders and concern from regulatory bodies regarding the threat to global financial stability has spurred activity to create better regulatory frameworks based on 'same activity, same risk, same regulation' (Financial Stability Board 2022). When this crypto winter has passed and tokens become a regulated but wholly new kind of digital asset – a cross between corporate paper and a loyalty scheme – there will be an opportunity to remake markets in a new and better way.

There is plenty of evidence that we are approaching this cusp. The management consultants McKinsey have pointed to a number of trends that support this view (Banerjee *et al.* 2023).

- Trading of digital assets needs digital *cash*, and there is already some $120 billion in circulation in the form of fully reserved stablecoins (e.g. USD Coin). Banks are experimenting with the tokenization of their reserves.

- Higher interest rates have changed the *economics* around short-term liquidity transactions such as repos and securities lending.

- Emerging *regulatory* frameworks are bringing regulatory clarity for digital assets, and even in the United States market participants are exploring various tokenization and distribution approaches, leveraging existing rules (a short-term patch in our view) by, as an example, limiting distribution of tokenized assets to accredited investors only

- Evolving *infrastructure.* Financial services organizations have been developing digital asset capabilities. The level of understanding of the technology and its promise has grown, and there is more experimentation (often through partnerships) underway, adding to the lessons learned all the time.

The ecosystem is steadily evolving, and there are good reasons for thinking that tokenization will gain traction and generate what McKinsey call 'meaningful' value for global markets over the next two to five years.

Tokens and transparency will see reputations established as an immutable history of participation in transactions, as we will discuss in part II of this book, so that good behaviour cannot be gamed and bad behaviour will be on display. Market participants will be able to assess and manage risk, and regulators will be able to look for patterns and connections. A counterparty will be able to see that your assets exceed your liabilities without necessarily being able to see what those assets or liabilities are.

With this architecture we will find ourselves in an era of 'ambient accountability'. This is because the transparency obtained by using this modern cryptography – such as homomorphic encryption and zero-knowledge proofs – can be used in interesting ways. These technologies open up the possibility of 'translucent transactions', where the technological architecture means constant verification and validation instead of periodic auditing long after the trades and exchanges have taken place. We will return to explore this concept in the specific context of digital currencies later on.

ICOs and origins

One of the first uses of tokens was, indeed, as money. People began to create cryptographic coins of one form or another and these became known as initial coin offerings (ICOs). Billions of dollars flowed into the first generation of ICOs.

A great many of the ICOs came from Zug in Switzerland (often referred to as 'crypto-valley') because the issuers used Swiss foundation law to create the tokens. This was why the opinion of the Swiss Financial Market Supervisory Authority (FINMA) was so important in those early days. It examined all kinds of tokens, not only ICOs, and looked to regulate them as appropriate. In its 2018 guidelines FINMA classified tokens into three categories: securities, utilities and payments. This was a useful way of looking at tokens, and it set the broad outline for how people look at the sector. The US Securities and Exchange Commission (SEC) made a similar distinction, although the SEC chairman Jay Clayton cautioned at the time that neither payment nor utility tokens would have safe harbour if they function as financial securities.*

The ledgers and tokens come together here in a new architecture for financial services. To recapitulate and emphasize the importance of this architecture we would point out that, once digital identities can exchange digital assets with confidence and trust, we have a functioning base layer for a new financial system – a system based on digital bearer instruments that require no clearing or settlement instead of the existing financial system based on electronic currency, accounts and fiat cash.

This more nuanced platform for the digital currency of the future is distinct from the frankly implausible wholly

---

* This is not the place to get sidetracked into a discussion of the ongoing legal disputes and prosecutions that abound at the time of writing. Suffice to say that the issue of whether something is or is not a financial security is beyond the scope of this book.

intermediary-free world of the bitcoin maximalists. A world of tokens is not a world without middlemen, but it could be a world in which the overall total cost of robust and reliable financial intermediation is substantially reduced.

A token taxonomy

As noted earlier, we use a simple taxonomy that divides tokens into two kinds: those with intrinsic value and those with extrinsic value, as shown in figure 10.

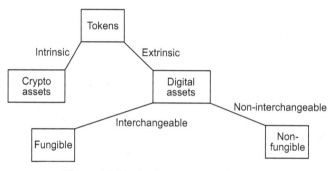

Figure 10. The basic taxonomy of tokens.

As this taxonomy shows, we consider digital assets in two categories: there are *fungible* tokens, such as pound coins, that are substitutable; and then there are *non-fungible* tokens, such as a concert ticket that you might buy with those pound coins, that are unique. These tokens and the DeFi protocols for exchanging them (more on these later) are at the heart of what is loosely termed web3. Frances Zelazny set out the relationship between the two plainly when she wrote that 'the metaverse is dependent on [web3]', and we agree (Zelazny 2022).

When it comes to digital assets, the crucial distinction between fungible and non-fungible tokens is so important that we must divert to it before we move ahead to discuss how tokens will be used in the Metaverse.

Fungibility

Fungible (from the Latin fungi, meaning 'to enjoy', via medieval Latin phrases such as 'fungi vice', meaning 'to take the place of') means that all tokens are the same and can therefore be substituted one for another. Alice owes Bob a quarter. It doesn't matter which quarter that she gives him to discharge the debt. Any quarter will do. Any quarter can substitute for any other quarter because they are all the same; that's how money is designed to work, and we think the same will be true of money in the Metaverse. This isn't true of bitcoins, of course, and it's one of the primary reasons that bitcoin isn't classified as money. Each bitcoin is unique and its history can be tracked through the blockchain, which is, as we are often reminded, an immutable public record of all transactions.

This lack of fungibility has major implications for criminals. In England, the High Court (in the decision of *AA v Persons Unknown & Ors, Re Bitcoin 2019*) has ruled that crypto assets such as bitcoin are considered to be 'property' capable of being the subject of a proprietary injunction against a cryptocurrency exchange. You can see what is going to happen here: the exchange will be required to identify who owns the stolen coins and the owner will then be the subject of legal action to recover them. This owner might have no idea about the origin of the coins and will not unreasonably say that they didn't know that the bitcoins they bought are the proceeds of a ransomware attack and may expect to keep them. That's not how property law works though. Even if you accidentally come into possession of stolen property, a judge can still force you to give it back to its rightful owner.

Laundry bills

In the mundane world of dollar bills we have the concept of 'money laundering' to describe what happens when dirty money is mixed with clean money.* But this doesn't work for bitcoin. The 'tainted' money stays tainted because of the immutable record.

---

* It's almost certain that every one of us has touched banknotes that have been involved in some criminal activity!

The recent takedown of ChipMixer is testament to the difficulty of laundering the dirty transaction history of cryptocurrency (Brewster 2023). ChipMixer charged a fee to clients to spread their cryptocurrency across different accounts, with the sole purpose of doing so being to complicate the law enforcement process. Analysis of the $3 billion worth of transactions that were processed found that close to a billion dollars had been involved in criminal activity.

We could well see a strange and interesting twist in the world of cryptocurrency that has no equivalent in the analogue world of notes and coins: black and white money, or clean and dirty money (an idea that goes back to the earliest days of cryptocurrency), in which some bitcoins will be worth more than others! Maybe a few years from now exchanges will be quoted two BTC–USD pairs: clean BTC at $100,000 and dirty BTC at $75,000. This doesn't happen for GBP–USD or JPY–EUR, which further underpins the point that, whatever bitcoin is, it isn't money.

In fact, if we develop a basic taxonomy of digital assets from figure 11, it leads us rather neatly into an organizing model: fungible tokens that can be used as money and non-fungible tokens that can be used as property. As we will see later, this is a categorization for the Metaverse, because digital assets are themselves a new form of property in the universe!

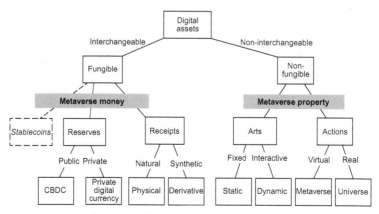

Figure 11. A basic digital asset taxonomy.

This is not the place for a detailed treatise on the future of fungible and non-fungible tokens, but it is worth taking a detour here to understand why their different behaviours are important and why it is that they make for a viable infrastructure.

Fungible Metaverse money

If we take the basic digital asset taxonomy set out in figure 11 and drive it down another level on the fungible side of things, we find ourselves looking at money from central banks (central bank digital currencies) and, more generally, at the world of 'stablecoins'.

Stablecoins

The wild and unpredictable historic oscillations in the prices of cryptocurrencies made them unsuitable for use as a medium of exchange, so people began to look at the idea of stablecoins that would have more predictable values. We think these have an important role to play in future commerce of all kinds, so we need to look into them in a little more detail.

To start with, we must first be clear on what a stablecoin actually is, because the word as used colloquially in fact refers to a number of different financial instruments, each with different characteristics. The basic split is between stablecoins based on algorithms and stablecoins based on assets, which may be money or some other suitable commodity. For the purposes of informed discussion, that means there are three different kinds of stablecoin, each of which might need to be approached in a different way. Figure 12 extends our earlier taxonomy for the purposes of this discussion.

This taxonomy gives us, essentially, three different kinds of fungible money to use in our metaverses: algorithmic stablecoins and stablecoins based on private assets or public assets.

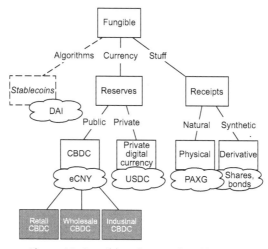

Figure 12. Fungible tokens and stablecoins.

Algorithmic stablecoins

First there are algorithmic stablecoins, such as the infamous Terra. These attempt to maintain their value against an external unit of account (e.g. the US dollar) by buying or selling assets. Terra isn't the only one of these to have found it difficult to maintain their pegs when under pressure. An algorithmic stablecoin called Iron collapsed before Terra did, costing investors a cool $2 billion when, according to the anonymous team behind Iron, it suffered a 'large-scale crypto bank run' (Osipovich 2022).

In fact, the idea of a cryptocurrency that has its value stabilized by algorithms is where the term 'stablecoin' originated. In practice, however, it has proved difficult for such algorithms to maintain stability in the face of external shocks. Attention has therefore shifted away from this mechanism, and the concept of stablecoins has been extended to digital currencies that have their value pegged to something external to their ledgers (as distinct from cryptocurrencies that have no value beyond their ledgers).

Asset stablecoins
Such 'asset-backed' stablecoins emerged early in the evolution of the space because market participants found it difficult to manage and minimize transaction costs with volatile means of exchange. It is important to note, however, that not all such assets were actually stable. The death spiral of the Terra stablecoin was a consequence of the economic model used that was widely anticipated by a great many well-informed industry observers, including the respected commentator Frances Coppola (who had been mocked by the Terra founder Do Kwon for being 'poor' when she suggested that the Terra model might not be sustainable in the long run) (see Birch 2022).

Then there are stablecoins that are receipts for some fungible commodity such as gold or for some other asset with independent value that can be traded: a square foot of office space in a particular building, say, or a square inch of the Mona Lisa, or a square mile of Wyoming ranch land. These are stable against the commodity but not necessarily against fiat currencies. A token that is one ounce of gold always has the same value in gold but not in dollars, since the value of gold varies against dollars.

Private. Then there are asset-backed stablecoins that have a reserve in fiat currency or high-quality liquid assets. These are what used to be called 'currency boards' before the term stablecoin was extended. When most people talk colloquially about stablecoins it is these fiat-backed tokens that they are thinking about. These are where we are going. As Coppola has noted, research shows that the only type of stablecoin that can guarantee to hold its fiat currency peg under all conditions (and therefore be actually stable) is one that is fully backed by hard dollars in the manner of a currency board (Coppola 2022).[*]

The dominant actually stable stablecoins are backed by US dollars – at the time of writing, the top three (with a combined

---

[*] By contrast, the stablecoins backed by algorithms cannot be guaranteed under all conditions and even those stablecoins that are over-collateralized in risky assets such as cryptocurrency cannot be guaranteed to hold their pegs under all conditions.

'market cap' of some $140 billion) were Tether, USD Coin and Binance USD – and there are many, many other stablecoins of various kinds out there. Circle has also launched a Euro stablecoin and Tether has just launched a Mexican peso stablecoin, and we are sure others will follow, but for the foreseeable future the dollar will dominate because the fact is that most people around the world still want to hold dollars, given that the dollar is the global reserve currency, while few people have a desire to hold yuan (and no one wants to hold, for example, rubles).

Public. Finally, there are stablecoins issued by central banks: the central bank digital currencies about which there is much discussion at present, not only in terms of national strategies for next-generation financial services but because the war in Ukraine and the consequent sanctions applied by the West have once again raised the issue of the US dollar's global dominance and the extent to which this benefits America both financially, because of the increased demand for dollars, and politically. The historian Niall Ferguson, a thorough scholar of the history of money, has described the soft power obtained through the dollar's dominance as being 'more valuable than boots on the ground'.[*]

Many observers think that China must be looking at the West's use of currency as a weapon against Russia with some alarm. Indeed, Benjamin Cohen, a veteran academic of international monetary relations, says that there is 'no question' that sanctions against Russia will further incentivize countries such as Iran, North Korea and Venezuela to diversify away from the dollar (Lockett & Kinder 2022).

Barry Eichengreen (professor of economics and political science at the University of California, Berkeley) has also written about this (Eichengreen 2022), pointing out that while the share of dollars in global identified foreign exchange reserves has been falling for a generation (it is now under 60% when it used

---

[*] If you are interested, Dave discussed this perspective in some detail in his 2020 book, *The Currency Cold War*.

to be over 70%), diversification has not been towards the euro, sterling and yen (the other long-standing constituents of the International Monetary Fund's special drawing rights basket). In fact, while a quarter of the shift has been towards China's renminbi, three-quarters has been into the currencies of smaller economies such as those of Canada, Australia, Sweden, South Korea and Singapore. All of these seem to me to be worthwhile candidates for their own stablecoins, perhaps with different (and competing) characteristics.

The point is that not all stablecoins are the same. In fact, dollar stablecoins seem to have performed as safe-haven assets during market turmoil, thus proving to be more trusted than cryptocurrencies, and they will surely perform the same role in the Metaverse.

Stable demand

Whether we are talking about US dollars or Canadian dollars or Singapore dollars, there is an evident market demand for stable-coins – if there was not, they would not exist. Professor Eswar Prasad, writing on the future of money, said that 'bitcoin, the cryptocurrency that started it all, may not have much of a role to play in this monetary future', because stablecoins of one form or another might well be more desirable to the average person than volatile tokens for speculators (Prasad 2022). He also suggested that, rather than leading to a proliferation of public and private currencies that compete on a level playing field, the emergence of digital currency could make economic power more concentrated than ever. If the currencies mentioned above are made available to citizens around the world, they might very well displace the currencies of many other nations. Similarly, the digital currencies issued by multinational corporations might replace weak fiat currencies by exploiting their ecosystems. In our view, these two scenarios are equally likely.

There is clearly a need, therefore, for proper regulation of stablecoins. Caveat emptor is not a solution. Jeremy Allaire, who founded Circle, the company behind the USDC stablecoin, put it this way (Pimentel 2022):

> I do not think it's sincere or high integrity for leaders to just say, 'Well, everyone knew the risks', because there were promoters and I think fairly intelligent people who indulged in this. Frankly, I'm very disappointed in a lot of people.

He is spot on here, and he is far from being the only power player that thinks this way. Reporting from Davos, Huw van Steenis, co-chair of the Global Future Council on Responsive Financial Systems at the World Economic Forum, wrote that he met a number of 'giants of the payment world' who said that the largest stablecoins are now not only hoping for regulation but actually arguing for such behind the scenes (van Steenis 2022).

So if stablecoins should be regulated, then what might that regulation look like? If you are talking about asset-backed stablecoins, then we would argue that a light touch is appropriate. As Morgan Ricks, a Vanderbilt Law School professor and former Treasury official, rather notably said (see Greeley 2022): 'There's nothing inherently dodgy about stablecoins, but there is something inherently dodgy about banking, which is why countries build elaborate regulatory regimes to protect deposits.' This is why banking regulations have to be rigorous (and expensive), but stablecoin regulations need not be, because stablecoin issuers do not create money as banks do. So long as the stablecoin issuers hold their reserves in safe assets, there is no problem.

The safest of all assets for a fiat stablecoin is central bank reserves. The fourth report in the IESE Business School's *The Future of Banking* series explored and reinforced the need for regulation around stablecoins, and it highlighted the key issue of whether non-banks should have access to central bank accounts (Duffie *et al.* 2022). This is an issue because, if a digital currency is to be a substitute for commercial bank deposits, then non-bank issuers must commit to guarantee the one-for-one convertibility with public money. The lack of access to central bank accounts and liquidity facility services complicates such a commitment, which threatens to jeopardize the stability of such alternatives.

Christopher Waller, à member of the Board of Governors of the Federal Reserve System, made a speech at the American Enterprise Institute in Washington DC in 2021 saying that he was sceptical that a Federal Reserve CBDC 'would solve any major problem confronting the US payment system'. He went on to note that appropriately regulated private sector stablecoins could be used to satisfy the demands of the DeFi sector for money that can be algorithmically traded for cryptographic assets. At the 2021 Financial Stability Conference, co-hosted by the Federal Reserve Bank of Cleveland, he also said: 'I disagree with the notion that stablecoin issuance can or should only be conducted by banks, simply because of the nature of the liability.' He then went on to talk about private sector innovation outside the banking sector, saying that it should be given a chance to compete 'on a clear and level playing field'. Interesting.[*]

Light touch
For what it's worth, we agree with both Professor Ricks and Governor Waller. There is no need to regulate stablecoin issuers as if they were banks (because they will not provide credit); instead they should be regulated in something like the way that the existing European electronic money regime works. This seems adequate for fiat stablecoins and, indeed, this is what the UK intends to do. The definition of 'electronic money' under the Electronic Money Regulations 2011 will be extended to include fiat-linked stablecoins, with the additional recognition that the holder of a stablecoin may not always have a relationship with

---

[*] It appears that recent proposals from legislators and regulators have shifted attention away from turning stablecoin issuers into insured depository institutions (which was one recommendation made by the President's Working Group on Financial Markets back in November 2021) and towards this lighter and more open approach.

the issuer. The holder's relationship may instead be with a third party (such as an exchange or wallet provider).

Federal Reserve Vice Chair Lael Brainard told the House Financial Services Committee that a 'CBDC could coexist with and be complementary to stablecoins and commercial bank money by providing a safe central bank liability in the digital financial ecosystem, much like cash currently coexists with commercial bank money'.

This is actually what we have today in some environments. When I go to Starbucks, for example, I have a choice between paying with cash (central bank money), with my debit card (commercial bank money) or with my Starbucks card (private money), and the system seems to work pretty well. I therefore think that Brainard is right to predict a similar mix for the short term, but in the longer term we are not so sure, because the need for value that can move between a panoply of metaverses will drive more (and more kinds of) stablecoins.

Non-fungible metaverse property

As already noted, the difference between fungible and non-fungible tokens is central to understanding the digital assets that are at the heart of the Metaverse. An interesting way to explore the difference between the two categories is to look at the work of the American artist James Stephen George Boggs. Mr Boggs is sadly no longer with us – he was taken to meet his maker back in 2017, at the age of 62 – but he has a small but important role in the history and future of money. Given the excitement around fungible tokens used for money, the non-fungible tokens (NFTs) we are about to discuss, and the general future of art and money in the Metaverse, here is a good place to look at Boggs's part in the story of money and reflect on the relationship between art and money.

Boggs entered the public consciousness for his drawings of banknotes. He began creating these drawings in 1984 when he drew a dollar bill and used it to pay in a restaurant. It was accepted at par, and a new chapter in the story of money was written.

Tokens and transactions

Here's how it all worked, as set out in his obituary in *The Economist*. Boggs would go somewhere and choose some goods or services and offer to pay for them with a drawing of a banknote. If the drawing was accepted, he would write the time and place on the back of the banknote, collect his change and the receipt, and complete the transaction. He would then sell the receipt to collectors. These collectors would use the receipt to find and obtain the banknote, and the receipt, the change and the banknote he had drawn were, taken together, like a token on a blockchain. They formed a proof of the banknote's value, confirmed by the transaction details as recorded. The banknote by itself was undeniably art. But the *tuple* of the banknote, the receipt and the change were something more than art.

Why? Well, as Steve Kaczynski and Scott Duke Kominers explained in a very good piece about NFTs for the *Harvard Business Review*, markets cannot operate without clear property rights: before someone can buy a good, it has to be clear who has the right to sell it; and once a buyer comes along, there must be a mechanism to transfer ownership from the seller to the buyer (Kaczynski & Kominers 2021). NFTs solve this problem by providing the mechanism to establish and transfer ownership in a decentralized manner.

This is actually a pretty radical step in the history of stuff, and the noted venture capitalist Andreessen Horowitz has provided a succinct explanation as to why this is the case (Rivera 2021). It begins by noting that fungible (i.e. interchangeable) and non-fungible (i.e. unique) tokens fill different niches.

Money is fungible, so, as we have seen, fungible tokens will be used for digital currencies (this is one of the reasons why bitcoin, whatever it is, isn't money) whereas non-fungible ones will be used to create a wide range of what Horowitz's firm a16z calls 'internet-native' business models centred on collectibles, rewards and achievements that deliver a sense of identity, status and belonging. And despite the fact that the initial NFT market was based on people selling pictures of chimpanzees with sunglasses on to each other for millions of dollars, there are many people (including the authors of this book) who think that NFTs will turn into a very serious business indeed.

One reason we think so is because, as Kaczynski and Kominers point out, the programmability discussed earlier means that NFTs can deliver utility both in digital spaces and in the physical world, which we find a very interesting characteristic with widespread applicability.

Tickets and transfers

A good example of this utility is event ticketing. Event tickets are unique and should not be cloneable or counterfeitable. They should belong to one and only one owner, and they should be able to be transferred between owners. NFTs are the perfect way to implement them, and this is something that we have ourselves tried.

We thought it rather interesting that Ethereum inventor Vitalik Buterin recently used this precise example to highlight his ideas about designing better markets to achieve fairness or 'community sentiment' – or, even better, 'fun' (Buterin 2021). But if event ticketing seems a little prosaic, there are even more interesting tokenization ideas out there. For example, there's the case of Alex Masmej, the 23-year old who tokenized himself. He created the $ALEX token, which would receive 15% of his income for the three years after the token was created. Token owners would be able to cash them in for Alex-specific fun. For instance, he will retweet you for 10,000 $ALEX. For only 20,000 $ALEX you can have a conversation with him. If you want an introduction to someone in his network, it's a whopping $30,000 $ALEX.

Rex Woodbury made a very important point about this at the time (Woodbury 2021). Talking about the shift in the generational perspectives on finance he said that if we expand 'everyone is an investor' to 'everyone is an owner', we then see what he called 'ripple effects' in the record-breaking 4.4 million businesses started in 2020, or in the 68 million Americans who freelance. As he asked, with some prescience, what if Taylor Swift had issued a token of herself before 'Kanye interrupted her onstage at the VMAs'?

Godfather

Boggs went on drawing banknotes to pay for stuff for many years. He had a golden rule, though. He would not exchange his bills for anything other than their 'face value', despite the fact that they resold for multiples of their face value. One of his bills sold for more than $400,000, and that was back when $400,000 was a lot of money.[*]

What especially fascinates is his battle with the US Secret Service. In America the Secret Service is charged with defending the integrity of the currency, so, naturally, they were not too happy with him. Boggs had to hire lawyers and he paid them with his drawings of bills. This led to what Jim Holt called the 'long comic project' of a legal battle between protagonists who were both able to fund their own challenges by literally creating their own money (Holt 1999).

What does the Boggs story tell us? Well, dollar bills are fungible and are therefore money. Bitcoins are not fungible and are therefore not money. The dollar bills that Boggs drew were not fungible and therefore they weren't money either. They could, however, perform a money-like function in certain circumstances. This helps us to understand more about both

---

[*] In England he was famously arrested and hauled before a judge to answer charges of forgery, but the jury loved his work and found him not guilty of all charges, presumably because no sane person would actually mistake a Boggs drawing of a fiver for one of the Old Lady's originals.

fungible and non-fungible tokens and the future of money in the Metaverse.

By the way, for this great service to the crypto community we think Boggs deserves to be remembered as a godfather of NFTs (Birch 2021).

Not your keys, not your Kings of Leon

With Mr Boggs to frame our thinking, let us now dive into the world of NFTs. You will probably remember your puzzled feelings when you first heard about them, bursting into the public imagination from the world of 'art'. Typical of the time was the anonymous guild of 'art digitalists' who bought an original Banksy and then set it on fire after digitizing the piece into an NFT (Wintermeyer 2021). The token eventually sold for $400,000 (although you can still have a copy of the artwork to use as your desktop background for approximately $0).

You may consider this more a piece of performance art* than a window into a new world that decentralizes Sotheby's out of existence, but it is undeniably interesting. Interesting because, putting trivially copyable artworks to one side, NFTs will indeed mean radically more efficient markets.

To see why, let us first remind ourselves of how tokens developed. Although tokens are not specific to Ethereum, they took off with the development of the ERC-20 standard back in 2015. ERC-20 defined a way to create a standard form of token using consensus applications on the Ethereum blockchain. ERC-20 tokens are simply structured data exchanged between these applications: a practical implementation of digital bearer claims on assets with no clearing or settlement involved in their exchange (making the marketplace for their trading more

---

* The author Bruce Sterling referred to it on Twitter as having a Paolo Cirio 'conceptual hacktivist feeling'.

efficient), thus creating a means to make the transfer of fungible value secure without a central authority.

As noted earlier, fungibility is a critical defining characteristic of money. All of the dollars in the world are the same, and any dollar can substitute for any other dollar. But all of the bitcoins in the world are not the same. They are non-fungible.

Similarly, a stalls ticket to see Hawkwind play at the London Palladium is not fungible. Each such ticket is unique. But if Alice wants to go and see Hawkwind, how does Alice know that her ticket is valid? How does the venue or the band or the purchaser on a secondary market? Right now there are event promoters, ticketing agencies, credit card acquirers, databases and barcodes to try to figure that out. But if Bob was a bad boy and sold his ticket to Alice and to someone else, and they both show up to watch the band, neither the venue nor the band nor other fans nor anyone else can tell which barcode is authentic and which is a copy. But what if the ticket isn't a barcode and is instead a non-fungible digital asset stored in my digital wallet?

Non-fungible fun

Non-fungible digital assets are a lot of fun, and virtual world markets for them existed before bitcoin, before the blockchain and before enterprise shared ledgers. Consider the obvious example of people playing massively multiplayer games such as World of Warcraft and the like. People buy and sell digital assets all the time. If Alice wants a magic sword or a laser cannon or a nicer hat for her avatar, she can buy it with real money. If you could copy magic swords to infinity, then they would have no value. So the number of magic swords is limited, and thus a market arises. So who says who the magic sword belongs to? If I pay you some real dollars for a non-existent virtual sword, who transfers the title for that sword? In the case of virtual games, it is obvious: it is Blizzard or CCP Games or whoever else is in the middle, running the game.

However, the technology of tokens means that Alice can now sell Bob the magic sword without having anyone in the middle. On Ethereum, for example, there are now a number of different ERC non-fungible token standards, the most notable being ERC-721, which defines non-fungible digital assets. ERC-721 hit the headlines (well, for people like us anyway) in 2017, when Crypto-Kitties took off. This is a game on Ethereum that allows players to purchase, collect, breed and sell virtual cats, and it became so popular that it caused so much congestion on the Ethereum network that it slowed down significantly.

Tokens mean that we can now exchange unique digital assets in a fully decentralized manner. These digital assets will very often be a means for controlling things in the real world without having anyone in the middle either. Since tokens might be a way to solve the 'ID for the internet of things' problem, they might also provide a means to link objects in the Metaverse to mundane objects. There will be more on this later, but for now, suffice to say that tokens deliver a virtual representation of things in the mundane that – as with their physical counterparts – cannot be duplicated. If we can link the digital asset of a Rolex watch to a physical Rolex watch, we can do some very interesting things.

The opportunities for new and disruptive businesses here are real and substantial. Here's an example, continuing the musical theme. A band is going to play a concert. There are 10,000 seats in the venue and 100,000 members of their fan club, so the band distributes the tickets to randomly chosen members of the fan club, who pay $50 each for them (this is all managed through smart contracts). And that's it. Now, the members of the fan club can decide whether to go to the concert, whether to buy some more tickets for friends, whether to give their ticket to charity or whatever. They could also put their tickets up for sale on eBay and the market will then clear itself. The tickets cannot be counterfeited or copied for the same reason that a bitcoin cannot be counterfeited or copied: each of these cryptographic assets belongs to only one cryptographic key ('wallet') at one time, and whoever has control of that key has control of the ticket.

For art's sake

An early experiment in this field came from the American popular beat combo Kings of Leon. The launch of one of their albums was accompanied by three different kinds of tokens: one included a special album package; one offered front-row seats for life at the band's concerts; and a third included exclusive audiovisual art (Beaumont 2021). We can see why fans might buy these, but we can also see why speculators might buy them: anyone might be tempted to part with a considerable sum of money for a lifetime front-row seat to the concerts of their favourite band, especially if they could simply and safely lend or trade those seats away at any time.

This is a really interesting experiment, and if you think that tokens (fungible or not) are going to be the basis of new financial markets, as we do, you should take a look at what's going on in the creative sector. Here, people are bringing art and money together in a way that Oscar Wilde could never have imagined when he famously said: 'When bankers get together for dinner, they discuss art. When artists get together for dinner, they discuss money.'

Brands and bits

Despite all of the nonsense surrounding NFTs and the 2021 collapse of the NFTs 'bubble', there is already real business there. The top ten NFT revenue-generating brands for 2022 are shown in table 4. As you can see, the list is dominated by Nike, which generated far more than all other top performers added together!

Table 4. Brand NFT revenues 2022.
(*Source*: Dune Analytics, August 2023.)

Brand	NFT revenue ($m)
Nike	185
Dolce & Gabbana	26
Tiffany	13
Gucci	12
Adidas	11
Budweiser	6
Time Magazine	5
Bud Light	4
Ao	2
Lacoste	1

Understanding decentralized finance

Digital assets that are bound to 'real world' value by regulated institutions present not only the mechanism for a *different* financial sector but an innovative approach to a *better* financial sector. This is not a technologist's perspective but the perspective of the financial markets. As Denis Beau, first deputy governor of the Banque de France, commented on overcoming inefficiencies in the sector, tokenization could be a way to 'answer the market's demands' (Beau 2023). Similarly, when he was chairman of the US Securities and Exchange Commission, Jay Clayton commented that 'everything will be tokenized', and the obvious corollary to this is that everything will be decentralized.

The view that tokens are the building blocks for the next generation of financial services has also been clearly set out by Fabian Schär in the *Federal Reserve Bank of St. Louis Review*. Schär explored the evolution of markets based on tokens that sit on shared ledgers of one form or another (Schär 2021). The trading of these tokens would be interesting enough in the existing market infrastructures, but this is not where we are going. We are heading into the decentralized finance era: an explosion of business models, institutional arrangements and transaction complexity that, when it settles, will leave us in a new financial world! As Schär's paper concludes, this protocol-based approach may contribute to a more robust and transparent financial infrastructure.

Decentralized finance

Decentralized finance, or 'DeFi', protocols are the new class of financial platforms powered by shared ledgers of one form or another and the tokens that sit on those platforms. These protocols eliminate the need for traditional intermediaries and give users direct access to financial products and services. Overall, the evolution of DeFi protocols will create a shift in the financial landscape, paving the way for a more transparent, accessible and autonomous financial system.

A spectrum of such services is available, including lending and borrowing platforms, trading platforms, insurance protocols and more. Notable examples include Uniswap, which is a decentralized exchange that facilitates peer-to-peer cryptocurrency trading using automated market maker technology.[*]

Yearn Finance, another DeFi protocol operating on Ethereum, offers users yield farming techniques to maximize investment returns. By automatically allocating user funds to the most lucrative opportunities, Yearn Finance streamlines the process and enhances users' returns.

---

[*] With around $120 million in trade volume as of April 2023, Uniswap stands as one of the most widely utilized DeFi protocols.

There are also decentralized insurance protocols, such as Nexus Mutual, which simplify the buying and selling of insurance policies, providing transparent and easily accessible insurance solutions as an alternative to traditional insurance companies.

Another significant DeFi protocol is Compound, which enables users to lend and borrow digital currencies through smart contracts on Ethereum. Interest rates fluctuate based on supply and demand dynamics within the platform.

An example: Compound

Let us use Compound as an example to show how these protocols work in practice. The functions provided by the protocol are as follows.

1. *Asset deposits.* Users can deposit supported cryptocurrency assets (such as ETH, DAI, USDC) into the Compound protocol. Each asset has its own interest rate, determined by supply and demand.
2. *Interest rates.* The interest rates for borrowing and lending are dynamic and are determined by the protocol based on the available supply and demand of each asset. If a particular asset has a high demand for borrowing, its interest rate will increase.
3. *Borrowing.* Users can borrow cryptocurrency assets by using their deposited assets as collateral. The maximum borrowing limit is determined by the collateral ratio, which is typically below 100% to mitigate the risk of default.
4. *Collateralization.* Borrowers need to maintain a sufficient ratio of collateral to their loan to avoid liquidation. If the value of their collateral falls below a set threshold, their collateral may be liquidated to repay the loan.
5. *Distribution of interest.* Users who deposit their assets earn interest in real time, which is automatically distributed to

their accounts. The interest earned can be withdrawn at any time.

6. *Governance.* Compound includes an ERC-20 governance token called COMP. Token holders can vote on proposals to make changes to the protocol, such as adding new assets or adjusting interest rates.

7. *Liquidity providers.* Market participants called liquidity providers can earn fees by supplying liquidity to the Compound protocol. They deposit assets into the protocol and receive cTokens (Compound's native interest-bearing tokens) in return. These cTokens represent their share of the deposited assets and earn interest over time.

8. *Redeeming assets.* Users can redeem their assets from the protocol by exchanging their cTokens back for the underlying assets. The redemption process withdraws the assets, along with the accrued interest, back into the user's wallet.

Using these functions, the Compound protocol provides a decentralized means for users to both lend and borrow cryptocurrency assets with transparent and automated interest rate mechanisms. At the time of writing, the protocol had some $1.2 billion total value locked.

The digital asset future

We will close this section with a model of digital objects for the Metaverse that are implemented as tokens, as shown in figure 13. We are interested in the tokens that are fungible to use as money and the non-fungible assets to use as property that can be exchanged for money, together with the decentralized finance protocols that are used to trade those tokens. When it comes to applications, while we may not be smart enough to pick the winners, we are smart enough to see that the uses of tokens in the Metaverse are manifold.

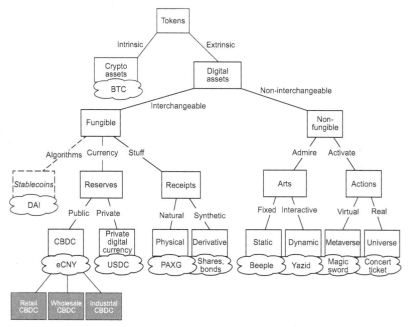

Figure 13. A full token taxonomy.

This taxonomy is sufficient to facilitate strategic discussion about both the building blocks of next generation business in the Metaverse and the financial services that will emerge.

Case study: Nike

In a bold move that set Nike apart from other brands venturing into the NFT realm, the sportswear giant acquired RTFKT: an influential creator-led brand with a strong presence in the NFT space. This gave Nike a strong position in the web3 universe, and it meant that the company could kickstart the brand's entry into the rapidly changing world of tokens and trading. The acquisition led to a fascinating fusion of physical assets with digital NFTs.

Nike launched the .SWOOSH brand for virtual apparel at the end of 2022, and in the spring of 2023 the company's first collection under the new label was launched: the Our Force 1 (OF1) Polygon virtual sneaker NFTs, designed to pay tribute to the iconic Nike Air Force 1. Nike sold $1.4 million worth of the digital shoes despite some technical problems with the launch.

Nike's motivation for developing .SWOOSH echoes Narula's sentiment that the Metaverse has the potential to be more immersive and fulfilling: 'Sports and culture are changing, so we want to build a future that's creative, inclusive, and brimming with unlimited possibilities. As more fans find new ways to express themselves in the games and social platforms they love, we'd love to invite more of our Nike community to help co-create these products alongside us.'

In mid 2023 Nike announced a partnership with EA that will bring select virtual assets created by .Swoosh to future EA Sports titles. Around the same time, Nike also teamed up with Epic games to create Airphoria: a themed game world in Fortnite. Players of Airphoria were able to purchase outfits for their avatars in the Fortnite Item Shop, and gamers who linked their Fortnite account to .SWOOSH gained access to limited edition virtual outfits created by Nike. In parallel, Nike made an Airphoria themed line of apparel available for purchase on their US website.

The benefits of aligning virtual and physical worlds was evident in .SWOOSHs community update in January 2024 (dotSWOOSH 2024): 'We're going to double-down this next year on more exclusive physical product – both in footwear and apparel – for those in our .SWOOSH community who buy our in-game wearables or digital collectibles.'

We can see one way that this may be heading if we pull together ideas from the industrial metaverse, 3D printing and virtual worlds. It is very plausible that when the cost of 3D printers is sufficiently low, people will select perfectly sized shoes on .SWOOSH and the eco-friendly materials needed to print them will be sent directly to the customer by Nike for home printing (Keane 2023). With Nike already promising that members of .SWOOSH will have the opportunity to create their own collections and receive royalties from their sales, it seems likely that the traditional design, manufacturing and distribution model could also change.

The ownership model for digital assets is also set to change. In the same .SWOOSH update, Nike acknowledges 'how important it is for you to have control of your digital collectibles and so in the second half of this year, we'll be allowing you to off-ramp your collectibles to your own wallet'. The company's clearly stated intention is to ensure that 'all creators benefit financially for the contribution of their art'.* Interestingly, Nike also makes it clear that they have no plans to run their own marketplace. Helpfully for the wider ecosystem, this will drive interoperability between creators, gaming platforms and market places.

---

* Nike will pay royalties to creators. See www.coindesk.com/web3/2023/04/17/nike-is-releasing-its-first-digital-sneaker-collection-on-swoosh/.

PART II

THE BUILDING BLOCKS

If we take the three core components of the metaverse identified above – that is, markets in virtual worlds, web3 assets and digital identity – we can assemble them to create a basic model of Metaverse transactions. As shown in figure 14 overleaf, the model immediately shows us the key building blocks that need to be in place in a useful metaverse: digital objects that can be traded using web3, identifiers that can control the trading of those objects, and credentials that enable the trading to take place in virtual worlds.

We already discussed the tools and techniques needed to implement these building blocks in part I. We have private keys and digital signatures and computers and all of the other necessary components. We already have smartphones that contain trusted execution environments capable of handling advanced cryptography. What we need is a way of deploying this strong security in a way that enhances privacy, which is where credentials come into play.

Let us now discuss how to turn those technologies into practical building blocks for a Metaverse suitable for work and play.

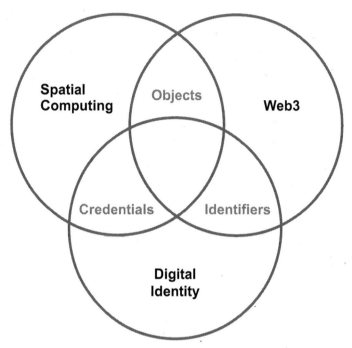

Figure 14. The key metaverse technologies.

CHAPTER 5

Digital objects

We looked at how digital assets can be implemented using tokens in part I of the book, and we established that digital assets are tokens that can be owned and exchanged but not copied. Now let us explore what these digital assets can be used for more generally, and let us introduce the wider concept of digital objects (which may or may not be assets) for the Metaverse.

What is 'crypto'?

Lee Reiners, the executive director of the Global Financial Markets Center at Duke Law School, has a firm line on digital financial

services. He is a former regulator and is of the general opinion that the crypto boom of recent memory had more to do with loose Federal Reserve monetary policy than with the inherent characteristics of such assets (Dogecoin, say, or CryptoDickButt #666). In fact, he thinks that crypto should be banned (Kozhipatt 2022).

He may well be right – we are not qualified to comment – but if we are going to ban it, we should probably work out exactly what 'crypto' is as a precursor to working out which digital assets should or should not become digital objects for trading in the Metaverse.

This step is necessary because we should be wary of using the very general term 'crypto' given the wide spectrum of instruments it has come to encapsulate (e.g. bitcoin, stablecoins, NFTs, DeFi, L2s and so on). If we're not precise here, the word 'crypto' will become less meaningful to the point at which it may in fact subvert discussion and undermine understanding of the whole topic. While we may be few against many, we will continue to distinguish between cryptocurrency and tokenized assets of one form or another, whether they are traded in a centralized market or a decentralized one.

We therefore undertake to try not to use the word crypto for these new kinds of digital asset. Instead we will stick to a clear taxonomy, based on previous work and on the Bank for International Settlements Cryptoasset Taxonomy. We will therefore distinguish between cryptocurrency (or 'unstablecoins' that are not pegged to any external asset or any kind) and digital assets (bearer instruments, exchanged without clearing and settlement). These digital assets can be divided into two basic categories that we can label

- stablecoins when they are backed by reserves of fiat currency and
- something else yet to be determined (we'll come back to this shortly) when it means tokens that are backed by real-world assets.

We will continue to use the word crypto in another context, however. The lawyer Charles Kerrigan wrote a fine article setting out that 'crypto isn't a what, it's a how – a way of doing things' (Kerrigan 2022). We think that's a really good take. So from now on, we will only use the general word crypto when we mean a way to exchange both fungible and non-fungible tokens directly and in a decentralized manner (i.e. in DeFi). But let's turn back to the problem of what to call these tokens: tokens that are some sort of digital asset that is kind of new and of which stablecoins are a specific subset. How should we begin thinking about them?

Perhaps the place to start is by observing that a useful Metaverse is one in which the rule of property holds, so that if you own something, it's yours. The advocates of digital property rights see computer code as being the virtual-world equivalent of the courts, contracts and correction facilities in the real world. Hence the mantra 'code is law' and the idea that the Metaverse can turn 'digital serfs into homesteaders', as Andreessen Horowitz put it (Harkavy et al. 2022).

This is an appealing perspective, given a legal framework rooted in another age, and it has been brought into sharp relief by the collision between NFTs and intellectual property law. Current copyright and trademark laws predate these kinds of digital asset by some years, which means that it's up to the courts to adjudicate disputes pursuant to existing laws until revised federal statutes are enacted. Well yes, but what might these revised statutes look like?

Proper property

The Law Society of England and Wales had a consultation concerning such matters. It noted that while the law[*] has to some extent been able to accommodate these new digital assets as objects of property rights, certain aspects of the law now need

---

[*] They mean the law of England and Wales, of course, not the concept of law in general.

reform to ensure that digital assets benefit from what the society terms 'consistent legal recognition and protection'.

The consultation observed that the law as it stands recognizes two different kinds of property. The first is 'things in possession', which means, broadly speaking, assets that are tangible, moveable and visible, such as a bicycle or a gold bar. The second is 'things in action', which means property that can only be claimed or enforced through legal action or proceedings, such as debt or shares in a company. The Law Society proposes adding a third category to allow for what they call new, emergent and idiosyncratic objects of property rights. We might be tempted (as you will see in part IV of this book) to label this category 'things in wallets', but the Law Society chose the more generic 'data objects'.

The reason for wanting to use the 'things in wallets' label is because it has connotations of personal control. Indeed, the lawyers say that in the case of these digital objects the factual concept of control (as opposed to the concept of possession) best describes 'the relationship between data objects and persons' – which is their way of saying 'not your keys, not your coins'.*

When it comes to the assets themselves, the Law Society says that the law should 'recognise and give effect' to the freedom of commercial parties to devise bespoke contractual arrangements. This includes systems in which the holder of a given token is regarded as having legal title to whatever it is that is somehow linked to the token. However, being lawyers, that is the beginning of the story rather than the end. They go on to say that holding a token should not necessarily be regarded as a 'definitive record of (superior) legal title' to the token. Or, in other words, code is not law.† And while that is admittedly a

---

* We agree with this general point: the owner of the token for a seat at the ball game is the person who controls the private key of the wallet that the token is in.

† To be honest, you wouldn't really expect them to say that code is law. What would they do all day?

case of turkeys voting against Thanksgiving or Christmas, they have a point.

The law is evolving and will adapt. We hope that it evolves reasonably quickly because leaving the public at the mercy of crypto-sharks and pretending that code is law is not a sound basis for healthy next-generation financial services. As the law evolves, regulators will be able to make informed decisions about what regimes might be desirable. We expect that, over time, this will help to address the 'caveat emptor' concerns – so well articulated by Circle CEO Jeremy Allaire – that we discussed earlier (Pimentel 2022).

So, we use tokens to implement digital assets, and those digital assets that are recognized as property in emerging legal structures are the digital objects that can be owned in the Metaverse.

Case study: Forever 21

In its November 2023 Digital Expression, Fashion & Beauty Trends update, Roblox reported that 56% of its cohort aged 14–26 agreed that 'styling their avatar is more important to them than styling themselves in the physical world'. An even higher percentage, 84%, confirmed that 'their physical style has been inspired by their avatar's style'. Combined, these two insights are likely to fuel further exploration and investment from fashion brands in virtual worlds and the Metaverse.

This is already playing out in the wake of the Apple Vision Pro launch, with some top-notch retailers and brands betting on increased sales from deeper engagement with their line of clothing. High-end fashion retailer Mytheresa is at the bleeding edge of this: Vision Pro owners can customize a 3D avatar to mirror their physical dimensions and then shop for beach wear on the island of Capri, say, or try on evening wear in lamp-lit nocturnal Paris.

Phygital fashion (a portmanteau of physical and digital) had humbler beginnings. In December 2021 fast fashion teen brand Forever 21 had a range of products for sale in its Forever 21 Shop City on Roblox. The most popular item by far was a knitted beanie emblazoned with the word FOREVER. Available in black and pale pink, it retailed on the gaming platform for just 70 cents. More than 1.5 million digital items sold within a year, dwarfing the $500 it cost to design and launch the beanie (Smith, A. N. 2022).

Off the back of this digital success, and one year after its foray into the Metaverse, Forever 21 marked its 'Meta-versary' by launching a limited-edition physical apparel range: the F21 Metaverse Collection. In its press release, the brand highlighted the importance of virtual product testing in creating the new range of physical items that were available in-store and online, starting at $14.99 (*Business Wire* 2022).

While this step already seems less groundbreaking just a couple of years on, Forever 21 was the first brand to release a digital clothing item in Roblox before selling the product at physical retail outlets (Tran 2023). It is not solely about tapping into customer engagement either, as there are also manufacturing efficiencies to be gained. In the words of Forever 21's chief marketing officer (see Smith, A. N. 2022): 'The work of going out and creating a product, talking to a factory, going through all that process – that's months and months and months of work. To create a product digitally, we can do that in days.'

CHAPTER 6

Digital identifiers

Digital objects need owners in a useful Metaverse. Both the digital objects and the owners of those objects must necessarily have digital identities. If these identities are to be portable across virtual worlds, they must be under the control of the citizen, consumer, business or other organization and not the platform operating the virtual world. One of the central complaints about the web2 world of today is that personal identity belongs to Facebook or Google or whoever.

However, the effective and convenient management of these identities is rightly seen as one of the current barriers to

mass adoption. We imagine that some form of custodial solution will become common. When a consumer purchases a new phone, their bank (as the obvious trusted and regulated entity) will download the relevant private keys into secure storage in the phone, which can then be used to authenticate access to the keys.

Remember the 3DID model of digital identity developed in part I of this book? Well, identifiers are about the left-hand side of that model – about the binding of digital identities to things in the real world. Credentials, as we will explore in the next chapter, are about the right-hand side of the model – about the binding of digital identities to things in the virtual world.

Things need identity

When we think about identity and identification we generally tend to think about people. Sometimes we think about companies, but most of the time regulators, lawmakers and the public tend to think about people. However, people are actually a rather small subset of the general category of 'things that will need to be identified in the always-on and always-connected world of the future'. Instead of just thinking about people and companies, then, we need a bigger picture to help us to deal with the Metaverse.

A simple way to proceed – and an approach that is sufficient for our purposes – is to begin by dividing the universe into two categories: things that exist and things that don't exist, or the mundane and the Metaverse if you prefer.

Things that exist are things like Alice, her toaster and her cat. Simple.

Things that do not exist need a little more exploration in order to see why economic avatars and digital objects need to be taken seriously. In his bestselling book *Sapiens*, the historian Yuval Noah Harari talked about the cognitive revolution, which he defines as the point at which 'history declared its independence from biology', because human beings gained the ability to think about things that do not exist. Things such as Citibank. He wrote that corporations do not exist in nature any more than Catholicism or human rights do. These are stories, and as 'modern business-people and lawyers are, in fact, powerful sorcerers ... the principal difference between them and tribal shamans is that modern lawyers tell far stranger tales'. Indeed, limited liability corporations are one of our species' most ingenious inventions. They are an important example of the things that don't exist that will need identities, but there are others. Artificial intelligences are a good example.

If our conception of the Metaverse reputation economy is even approximately right, then, as we shall see, the ability to recognize all of these things (that is, things that do exist and things that don't exist), to form relationships with them and to produce communicable reputations from these relationships generates a workable paradigm. We can then use this paradigm to think clearly about problems and to communicate effectively to create practical solutions.

Things that don't exist

Things that don't exist can quite easily be divided into two groups, building on the distinction that Harari talked about, into things that are legal constructs and things that are not legal constructs. There is therefore a distinction between the identity of the company – an identity that can take part in contracts and transactions – and the identity of a 'smart' 'contract', which is something entirely different.

We can certainly imagine a future in which certain kinds of artificial intelligences are given legal personhood and the ability to form contracts, but we cannot imagine a future in which (as was proposed to the legislature of Malta) apps on a blockchain are afforded the same status (Ganado & Tendon 2018). That really is a discussion for another day though.

Trust frameworks

It is clear that these different kinds of identities must be able to interoperate. My online identity should be able to recognize your company's online identity. Alice's toaster should be able to recognize its authorized users. Bob should be able to understand the reputation of a financial services wealth management AI and give consent for it to access his bank account. The stadium in the Metaverse should be able to admit avatars who possess a special bracelet. Avatars and objects have to be able to interact with each other.

For this to happen there have to be trust frameworks. A trust framework is a set of standards, guidelines and agreements that define how different entities within a system or network establish and maintain trust among themselves. In the context of digital identity, a trust framework outlines the rules and mechanisms that enable different organizations, platforms or services to trust and authenticate each other's digital identities. This is crucial for enabling secure online transactions, access to services and data sharing. Trust frameworks often include specifications for identity verification processes, authentication methods, data protection measures and legal agreements.

There is no need to try to create one trust framework for the Metaverse (or even for each of the metaverses), and within a given framework there may be very many different kinds of identities but the framework will establish the standards and mechanisms for interoperability. Should Alice be able to log in to create an account with British Airways using her bank identity? Probably, yes. Should she be able to log in and create a bank account using her British Airways identity? Probably not.

In some countries and in some cultures the idea of having a single trust framework and a single identity within that framework is seen as being the natural way forward because, apart from anything else, it is the simplest and cheapest way to proceed. But for a variety of reasons we are unconvinced that this is the right approach. We need a much more sophisticated infrastructure to simultaneously deliver goals for privacy, security, practicality and cost effectiveness.

Case study: Pan-Canadian Trust Framework

The Pan-Canadian Trust Framework is designed to enable a transition to a fully digital ecosystem that is beneficial to all Canadians and businesses (Bouma 2019). It defines the two main types of trusted digital representation needed in that ecosystem:

- trusted digital identities of persons and organizations; and
- trusted digital relationships between persons, between persons and organizations, and between organizations.

The framework is designed to serve the needs of different communities who need to trust digital identities, across the public and private sectors, and it allows for the interoperability of different platforms, services, architectures and technologies working together as a coherent whole.

It supports the acceptance of trusted digital identities and relationships by defining a set of agreed-on standardized trusted processes (21 in total) that can be mapped to existing business processes, independently assessed using conformance criteria, and certified to be trusted and interoperable within the many contexts that comprise the digital ecosystem.

Overall, the Pan-Canadian Trust Framework aims to create a unified approach to digital identity and authentication, enhancing the security and convenience of digital interactions for Canadians while also respecting their privacy and rights. There are similar frameworks in Australia, New Zealand, the UK and other countries.

Sovereignty of identity

We will use a straightforward classification of digital identities based on the creation of the digital identity itself. This gives us a taxonomy, as shown in table 5, that distinguishes between 'sovereign' identities created by service providers (whether private or public) and 'self-sovereign' identities created by the real IDs (well, the owners of the real IDs) . We further divide the digital IDs that are not created by the end user into sovereign identities that are used only by their creators and 'trans-sovereign' identities that are used by others beyond the creators.

Table 5. The three families of digital ID.

Category	Implementation	Example
Self-sovereign	Decentralized	dgwbirch.eth
Trans-sovereign	Distributed	ConnectID
Sovereign	Centralized	Aadhar, Google ID

This taxonomy is based on the bindings discussed in the earlier discussion about the 3DID model. First, there is the binding between the digital identity and the mundane identity (of a person, in this instance), where the taxonomy recognizes the fundamental difference between doing this yourself and having someone else do it for you. If you do this, the digital identity is self-sovereign. If someone else does this, it is not. Second, there is the binding between the digital identity and the virtual identity. If that binding is only used by the organization that bound the digital identity to the mundane identity, then this is a sovereign identity. My Barclays Bank identity is a sovereign identity. I can only use it to get into Barclays Bank. It doesn't mean anything to anyone else and I can't use it to get into Citi or Carrefour or Qantas.

If the binding can be validated and used by other organizations, then this is what we have labelled a trans-sovereign identity – a category that includes federated identities. Until recently, only the sovereign and trans-sovereign options were out in the marketplace but there is now a third option: the self-sovereign identity (Hori 2021).

Sovereign identity

Most of the identities that we use today are sovereign identities. A passport is an obvious example. The government issues the passport and only the government can tell you whether a passport is valid. The only credentials that the passport can attest to are attributes put there by the government (e.g. your date of birth). You can't use your passport to log in to your bank, although you can use your passport to obtain another sovereign identity (i.e. your bank's sovereign identity) to get access to other 'realms'.

When it comes to the Metaverse it is really not clear who, if anyone, would be responsible for a Metaverse sovereign identity. Some strategic thinkers are already looking at this problem though. The Chinese state-owned telecoms operator China Mobile has already proposed a 'Digital Identity System' to the International Telecommunications Union. The proposals call for a kind of Metaverse driving licence, with 'natural' and 'social' characteristics that include a range of PII including occupation and 'identifiable signs', along with other attributes (Volpiocelli 2023). They suggest this information be 'permanently' stored and shared with law enforcement 'to keep the order and safety of the virtual world'.*

We need a means to take credentials associated with sovereign identity and use them in the Metaverse, of course, but the special case of a virtual identity of Alice's that is a homonym of her physical identity Alice (e.g. her passport) should be seen as just that: a special case. Generally speaking, we do not see sovereign identities at the heart of the Metaverse.

---

* The proposals give the example of a user called Tom who 'spreads rumours and makes chaos in the metaverse', and they note that the proposed system would allow the police to promptly identify and punish him.

The idea of credentials from the physical world being used in the Metaverse is as old as the term itself. In Stephenson's *Snow Crash*, avatars are not allowed to change their height; your avatar is proportionally the same as your 'real world' self: it is a credential that visitors must take into the virtual world with them, to 'prevent people walking around a mile high'.

Trans-sovereign identity

The trans-sovereign – or 'federated' – model has its roots in convenience. Rather than setting up a new account and creating yet another username and password every time Alice wants to access a new service online, she uses an existing authentication mechanism.

The example that most people are familiar with is social logins: when we create an account on a new website or app using our Google or Facebook details, we are reusing the credentials that these organizations issue and manage on our behalf. It is convenient, it is free to the end user, and, until relatively recently, no one appeared to mind very much that the trade-off for using these services was that the data association with the transaction was monetized by the credential providers. There is an inexplicit trade-off: if you use social logins, you pay with your data, and therefore the cost of using the service is your privacy.

The other prevalent trans-sovereign model is where a group of participants come together to offer federated identity services under a trust framework. The trust framework comprises a set of multilateral agreements with technical, operational, business and legal guidelines that ensure interoperability among different service providers. Sweden, Norway, Denmark, Belgium and Australia all provide powerful examples of financial services providers coming together to build and operate this type of trust framework. Within these types of framework, Alice uses her bank-issued credentials to create an account with a real estate agent online. Thereafter, she can share a range of attributes (name, address, date of birth) that have been verified by her bank.

By and large, the promise of trust frameworks is that they offer greater privacy to the end user. And while convenience has historically trumped security and privacy for the vast majority of people, there are strong signs that this sentiment is changing. Following Apple's decision in early 2021 to let customers 'take control over their data' (Apple 2021) – by limiting the data-tracking ability of apps in the AppStore – Facebook blamed its steep fall in earnings in one quarter on these new privacy settings on the iPhone (Gilbert 2022).

Self-sovereign identity

The idea of user control over attestations about 'identity' and data has been around for a couple of decades, starting with the notion of persistent identities that could move across communities. A high-level reflection on the journey across these decades – viewed through the prism of the Internet Identity Workshop – might be that the evolutionary stages were from centralized designs rooted in identity and access management, through more federated options, and on to more 'user-centric' designs.

In recent times, the concepts behind the user-centric designs began to evolve further in response to criticism that the user was not really in control of their identity, no matter how user-centric the design was. As industry observer Doc Searls put it (Searls 2013): 'User-centric identity (with its identity providers and relying parties) is framed in administrative terms. They do not start with the sovereign individual, and are not driven by that individual.' From here, the concept of self-sovereign identity (SSI) emerged.

Many of the terms used today by SSI enthusiasts can be found in the late Kim Cameron's long-established 'Laws of Identity', demonstrating that this is not new thinking – that said, it is clear that there are other macroeconomic factors in play that are triggering a new wave of interest in the concept (Cameron 2005). In 2016 Christopher Allen produced some principles for the term 'self-sovereign identity', and these are summarized in table 6.

Table 6. Principles of self-sovereignty.

Principle	Definition	Notes
Existence	Users must have an independent existence	Any self-sovereign identity is ultimately based on the ineffable 'I' that is at the heart of identity. A self-sovereign identity simply makes public and accessible some limited aspects of the 'I' that already exist.
Control	Users must control their identities	Subject to well-understood and secure algorithms that ensure the continued validity of an identity and its claims, the user is the ultimate authority on their identity. They should always be able to refer to it, update it or even hide it. They must be able to choose celebrity or privacy as they prefer. This doesn't mean that a user controls all the claims on their identity: other users may make claims about a user, but they should not be central to the identity itself.
Access	Users must have access to their own data	A user must always be able to easily retrieve all the claims and other data within their identity. There must be no hidden data and no gatekeepers. This does not mean that a user can necessarily modify all the claims associated with their identity, but it does mean they should be aware of them. It also does not mean that users have equal access to others' data, only to their own.
Transparency	Systems and algorithms must be transparent	The systems used to administer and operate a network of identities must be open, both in how they function and in how they are managed and updated. The algorithms should be free, open source, well known, and as independent as possible of any particular architecture; anyone should be able to examine how they work.
Persistence	Identities must be long-lived	Preferably, identities should last forever, or at least for as long as the user wishes. This must not contradict a 'right to be forgotten'; a user should be able to dispose of an identity if they wish, and claims should be modified or removed as appropriate over time. Doing this requires a firm separation between an identity and its claims: they can't be tied forever.

Table 6. *Continued.*

Principle	Definition	Notes
Portability	Information and services about identity must be transportable	Identities must not be held by a singular third-party entity, even if it's a trusted entity that is expected to work in the best interests of the user. Transportable identities ensure that the user remains in control of their identity no matter what, and can also improve an identity's persistence over time.
Interoperability	Identities should be as widely usable as possible	Identities are of little value if they only work in limited niches. The goal of a twenty-first-century digital identity system is to make identity information widely available, crossing international boundaries to create global identities, without losing user control. Thanks to persistence and autonomy, these widely available identities can then become continually available.
Consent	Users must agree to the use of their identity	Any identity system is built around sharing that identity and its claims, and an interoperable system increases the amount of sharing that occurs. However, sharing of data must only occur with the consent of the user. Though other users such as an employer, a credit bureau or a friend might present claims, the user must still offer consent for them to become valid.
Minimalization	Disclosure of claims must be minimized	When data is disclosed, that disclosure should involve the minimum amount of data necessary to accomplish the task at hand. For example, if only a minimum age is called for, then the exact age should not be disclosed; and if only an age is requested, then the more precise date of birth should not be disclosed.
Protection	The rights of users must be protected	When there is a conflict between the needs of the identity network and the rights of individual users, then the network should err on the side of preserving the freedoms and rights of the individuals over the needs of the network. To ensure this, identity authentication must occur through independent algorithms that are censorship resistant and force resilient and that are run in a decentralized manner.

We think these principles are an excellent guide to the requirements, goals and constraints of an SSI infrastructure, and it is clear that the technologies being explored to implement this self-sovereign view of identity are evolving rapidly and in interesting directions. SSI extends the use of public key cryptography and, in particular, digital signatures beyond the identity management of web servers (through SSL) and makes it useful to end users via digital wallets (Glöckler *et al.* 2023). This kind of identity management, based on public key certificates, has been standard practice in the cryptographic world for decades.

SSI looks to apply this approach to the identities of people, things and companies to deal with the security, usability and efficiency challenges of the open internet, and it provides an alternative to the privacy issues and lock-in effects related to the data silos of trans-sovereign identity providers. At a high level, the infrastructure comprises the following.

- *Digital wallets.* An individual creates a digital wallet, often in the form of an application, where their identity information is stored. This wallet holds decentralized identifiers and credentials (and, in the more general case, other digital assets such as fungible and non-fungible tokens, but more on that in part IV).

  » *Decentralized identifiers (DIDs).* In the SSI model, each identity is assigned a DID: an identifier that is created, owned and controlled by the subject of that digital identity. While DIDs were initially envisaged as being stored on some sort of distributed ledger, to aid discoverability and tamper resistance, more recent DID methods (such as did:web and did:key) do not depend on blockchains or other such data structures.

  » *Verifiable credentials.* These are digital statements made by issuers about a subject, and they are central to transactions in the new economy. They are explored in some detail in chapter 7, but to introduce them here one might imagine a university issuing a verifiable credential stating that someone has a particular degree. The holder of this credential (the graduate) can then share this with others, and due to cryptographic proofs the receiver can verify its authenticity.

- *Trust framework.* While SSI removes the need for centralized control, there is still a need for some kind of framework. This means that there will be recognized entities that issue verifiable credentials (like the university in the previous example). A given entity's reputation or the trustworthiness of its credentials might be based on various factors, including public reviews, audits or adherence to certain standards. It would take a whole dedicated book to explore such frameworks in detail, but there are examples in place already that show how this can be done (e.g. the Pan-Canadian Trust Framework discussed earlier).

- *Transactions.* When an individual wants to perform an online transaction, such as logging into a website, the ceremony will use their wallet. The website will challenge the individual to prove certain aspects of their identity, and the individual can respond by providing the necessary verifiable credentials or proofs.

- *Privacy by design.* Since users can selectively disclose information, and the actual data often remains 'off-chain' (i.e. it is not stored on the ledger where the DIDs are stored), SSI models inherently support greater privacy. Furthermore, because DIDs are pseudonymous, they can be rotated or changed, adding an additional layer of privacy.

The adoption of SSI offers numerous benefits, including enhanced privacy, reduced reliance on centralized authorities and a more user-centric approach to digital identity. However, widespread adoption requires overcoming challenges related to interoperability, scalability and establishing widely accepted trust frameworks. Our view, as you will see in chapter 10, is that consumers and businesses will find it difficult to manage DIDs and credentials themselves, so perhaps a more likely route to the mass market is custodial SSI, where the DIDs and credential are actually managed by regulated institutions rather than by individuals themselves.

The use of standardized verifiable credentials (VCs) is already being explored in different sectors, including travel (as we will explore later) and banking. For example, HSBC Labs is prototyping a DID solution for internal account opening powered by Polygon ID. When a customer opens an HSBC account, the bank conducts KYC and creates a VC that can be used later for a number of transactions, including logging into an HSBC account, purchases, applying for a loan, carbon credits and much more.

This HSBC ID could draw on any number of identity issuers, from government agencies and credit bureaus to telcos and utilities. With this customer identity wallet, users would also be able to provide their personal information (such as date of birth, passport number and so on) to establish trust, prove eligibility or complete a transaction.

Ben Chodroff, the head of HSBC Lab, has highlighted the use of open standards for this work, saying that 'as more regulated financial institutions embrace open standards for decentralised identity, it will help to create a safer and more efficient customer experience' (Polygon 2023).

Trust over IP

In the words of the Trust Over IP Foundation[*] (ToIP): 'As developer communities began implementing Verifiable Credentials

---

[*] See https://trustoverip.org/.

over secure connections, they recognized this new model could underpin an entire layer of Internet-scale digital trust.' There is nothing controversial in that, and the same is true of ToIP's follow-up statement: 'As is usually the case, their initial efforts focused primarily on proving the technology side of things.' We have sat in enough rooms over the years discussing new projects and hearing the 'technology is the easy part' line to know that making the bits and bites work is only part of the equation.

This is certainly true when you start to think about international use cases. For a start, different jurisdictions have different rules and regulations covering open data regimes and digital identity, and as we are often reminded, identity is culturally specific. Most Europeans have little to no sympathy for the long-standing suspicion of mandatory government ID in the UK and Australia, for example.

There are sufficient InterOp Plugfests – where developers in various different global standards communities build prototypes to demonstrate that their software works with that of others – for us to think that the technology part is well on the way to being solved. We believe, though, that without some guardrails to provide the 'narrow waist' of governance interoperability, the adoption and scale we are looking for will take several more years.

This is exactly where ToIP comes in. The foundation's mission is to align the technology layers with what they term the 'human accountability' of the business, legal and social layers that make up governance. Combined, these two halves form a complete framework for digital trust infrastructure, known as the ToIP stack (see figure 15).

Specifically, the governance stack defines roles, responsibilities and rules for all participating entities and mechanisms for ensuring compliance with the agreed standards and policies. Importantly, it also provides standardized mechanisms for dispute resolution and enforcement.

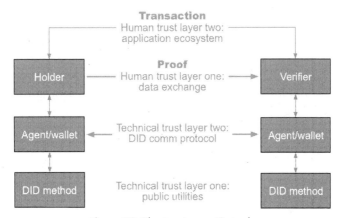

Figure 15. The trust over IP stack.

We are aware that governments and private sector entities tendering for services have made reference to ToIP, which is a positive step towards ensuring interoperability between different legal frameworks, alongside technical frameworks.

Case studies: global perspectives

The Bill and Melinda Gates Foundation talk about the need for what it calls a 'digital public infrastructure' (DPI). The foundation says that a strong DPI has three foundational systems – identity, payments and data exchange – that together can make life easier in important ways. It highlights such an infrastructure as a way to reduce poverty in emerging economies, but the truth is that developed economies (and the Metaverse) need a DPI too. It is interesting, therefore, to look at some examples of how identity is being deployed in DPI around the world to see what lessons can be learned to help the Metaverse develop its own infrastructure(s).

India

The International Monetary Fund (IMF) similarly talks about the need for a DPI that is built up from digital identity, the payments system and a data exchange layer. It agrees that a DPI has the potential to support both the transformation of the economy and inclusive growth. The IMF highlights the particular example of India's foundational DPI, the so-called India Stack, and shows how it has been harnessed to foster innovation and competition, to boost financial inclusion and to improve government revenue collection. India's DPI contains powerful lessons for other countries embarking on digital transformation, in particular a design approach that focuses on shared building blocks and on supporting innovation across the ecosystem through APIs.

Aadhaar, the canonical example of sovereign identity, is the biometric identification system for all Indian residents and is used for all purposes from air ticket booking, to ration cards, to opening bank accounts (Arthi et al. 2023). Aadhaar was developed because of a basic need to provide access to public services and government benefits in India. Before Aadhaar, it was assessed that about a third of subsidized fuel and almost two-thirds of subsidized food distributed under government programmes never reached the intended beneficiaries! When it comes to mitigating abuse and fraud, Aadhaar saves the Indian government in the region of a billion dollars per annum.

Beyond this basic use case, though, the scheme has transformed India through financial inclusion. When linked with a bank account, the twelve-digit Aadhaar number is a 'payname', and it is adequate to transfer any payment to a person's bank account, removing the need to give details such as name, bank account number or bank branch details to a payer. Individuals are also empowered as they can decide which bank account they receive funds into under a scheme called direct benefit transfer. By 2022, more than 750 million Aadhaar numbers had been uniquely linked with bank accounts, and usage continues to grow.

The scheme is not without challenges, though. Aadhaar transactions currently require network connectivity in order to be verified. For transactions in rural areas, this leads to high costs for each transaction and also to high fixed IT and network costs. There are also ongoing security and privacy issues. According to a report by the US-based cybersecurity firm Resecurity, a serious data breach in 2023 resulted in the personally identifiable information of 815 million Indians being put up for sale on the dark web. Resecurity reports that details such as Aadhaar and passport information, along with names, phone numbers and addresses, are available for sale online (Mistra 2023).

Australia
ConnectID – a digital identity scheme developed by Australian Payments Plus – is a recently launched example of trans-sovereign identity. ConnectID operates the trust framework, and the identity providers at launch were the major banks. ConnectID is interesting for two main reasons: it starts to explore the relationship between government and private sector providers; and its design and use of open standards provides a pathway for more portable self-sovereign identity.

ConnectID is the first non-government scheme to successfully achieve accreditation under the Australian government's Trusted Digital Identity Framework (TDIF). The TDIF creates standards, rules and guidelines for digital identity providers, and its longer-term intention is to enable citizens to be able to log into federal or state-based government services with an identity provider of their choice, be that one from the public or the private sector. The government also has in its sights that citizens will be able to access private sector services using their federal or state-issued digital ID. Before a private sector entity can offer their customers this convenience, they need to be accredited under TDIF. There is a healthy debate about this because, although technical accreditation has been achieved, there is no legislative framework to support the use cases as yet – but it is coming.

Australia has no mandatory government-issued identifier, and the introduction of a digital ID requires the passing of the Digital ID Bill. The inquiry into this bill by the Senate Economics Legislation Committee was publicly streamed and included representation from public and private sector entities, including ConnectID and NAB, a founding member of the bank-led scheme.

We think the opening statement to the committee from Brad Carr, NAB's 'Executive, Innovation & Partnerships', is worth reproducing in full because it resonates with some of the lessons from Sweden. Although Sweden began its journey twenty years earlier, both countries are considering the importance of competition and choice.

> In considering Digital ID, there are three key points I'd like to raise.
>
> Firstly, choice. We believe it's important that Australians have choice, both (a) whether to use a Digital ID service or not; (b) and if they would like such a service, a choice of verifier. Our mantra is that Australians should be able to 'trust who you choose, and choose who you trust'.
>
> Secondly, minimizing sharing of data. Reducing the amount of personal information being shared each and every day can help tackle important issues such as fraud and scams – which thrive on criminals exploiting the loss of personal information.
>
> Thirdly, private sector participation. We would like to see the committee closely consider the proposed phasing, to allow the private sector to fully participate in the Digital ID ecosystem sooner.
>
> Australians need to have access to Digital ID services that they can utilize readily, safely, with choice, and with trust.

If we look forward a few years, we can imagine that, as an Australian citizen, Alice might be able to select a credential issued by the federal government to lodge her tax return and a credential issued by her bank to apply for part ownership of a koala sanctuary.* The choice of which credential Alice uses will be shaped by a number of things: which credentials are accepted by the service provider; what degree of privacy is assured; and perhaps, over the longer term, price. While the general rule of thumb is that individuals do not pay for identity services, we can see this evolving over time. Alice may wish to use a particular credential because of related benefits, but the company providing the service that Alice wants to access may prefer her to use a particular credential because the issuer of that credential offers a lower transaction fee.

We are yet to see competition for identity services between public sector and private sector entities, but it is likely to evolve, and it is particularly interesting in the Australian context because of existing regulation relating to payment card interchange fees. It seems possible that some form of regulatory framework for pricing identity transactions may be required. Alice may decide to use the credential equivalent of her Amex Platinum Card, and she may be comfortable to pay a premium to do so.

We do not see this as a uniquely Australian position either. The dominance of private sector identity services is understood to be a significant driver in the rollout of the European Digital Identity Wallet. And while BankID in the Nordics, with more than 8 million users, is often held up as a poster child of success, the Swedish central bank has a slightly different perspective. In a report on payments safety and efficiency, the Riksbank observes that (Sveriges Riksbank 2022b):

> It is the banks that issue BankID and they decide who can access the service and how it can be used. This means that it is the banks that decide whether we are who we say we are. Physical ID documents, such as passports and

---

* See https://bricklet.com.au/co-own-a-koala-sanctuary.

driving licences, are the responsibility of the state. This should also be the case for digital ID. A government e-ID is therefore needed. Such an ID could foster competition in the payments market and would provide equal access to e-ID for all.

While we think that the point about the banks deciding whether people are who they say they are is a little more nuanced (because we think in many cases the banks will target the 'what' rather than the 'who'), the point is not lost.

Coming back to the second reason that ConnectID is interesting, this hinges on the fact that it positions itself as an exchange between identity providers and service providers (different merchants or government departments, for example) that need to verify who they are dealing with. As an exchange, ConnectID never sees or stores the identity data. ConnectID's trust model is predicated on peer-to-peer communication directly between the 'identity provider' and the 'relying party', enabled by OpenID Connect (OIDC).* OIDC leverages OAuth 2.0 (the industry standard for apps and websites to access information they need from other services) to enable secure user authentication across different applications and platforms. It simplifies the login process, enhances security and respects user privacy, making it a popular choice for modern web applications and services. OIDC also powers social logins (sign in with Facebook, Google, etc.), and we think its widespread adoption is interesting because it provides a pathway to self-sovereign identity.

In June 2022 the OpenID Foundation published a white paper on its work on VCs. Importantly, the work was – and continues to be – conducted in liaison with the Decentralized Identity Foundation and the International Organization for Standardization, working in conjunction with W3C. The practical

---

* See https://openid.net/developers/specs/.

implication of this is that the OIDC protocols will support the presentation and verification of VCs. This evolutionary – rather than revolutionary – approach to more portable identity appears very likely to succeed.

CHAPTER 7

Digital credentials

The fundamental enabler for trust in the Metaverse is credentials not identity: it's not about who you are, it's about what you are. Here are a couple of examples from the UK to help frame this statement.

In 2022 a woman who took around 150 driving tests for other people was jailed for eight months (*BBC News* 2022). It seems to us that if the driving licence test centres are incapable of determining the correct identity of their customers, there is absolutely no possibility of (for example) volunteers at polling stations validating the identity of voters (the UK now

has voter ID laws) or HR departments verifying the credentials of applicants.

We can further illustrate the problem of having no digital identity infrastructure with the story of a pilot who was sent to prison in Britain for lying about his flying experience to get a job with British Airways. The fraudulent flyer entered false details and altered entries in his flight logbook so that he could appear more experienced than he actually was (*Sky News* 2022). He got the job and was working for the British Airways subsidiary BA CityFlyer and former Irish regional airline Stobart Air for two years before he was found out. Two years!

Now, it's one thing to lie about one's credentials to get a job flipping burgers ('No, I have never been convicted of possession of a deadly weapon') or as a member of parliament ('I am unfamiliar with the use of cocaine'), or as the CEO of an internet company ('Yes, I have a computer science degree'), but surely it is quite another thing to lie about being able to drive, or about being a police officer, or about having qualified as an anaesthesiologist or a pilot! How can you transact with someone in a metaverse without being able to establish their credentials? In the absence of any other familiar physical cues, you will need to see proof. But what does that mean?

Proof points

How, then, can someone prove that they are a police officer or a pilot? The police in London were thinking about adding QR codes to their identification cards so that women and girls could scan the cards with a smartphone to confirm the officers' identities, but that isn't a real solution. QR codes are too easy to copy, and in any case, there are currently at least 2,000 British police identification cards that are missing and could be used by anyone, since there is no authentication.

The lack of any identity infrastructure can be seen in the out-of-control fraud we see around the world. Losses from identity-fraud schemes, in which fraudsters use stolen payment credentials for their own gain, continue to soar. The fact that Miami street gangs are now competing to control identity theft instead of boring old guns and drugs tells us that we are long overdue the introduction of a practical identity infrastructure (Fabiani 2022).

Verifiable credentials

The general problem statement here is, as you will have noticed, not about proving who you are but about proving what you are. I need to know you have a line of credit, a pilot's licence or a diploma from a top ten dental school. I do not care who you are unless something goes wrong, in which case law enforcement or professional bodies take over.

Clearly, this system does not work properly in the mundane world. Consider the example of an acquaintance of ours who went on holiday to Egypt and, a couple of days after his arrival, was afflicted with an intestinal disorder.* Confined to his hotel room, he called down to reception to seek medical assistance. In time a chap arrived to examine him, diagnosed a common gut infection and hooked him up to a saline drip to prevent dehydration. The treatment worked and after another day or two of solitary, he was able to leave the hotel and go sightseeing again.

When he returned home he filed a claim with his insurance company, including a copy of the bill he had paid for the medical assistance while on vacation. The insurance company refused to pay up, because it turned out that the person who had examined him and put him on a drip wasn't a doctor: he was just a friend of some guy at the hotel (Birch 2020b). He had no medical qualifications at all but had developed a nice sideline in treating victims of a common illness.

---

* Note: personal details have been altered to preserve privacy.

Here, then, is most definitely a problem looking for a solution, in both the mundane world and the Metaverse, and we already know what the solution is: verifiable credentials.

Why VCs? Well, there was a post on Twitter in the midst of the coronavirus pandemic that explains this perfectly.[*] It quoted an emergency room doctor in Los Angeles asking for help from the technology community. It said: 'We need a platform for frontline doctors to share information quickly and anonymously.' It went on to state the obvious requirement that what is required is 'a platform where doctors can join, have their *credentials* [our emphasis] validated and then ask questions of other frontline doctors'.

Who the person on that platform is does not matter. What the person is, however, is fundamental. The credentials, not the identity, are the key.

Mass market credentials

It should be quite straightforward. You walk into the doctor's surgery and there is a certificate on the wall. You tap the certificate with your phone (or scan a QR code on the certificate) and your phone either shows you a picture of the doctor if the qualification is valid or a big red cross if it is not valid. If the process is anything more complex than that, it cannot help the general public.

The UK is undoubtedly taking some steps in the right direction. For example, the Post Office and Yoti have become the first government-approved digital ID providers, allowing UK citizens to prove their identities with an app instead of physical documents for the specific purposes of applying for a job or renting a property. In Europe, there are multiple trials underway, under the umbrella of the European Blockchain Services Infrastructure, involving post offices, banks, universities and retail outlets

---

[*] See https://twitter.com/nicoleperlroth/status/1239723703706869761.

on a range of use cases including interoperable cross-border services for IP management, track and trace supply chains, and VCs for education and the workforce.*

Given the evolution of smartphones, contactless interfaces and VC standards, we are taken beyond the familiar tap-to-pay world that people already seem very comfortable with and towards what Jerry Fishenden calls the 'tap-to-prove' world, which we need to get to as soon as possible. As Fishenden points out, Apple already provides various layers of anonymity in payments and in other areas (such as its iCloud Private Relay service), so 'surely it can't be long before it does the same with identity', enabling us to 'tap to prove' rather than 'tap to pay'? His point is that this would deliver secure, private identity services in both the face-to-face and online worlds (as with Apple Pay, which we both use all the time). Additionally, where necessary it could create automatic pseudonyms for credentials, just as it now does with email addresses (Fishenden 2022).

We are rather taken with the tap-to-prove formulation, because it introduces the possibility of a standardized mechanism for demonstrating credentials not only at the technological level but also at the human level. It makes for a recognizable 'ceremony' of making a claim.

Identity experts often talk about the need for a ceremony. By this they mean that the actions that two people need to take in order to engage with each other are well known to each individual, so the ritual is familiar and provides confidence in the outcome. If you have to do something different in the bank, in the supermarket, in the sports stadium, on the web and everywhere else, then fraudsters can take advantage of

---

* In one of the first projects to be announced, Howest University students have been issued with a VC that they store in their KBC bank app. The credential, which will be accepted across Europe, confirms their status as a student, and it will provide access to retail offers and benefits for students. Interestingly, in terms of the value proposition for the bank, a student doesn't need to be an existing customer of KBC to use the service, making it a very smart customer acquisition tool also.

the uncertainty. If, on the other hand, the same 'ceremony' is applied in all circumstances, then not only are you able to do it automatically, but your suspicions are aroused if someone asks you to do something out of the ordinary.

This is what we mean by an identity ceremony: something simple and familiar and repetitive and satisfying when you are required to prove something about yourself. If you go into the bar, you tap your phone on the doorman's phone and the doorman gets confirmation that you are over 21 and you get confirmation that the doorman is licensed by the city to perform such a function. If you go to see a doctor when you are on holiday, you tap your phone on the doctor's phone and the doctor gets your insurance details and you get confirmation that the doctor is licensed to practice. If you go to watch a soccer game, you tap your phone on the turnstile and the gate gets confirmation you have a ticket and are not banned from the ground while you get confirmation that your loyalty points have been awarded.

In all of these cases the familiar 'dance' results in actual security, with keys and certificates under the hood so that consumers never have to deal with them. If something is out of the ordinary – a qualification shows up red when it should be green, or whatever – both parties will notice immediately. It is one thing to have the digital identity infrastructure that we need to function in the modern world, but it is quite another to make it deliver for the populace. Identity ceremonies are a way to do this.

What we therefore need is the ability to extend ceremonies into the Metaverse so that economic avatars can easily determine whether counterparties have the necessary credentials to enable an interaction. One key requirement for this kind of ceremony is that there is no need for special hardware or devices. We should be able to present and verify credentials using whatever devices we are using to interact: whether that is goggles or a browser, a smartphone or a smart watch.

The missing piece

So we now have digital objects and digital identities, and digital credentials are the final missing piece of the transaction jigsaw. The Metaverse economy is an economy in which the fundamental enabler of economic activity is not identity but persistent and digitally verifiable credentials – again, it's not who you are but what you are. Trust will be built around the presentation of credentials, and more specifically around standardized VCs such as the ISO 18013-5 standard for mobile driver's licences and W3C verifiable credentials. That is, if you present your driving licence to someone, they can cryptographically verify that it is not a fake and that it really was issued to you.

There are a wide variety of potential implementations. Puja Ohlhaver of Flashbots, Glen Weyl of Microsoft and Ethereum progenitor Vitalik Buterin have, for example, outlined a kind of non-transferable NFT – something they call soulbound tokens – that could be used as a sort of living, transparent and immutable curriculum vitae (Weyl et al. 2022).

By contrast, Tim Sweeney, the CEO of Epic Games, has pointed toward the field of zero-knowledge proofs (ZKPs) – which give you the ability to verify that something happened without receiving any private details about it – as a powerful mechanism for delivering both privacy and security in a decentralized system. 'I think that's going to be the backbone of a large part of the next century in technology,' Sweeney said. There is groundbreaking work going on right now to bring ZKPs and VCs together, and it seems to show that general-purpose ZKP credentials are already practical and can easily provide for digital wallets, for instance, to facilitate new design options that previously were not accessible because of the threat of man-in-the-middle attacks (Babel & Sedlmeir 2023).

Tokens and VCs are often spoken of interchangeably because they uniquely identify entities in the digital world, but they are not the same thing at all. For one thing, as noted earlier, a fundamental characteristic of a token is that it can be transferred. We feel it may be best to use them for the purposes for which they were invented: NFTs for recording the ownership of and transfer of value, as well as representing assets in digital form; and VCs for recording attributes relating to entities.

Case study: carbon credits

One area in which this distinction between tokens and VCs is becoming helpfully clear is in the voluntary and compliance carbon markets. The carbon markets allow carbon emitters to offset their greenhouse gas (GHG) emissions by purchasing carbon credits created by projects targeted at removing or reducing GHG emissions. In some markets, allowances can be sold – such as in the EU Emissions Trading System, where companies trade 'excess' carbon emissions allowances to companies that emit more than their allocation. Whether or not you are a proponent of the view that climate change is mainly caused by human activities and can be addressed by reducing carbon emissions, there is no denying that the carbon markets are big business. And it's business that is being rapidly tokenized because of the requirement for improved transparency and accountability to combat greenwashing. Tellingly, a recent global survey found that 59% of executives admit to overstating or inaccurately representing their sustainability activities (something known as greenwashing). When you understand that 85% of that same group acknowledge that consumers are more likely to do business with sustainable brands, their motivation for overstatement is clear, if not excusable (Keeble 2023).

It's not simply about consumer preference, however. Carbon offsets are rapidly emerging as an investable asset class because of the view that regulated instruments (such as carbon taxes and caps on emissions) alone will not be sufficient to meet net zero targets by 2050. Net zero refers to a future state in which any GHGs produced by human activities are balanced out by removing an equivalent amount of GHGs from the atmosphere. The intent to reach this state was ratified by signatories of the United Nations 2015 Paris Agreement (basically, most of the world), and some nations have implemented requirements and regulations on enterprises as part of their efforts to meet their Paris Agreement commitments. The general view is that, in order to meet these commitments, public and private companies will need to reduce their own emissions as much as they can and that regulated carbon markets will be insufficient, which will create demand for carbon offsets in the voluntary carbon market. Bloomberg puts the value of the offset market at half a trillion dollars annually by 2050, provided some of the inherent challenges are addressed (BloombergNEF 2023).

This is the opportunity that organizations such as Hedera – which provides carbon neutral distributed ledger technology – are targeting.[*] As Hedera's chief policy officer puts it, 'the opacity surrounding carbon markets and green debt has undermined the confidence in climate finance mechanisms to deliver tangible sustainable outcomes' (Rubin 2023). Hedera's contribution is to put 'the balance sheet of the planet on the public ledger' in order to establish a single source of truth that 'facilitates cross-sectoral cooperation and decision-making processes that are cost-effective and rooted in real-world impact'.

To deliver on this, Hedera created Guardian, an open-source platform that uses Hedera's public distributed ledger network to mint policy-based tokens. Guardian acts as a rules engine for complex multiparty workflows and provides a set of guardrails for asset creation. Users of Guardian digitize carbon market methodologies, which empowers actors across defined roles to submit data corresponding to those rulesets. After a workflow has been completed, a credit is issued and all of the rules and related information are cryptographically linked to the

[*] See https://hedera.com/guardian.

asset in the form of a verifiable presentation. Guardian also acts as a coordination tool to produce 'auditable, traceable, and reproducible records that document the measurement, reporting, and verification (MRV) process and lifecycle of carbon credits', and it enables their retirement when claims are made on the public ledger. Hedera's vision is that organizations delivering carbon projects will deploy their own instance of Guardian to provide cradle-to-grave transparency to all project stakeholders – and it's a vision that is playing out successfully. In September 2023 ALLCOT IO, the digital arm of established climate leader and project developer ALLCOT, undertook to onboard ALLCOT's 500 million tonne portfolio of carbon credits to the Guardian ecosystem (Geisenberger 2023).

Alongside the carbon tokens that it mints, Guardian publishes a 'trustchain' of signed data as VCs to allow independent verification of supporting MRV data originating from multiple parties and sources. These VCs have selective disclosure capability to support public discovery, without disclosure of confidential or private information. A selectively disclosed version of the verified data is published to IPFS (an open access distributed file storage system), which enables public discovery. The verifier can then request further information by presenting their own credentials, as a VC Presentation Request (a standardized request within the W3C VC specification) to gain access to the sensitive information.

Additionally, Guardian can support authentication via a DID, and the presentation of VCs for authorization via a Self-Issued OpenID Provider flow. A simplified use case might see an environmental, social and governance auditor[*] logging into a Guardian instance with VCs issued by a governing audit body, allowing the project company to decentralize the management of auditors to trusted entities.

[*] See Verra for an example of a carbon market validation and verification body: https://verra.org/validation-verification/.

PART III

THE SERVICES

Having used our model to explore the building blocks needed to deliver transactions in the Metaverse, it is time to delve further into the transaction environment to see what services need to be built from these blocks and therefore what opportunities for new products and services might arise as the Metaverse evolves. Looking at the intersections across the model, we see opportunities presenting themselves in the trading of digital objects (the transactions), in the market for those objects (which we see as a reputation economy) and in the secure ownership of those objects.

These services, as shown in figure 16 overleaf, provide a surface for a new economy and, therefore, for new financial services. With these services in place, the costs of financial intermediation in that economy should be substantially lower than they are in the current economy, and it will therefore in time become the dominant financial sector.

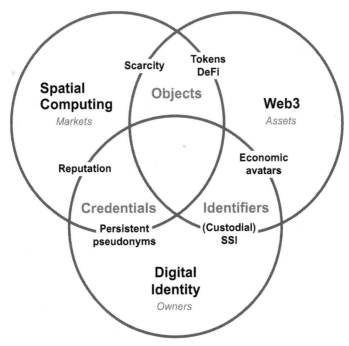

Figure 16. Services provided by the key technologies.

CHAPTER 8

Trust and transactions

Way back in March 2005, at the Consult Hyperion Digital
Money Forum, the computer games expert Richard Bartle
(yes, the Richard Bartle from Cyberia) gave a presentation on the
emerging economies in virtual worlds. At that time the science
fiction massively multiplayer game EVE Online had 200,000 players (it now has some 10 million). Richard memorably described
those economies as being based on 'people buying things that
don't exist from people who don't own them'.

He was right, of course, but as it turned out, buying things
that didn't exist from people who didn't own them was a big

business (and 'exist' is in the eye of the beholder). In his 2014 book *Wildcat Currency*, Edward Castronova, one of the first economists to study virtual worlds in detail, wrote that it was a mistake to think of some money as 'real' and other money as 'fake', 'play' or 'virtual' because 'the value of money has always depended on what people think'.

Indeed. Just because money is virtual, that doesn't mean it's not useful and desirable. When you consider the billions of dollars already being spent on in-game purchases for skins in Fortnite, it is possible to see (at least in outline) just how big the burgeoning Metaverse economy could be.

In this Metaverse there are digital objects that cannot be replicated, and some of these are digital assets (that is, they have value to someone). You might remember that in *Star Trek*, where there are replicators, the only thing that cannot be replicated is 'gold-pressed latinum' (which is why the Ferengi use it as money). Setting aside the hippy nonsense about post-scarcity and the end of economics, the Metaverse is the Star Trek version of the universe: almost everything can be copied, but the things that cannot be are the things with value.

Now you can see why we refer back to Bartle's memorable comment. When you bring tokens into virtual worlds, you now have the means to implement digital assets that work like physical assets – and these objects can be linked to digital identities. In other words, there is an economy of people buying things that don't exist from people who *do* own them.

Those early virtual worlds did involve economies of sorts, but in such environments the game owner can create and destroy value at will by increasing or decreasing the number of magic swords or gold mines or asteroids that exist in the game. They were play markets, and while some people certainly did earn real money from them, they did not evolve into real economies. They did, however, give other valuable insights into the future, and one of those insights was about the very nature of work itself.

We are now at the point where 'almost all contemporary games contain some mimetic elements of work and market exchange' (Adler-Bell 2021), which suggests that computer games no longer offer fantasy, an escape from the day-to-day, or what anyone might think of as 'play'. Sam Adler-Bell says that such games are attractive because they offer *rules* that are 'a rationality otherwise missing from the contemporary wage labour process'. They have become, in the words of Vicky Osterweil, utopian work simulators (again see Adler-Bell (2021)).

The work, however, is real. As is the economy that provides context. Matthew Ball identifies a real economy – the space we have described where economic avatars (i.e. individuals and businesses) are able to create, own, invest, sell and be rewarded for their 'work' – as a defining characteristic of a metaverse. He is correct. And this real economy depends on property rights (Ball 2020).

The nature of the economy is critical. If everything belongs to the state (or to Blizzard or Electronic Arts or Sony or whoever), then you don't have an economy, you have serfs tilling the fields for their Dear Leader. But once you have secure property rights, you have a modern society. As Richard Pipes wrote in his book *Property and Freedom*, which interestingly contrasts the evolution of property rights in England and in Russia, 'while property in some form is possible without liberty, the contrary is inconceivable' (Pipes 2000).

Objects and scarcity

Scarce digital objects are the property in this new economy. As has been nicely summarized by *The Economist*, property rights classically entail three elements: *usus, fructus, abusus* – that is, the right to use property, to profit from it and to dispose of it. The reason for people's excitement about the Metaverse is because of those rights. In virtual worlds you have a command economy run by platform dictators who can take your stuff away at the press of a button. But tokens turn the personae of virtual worlds into economic avatars in a metaverse empowered to use, profit from and dispose of property. This reinforces a point made by Kayvon Tehranian, a founder of the NFT marketplace Foundation, who said (see Babel & Sedlmeir 2023): 'Property ownership is a tool. It works. It brings financial incentives.'

With tokens for money and tokens for digital objects in place, we have that real economy that Matthew Ball referred to. From our perspective, the excitement is not about the graphics, it's about the GDP. To give a simple example of both of the kinds of digital object that are in use (i.e. fungible and non-fungible tokens), think of NFTs as tickets for a seat at a sporting event, and think of the coins used to buy those seats as fungible tokens (i.e. money).

DeFi and markets

In the Metaverse, where tokens of all kinds are bought and sold in transparent marketplaces and where the laws of supply and demand can operate under the sunshine of privacy-enhancing digital identity services, there is what we might truly call a new economy. And while, right now, these new token-powered economies seem to be founded on art and music, the fact is that the first financial services are already up and running within them.

DeFi is real, whatever happens to cryptocurrency

In the middle of 2022 the *Wall Street Journal* said that 'the crypto party is over' (which is surely the case) and went on to compare the current shakedown with what happened at the end of the 1990s, with the collapse of the first wave of internet companies (Driebusch & Vigna 2022). Investors were fundamentally correct during that bubble: the internet was the future. But that didn't stop many of them from losing 'boatloads of money' as companies failed. If this comparison is valid, then what will be the core of the next generation of behemoths to arise from the embers of the crypto craze to rival the 'web2' giants that dominate the landscape today?

A pointer to the answer is available. In one of Jamie Dimon's recent annual letters to JPMorgan Chase shareholders, he said that 'DeFi and blockchain are real' (Shevlin 2022), which caused some comment in crypto circles given his previous claim that: 'I don't care about bitcoin. I have no interest in it.'

A paradox? No. We think it is possible to believe that tokenization will be huge and that DeFi protocols will have a serious role to play in the next generation of financial services while simultaneously being sceptical that cryptocurrencies will have a major role.

Actually, this has long been the view of some serious players in the financial services mainstream. Larry Fink, the CEO of Blackrock, called tokenization 'the next generation for markets'. If you think of tokens as bitcoin or as pictures of chimpanzees with sunglasses on, you probably think that the man who runs the world's biggest asset management company (with $7 trillion under management) is going out on a limb here. But if you think of tokens as digital assets that can be traded via protocols, you may well agree with us that his view is spot on. It may sound hyperbolic, but we are sure that the future will be tokenized.

Fink's perspective is not ideological. His view of a new kind of financial market infrastructure of fungible and non-fungible tokens that are exchanged through decentralized financial services will provide 'instantaneous settlement' and 'reduced fees'. Tokens as bearer instruments. The token for $100 or for a seat at a Rangers game is either in Alice's wallet, in which case it is hers, or it is in Bob's wallet, in which case it is his. There is no clearing or settlement, no reconciliation and no question of authenticity.

The idea that tokens are central to the future of finance is not new to various other serious players who understand financial markets either. Jonathan Larse, head of the Ping An Global Voyager Fund, said on stage at Money20/20 Asia in Singapore that tokens in finance are 'a much bigger story than cryptocurrencies', and he suggested that institutional strategies and scenario plans should be updated immediately to take into account the new technology. His focus was on three key characteristics that he saw as driving the new asset class: transparency, universal access and the ability to reduce 'frictional costs'.

Access is important, of course. Reducing frictional costs, and thereby reducing the overall cost of financial intermediation in society, would be a good thing for all of us as well. But that point about transparency is central to our vision of new financial markets. While talking about using decentralized finance to reduce risk in the financial system, David Solomon, the CEO of Goldman Sachs, said that the technology was about making the financial system more transparent. The St. Louis Fed, in a report on decentralized finance, similarly described an infrastructure based on open protocols, with agreements that are enforced by code and transactions that are executed in a secure and verifiable way (Schär 2021). It predicted that such an infrastructure could mean an interoperable financial system with 'unprecedented transparency, equal access rights and little need for custodians, central clearing houses, or escrow services'.

In a January 2023 working paper, the Bank for International Settlements set out their view that DeFi harnesses innovative technology that might shape the future financial ecosystem. This innovation can be traced back to the following three fundamental characteristics, which are of interest well beyond cryptocurrency markets.

1. The algorithmic automation of financial activity, such as market-making, to support the pooling of assets of small-scale and large-scale actors alike. In the best case, such algorithmic services might reduce inefficiencies while being transparent to all parties, and they should also allow users to retain full control over their funds.

2. A novel form of competitive financial engineering, reinforced by what are known as 'DeFi compositions', where financial service providers can combine the financial functions of several DeFi protocols to offer novel, complex and deeply nested financial products without being dependent on any single intermediary. This is possible because DeFi protocols are, in essence, computer programs that can automatically call on other computer programs.

3. DeFi could be a blueprint for how technology can enable new forms of openness to the financial sector. One could envision making use of the underlying technology in the current financial system to provide stability and scale for programmable finance ecosystems.

Again, that point about openness resonates with us. Now, transparent does not, of course, mean that everyone will be able to read everyone else's data, but it does mean that the new technologies will enable everyone to see that they can trust everyone else – the financial markets version of the difference between showing people your date of birth (bad) and showing people a credential from a regulated financial institution that states that you are over 21 (good). You can prove things about data without sharing the data – a concept we keep returning to because it is so central to both the universe and the Metaverse.

The new environment

Fink, Larse, Solomon and the St. Louis Fed all know what they are talking about, and we need to take their points about transparency on board to start thinking about how the emerging regulatory environment for digital assets can be different from, and more efficient than, the existing regulatory environment. Using the privacy structures that will be discussed in chapter 9 we can make markets that work in a very new way. We can make markets in which, for example, organizations can be sure of the solvency of counterparties by computing that their assets exceed their liabilities without being able to discover what any of those assets or liabilities actually are. No need for meaningless 'attestations' or after-the-horse-has-bolted audits: financial markets that are built on the pillars of tokens, transparency and trust will indeed be the next generation.

It seems to us that – whether cryptocurrencies survive the coming storm of regulation, central bank digital currencies, instant payments and digital identity – institutional markets will ultimately use the new infrastructure to trade bonds, gold and carbon in digital form. It won't only be commodities that are tokenized and traded without clearing and settlement. Banks will tokenize all forms of collateral, such as title to property, using the technology. As the Bank for International Settlements set out in a bulletin in June 2022: 'DeFi lending must engage in large-scale tokenization of real-world assets unless it wants to remain a self-referential system fuelled by speculation.'

This will be a whole new financial services sector, and it will be an important one. Since, as *The Economist* pointed out in an article titled 'DeFi land' in 2021, tokens can be digital representations of nearly anything, 'they could be efficient solutions to all sorts of financial problems'. Apart from anything else, tokens mean a lower-cost trading environment, which is why the big players want to use them as soon as the regulatory environment is stable.

The transition to DeFi

If the concept of future decentralized markets operating in virtual worlds seems a little far-fetched, note that, when speaking at Consensus 2022, Tyrone Lobban (head of Onyx Digital Assets at JPMorgan) described in detail the bank's institutional-grade DeFi plans and highlighted how much value in tokenized assets is waiting in the wings (Allison 2022). He said that tokenized assets ranging from US Treasuries to money market funds could all be used as collateral in DeFi pools, bring trillions of dollars of assets into DeFi, 'so that we can use these new mechanisms for trading, borrowing [and] lending, but with the scale of institutional assets'.

Financial institutions welcome this development. Here's Thomas Zschach, chief innovation officer at Swift (see Swift 2022): 'Financial institutions today don't typically engage with permissionless digital assets, because of their unregulated status and anonymity... But many financial institutions, central banks, market infrastructures, and others including SWIFT are experimenting with digital assets – particularly CBDCs and tokenized assets.'

Why? Well, SWIFT says it is to uncover new opportunities to increase efficiency, reduce costs, encourage financial inclusion and continue to bring more value to their communities. This is not a unique perspective. It is why forward-thinking financial institutions are looking at DeFi: not because of ideology, but because of money.

One thing that the advent of institutional DeFi will require is digital identity infrastructure because of the need for KYC and so on in legitimate markets. This has already started to happen here and there (e.g. in Aave Arc) but we need a scale identity infrastructure if we are going to connect DeFi with the 'real world', so to speak. Lobban's view is that the way forward is to use digital identity building blocks such as VCs. These are the key to scale solutions and, as Lobban says, 'since verifiable credentials are not held on-chain, you don't have the same overhead involved with writing this kind of information to blockchain, paying for gas fees, etc.'.

Indeed. And VCs have another important benefit too, as we will see in the next chapter.

Seeing clearly

Transparency is one of the key reasons we should all want to see a renewed and reinvented financial sector. Look at some of the recent problems in the world of finance, such as the collapse of Wirecard. Corporate accounts included assets that simply did not exist. Since auditors and the regulators and the board were unable to prevent criminality on a grand scale here, it is reasonable to ask whether technology might have been able to do a better job. Well, we think the answer is yes, and we think tokenization is part of a consistent vision of just how it might do so. If someone claims to own one-thousandth of the Mona Lisa, it is easy for you to check on the digital asset platform to see that the token representing one-thousandth of the Mona Lisa is in that person's wallet. You don't have to rely on auditors or other middlemen.

Many people we have spoken to in the financial sector reiterate the point about transparency, saying that it transcends specific DeFi applications but encompasses industry-level transparency for the entire community conducting DeFi transactions. This is because information on how various assets and wallets are performing is completely visible to all. This seems a key perspective to us: state information is available to all market participants, not just those in the know. This increases everyone's ability to understand (and regulate) what is going on in the markets.

As was evident from the start of the crypto polar winter vortex, DeFi has some significant advantages. DeFi protocols control loan books with the lending standards, counterparty addresses and liquidation levels being completely transparent. Depositors can access all of the information they might want in order to determine the health of DeFi protocols before they invest – and, because collateral is automatically liquidated when the value of that collateral drops below a certain level, there are no bad debts.

Transparency, however, does not mean that everything should be visible to everyone all of the time. A Wharton School paper on 'DeFi beyond the hype' noted that there may well be some tension between the increased auditability and transparency of shared ledger records and the privacy of stakeholders

(Gogel 2021). It is one thing for me to be able to examine your loan book on a shared ledger somewhere to determine that you are solvent, but it is quite another for me to know who your counterparties are (as long as I know that someone knows who they are). Business cannot work like that. Secrecy is necessary for business to function at all! Not only is it important for businesses to protect the privacy of their customers and suppliers, but they also want to avoid revealing strategies to competitors or alerting potential competitors. Anonymity does not work for markets, but complete transparency does not work for market participants. What is needed is privacy, and this, as we will see, is where the Metaverse may have the potential to outperform the mundane.

CHAPTER 9

Privacy with credentials

Recently published research from the University of California, Berkeley has put the need for privacy under the spotlight (Nair *et al.* 2023). Researchers found that the three data points required to track an individual in a game – one on the head and one on each of the hands – are sufficient to uniquely identify an individual. Here's lead researcher Suraj Nair:

> Moving around in a virtual world while streaming basic motion data would be like browsing the internet while sharing your fingerprints with every website you visit. However, unlike web-browsing, which does not require anyone to share their fingerprints, the streaming of motion data is a fundamental part of how the metaverse currently works.

The solution to this is likely to be a combination of better data regulation and clear guidance around the adoption of privacy-preserving technologies such as VCs so that when someone moves from one virtual world to another, they are not immediately identifiable. What is more, as we will see, the flexibility and granularity of VCs give us the ability to bring selective and progressive disclosure to transactions, ensuring that private data is protected and that the interactions are supported with the bare minimum information being shared.

Persistent pseudonyms

For web3 to work, digital identity is needed. For reasons of privacy and practicality, digital identities should be provided as persistent pseudonyms. A visionary in this field is Philip Rosedale, who founded Linden Lab (the home of Second Life) a generation ago. He has spent more time in the proto-metaverse than pretty much anyone else on the planet. He says that persistent pseudonyms are at the heart of the metaverse and that 'true names, for so many reasons, are not what we want to go toward, because not everybody wants to use their true name or true face' (Olson & Peers 2022).

Solving identity paradoxes with pseudonyms

As Dave set out in some detail in *Identity Is the New Money*, the use of pseudonymous virtual identities (giving a persona not only to people but also to both real and virtual 'things') is a basic means of making digital identity work for individuals, businesses and governments alike. We look back here to John Clippinger's notion of 'negative identities', which he defined as persistent but anonymous online identities that are never revealed in full but are revealed *just enough to enter into a relationship* (Clippinger 2007). As Clippinger said, the merchant doesn't need to know your name to sell you shoes. Clippinger also said that 'negative identity should become the default identity online' – a sentiment we strongly agree with.

Rather than 'negative identity', though, we will use the structured formulation of 'pseudonyms with credentials', as discussed in part II . A pseudonym is an identifier – a name in the simplest case – that is not the real identity of something but that is persistent and linked to the real identity. Robert Galbraith was J. K. Rowling's pseudonym for writing her Cormoran Strike crime novel series. It was a pseudonym because someone knew that Robert Galbraith was J. K. Rowling while almost everyone else did not. A pseudonym can be connected with credentials to form a persona, rather like an avatar in a computer game: not just an identity, but an identity with some attributes.

Pseudonyms are not a mechanism for committing crimes or escaping responsibilities. Two–way pseudonymity (between, for example, a shopkeeper and a person using a chip and PIN card to purchase something in a shop) means that we can have transactions in which the counterparties are unaware of each other's real identities yet engage in legal transactions with accompanying legal certainty. This kind of conditional anonymity has long been known to be socially useful (see Grijpink & Prins 2001) and has always seemed to us to be the core of the architecture that we need to implement a practical identity infrastructure that works for the new economy (see Birch & McEvoy 2007). The idea of persistent pseudonyms as the anchors for relationships is the core of the business processes that will use that architecture.

We proceed, therefore, on our assumption that if identity infrastructures are to serve the needs of our information society, their focus must be moved away from the identities of individuals to become more supportive of pseudonymity (Clarke 2001), giving people a means of engaging in economic and social transactions without having to give away everything about themselves in the process. This leads us to think of transactional identity as being akin to menu selection, so that, as Jaron Lanier puts it, people can select between 'economic avatars' (Lanier.2013).

A key reason why this is so desirable is that it gives us a means to introduce some control over our privacy into the transactional world. If we make pseudonyms central to the new identity narrative, we have a solution that is enabling as well as enhancing, and this means that some apparently difficult problems (e.g. access to adult services) can be solved.

The reputation economy

Persistent pseudonyms that transact using tokens on the basis of their credentials deliver the 'reputation economy' so long talked about by both science fiction writers and privacy advocates. The tokens and credentials work together: NFTs are about demonstrating the rights of ownership, fungible tokens are about bearer instruments, and VCs are about demonstrating the reputation of owners.

Here's an example (again using sporting tickets) to show how a reputation economy might work in practice. A ticket for a seat at the Champions League final is an NFT. It is absolutely unique and there are no copies or clones allowed if the system is to work. For the sake of discussion, let us assume that some of these go to the clubs, some go to corporate sponsors and some go to various dignitaries. Each of these is allocated through multiple tiers of distribution until an actual ticket ends up in the hands of an actual fan.

Now imagine a decentralized alternative. The venue mints the NFTs for the event and then sends these over to the wallets of the supporters' clubs, those of the sponsors, and so on. Basically, that's it. That's all they have to do.

Neither the stadium nor the clubs nor the police nor anybody else has to worry about counterfeit tickets in this alternative vision because they simply don't exist in the NFT environment. The tickets can be bought and sold and transferred between wallets by means of DeFi protocols with no further central co-ordination required. When a fan turns up at the stadium they either have the NFT for a seat on the night or they do not. Simple!

Well, not quite. As always, the complicated part is identity.

The stadium is private property and it is under no obligation to allow entry to one and all. It might, for example, require that fans with a Liverpool ticket belong to the official Liverpool Supporters Club. Why? Well, because some people are banned from stadiums. In that case, even if a banned fan buys an NFT for a game at an English football stadium, they will be denied entry because no supporters club will issue the necessary credential that is needed to get into a ground, since in order to issue this credential they will have to scan the list of banned supporters. You can easily imagine the supporters club app on the phone connecting once a week, say, to obtain an IS-A-SUPPORTER credential that is valid for a week. No credential, no entry.

Note that the entire transaction from buying the ticket to getting into the ground does not require the fan to divulge their identity to the stadium. Their personal information cannot be stolen (see, for example, the case study on the Optus hack later in this chapter) because it is never gathered.

Know Your Employees

Reputation is not only about business partners of course. In the financial services world we spend a lot of time thinking about KYC regulations because of the colossal expense of implementing them and the massive penalties for getting them wrong. It has been clear for years that the system is broken, but it is not only broken when it comes to dealing with customers, it is also broken when it comes to dealing with employees.

Compliance

If you are involved in any way at all in moving money, you will be aware of the Financial Crimes Enforcement Network (FinCEN). It is a bureau of the US Treasury that was created in 1990 to combat money laundering, terrorist financing and other financial crimes through the collection, analysis and dissemination of financial intelligence. It works to achieve this mission by administering and enforcing the Bank Secrecy Act and other anti-money laundering (AML) laws and regulations. When it comes to moving money, the cost of shifting the electrons around is nothing, frankly, compared with the cost of compliance, and many new businesses have set sail only to founder on the reef of due diligence.

In many ways, compliance is a moat that protects incumbents from competitors. As any fintech entrepreneur knows, it is a headache to deal with compliance, and the costs continue to escalate. Digital identity must be one of the keys to getting these costs under control, and indeed Jimmy Kirby, FinCEN's acting deputy director, spoke in early 2023 about the need for digital identity, stating that FinCEN is 'pragmatically focused' on protecting the US financial system from illicit finance threats (Orrick, Herrington & Sutcliffe LLP 2023). According to Kirby, financial institutions must establish with confidence who their customers are on the front end and *throughout the customer relationship*. It's not good enough to do the KYC check and then forget about it, which means that the cost of compliance is growing and digital solutions are desperately needed.

This is why what Laura Spiekerman from Alloy calls the 'perpetual KYC approach' is so important (Spiekerman 2023). What she means by this is automated recurring checks based on specific triggers: an update to a customer's personal data, say, or a transaction that sets off a risk alert.*

---

* Cryptocurrency players are subject to the same concerns as mainstream financial institutions and we do not doubt they take the rules just as seriously. Coinbase, for example, requires onboarding individuals and entities to provide identifying information, including their name and country of residence, which is then checked against lists of sanctioned individuals or entities. It also uses 'geofencing controls' to prevent access to Coinbase from places including Crimea, North Korea, Syria and Iran, and it says that it routinely subjects its sanctions compliance programme to internal testing and independent audits by third parties.

That is all about onboarding customers, of course. But it appears that some companies do not apply the same rigour when it comes to figuring out who employees are or onboarding new business partners. The key point is that digital identity isn't needed only to support due diligence around customers: Know Your Employee (KYE) is just as important an opportunity as KYC, Know Your Customer's Customers, Know Your Business, and so on. All of these need to be established with continuing confidence, and they are all currently a mishmash of scans of utility bills, pictures of driving licences and pointless box ticking.

When it comes to employees, for example, some of those new hires might not be simply exaggerating about their expertise on their résumés, they might be acting on behalf of a foreign power! In a recent case, the Feds charged a representative of the Foreign Trade Bank of the Democratic People's Republic of Korea for money laundering conspiracies designed to generate revenue for North Korea through the use of cryptocurrency. According to court documents, North Koreans applied for jobs in remote IT development work and passed employment checks by using fake – or fraudulently obtained – identity documents. These workers would then request payment in cryptocurrency and whisk their earnings back to the motherland (US Attorney's Office, District of Columbia 2023c).

Running a business in the Metaverse will require some pretty serious thinking about employee identification, credentials, authorizations and relations, so KYE would clearly benefit from digital infrastructure. The last time Dave was asked for documents for an employment check – to tick a box confirming that he had the right to work in the UK despite having been born in the UK, having more than one paid employment in the UK, and paying tax in the UK – he was required to send a picture of his passport by e-mail to an HR department. Now, while HR departments are famed for their strong cybersecurity practices, Dave was a little concerned about personal information being exposed (especially when digital alternatives have been demonstrated).

This is a reasonable concern, as the fallout from the Optus data breach in Australia explored in the case study later in this chapter has clearly demonstrated. People can get up to no end of mischief with a copy of your passport and your personal details.

Digital identity hopefully provides a way forward here, even though KYE is very different from KYC because of risk tolerance (Hoffart & Settle 2023). While advances in digital identity management around customer identification, authentication and authorization add to the corporate toolbox, there is a fundamental difference in deployment because the tolerance for consumer fraud is non-zero; the optimal tolerance for internal corporate crime is zero. Companies can reuse KYC technology (e.g. digital onboarding) for employees but in a more rigorous process.

KYE as a vector
It is interesting to see how KYE is moving forward though. The authors took part in a digital identity design sprint day hosted by National Australia Bank in Melbourne in 2023, and it seemed to both of us that the most attractive of the use cases explored (in the context of commercial opportunities that might arise from using bank-issued digital identities) was indeed KYE. There were some start-ups there that were already delivering services in this space and looking to improve their offerings by integrating digital credentials of some kind, and we know that that approach works.[*]

Given the scale of the KYE problem, it is clear that a shift to VCs for employee onboarding is a win–win, and it makes sense to provide candidates and employers with the necessary infrastructure to provide specific characteristics (e.g. this person has

[*] Here we must note that ConnectID, as an example, worked with Australian fintech Meeco, a state government and an engineering and technical services company in a pilot to demonstrate the commercial benefits of digital identity and VCs in workplace onboarding. Instead of presenting the originals of physical documents, or digitized copies of physical documents, employees digitally asserted their identity by presenting a VC, all from a wallet application on their phone.

a valid welding certificate) without giving away personally identifiable information.

The European Union has four large-scale EU Digital Identity Wallet pilot projects running at the moment, and it intends to launch such a wallet to 450 million European citizens next year. This will give those citizens the ability to store digital identity credentials including their national ID, their driving licence, their qualifications and their bank details, and there is no reason why other jurisdictions might not develop similar infrastructure.

Hopefully, with new energy being directed towards digital identity wallets, VCs and (custodial) self-sovereign identity, this specific problem of KYE can be tackled quickly, efficiently and to the mutual benefit of all stakeholders, and it can end up serving as a vanguard for mass market digital identity solutions. KYE and the need to hire and fire in the Metaverse might prove to be an important vector for digital identity in the mass market.

Case study: Optus breach

There are a huge number of grand-scale data breach cases that we could have chosen to make the point about how not to manage personal information in the Metaverse, but we thought that the well-known case of the Optus breach in Australia in 2022 was an excellent illustrative example. Hackers stole the names, dates of birth, phone numbers and email addresses of a large number of Optus's customers, and for a subset of customers they also stole addresses and ID document numbers (such as driving licence and passport numbers).[*]

The breach was serious for Optus, which suffered reputational damage in the form of increased churn as well as an exceptional expense amounting to A$140 million for a customer remediation programme. It was more serious for

---

[*] Around ten million Australians had had their personal data looted and three million of them had their passport and driving licence data accessed.

customers though, especially the ones who can no longer use their passports for identification purposes when using the Australian national Document Verification System. This happened because Optus asked the federal government to block the exposed passport numbers from being used for access to government departments, health and welfare payments, as well as access to banking and other institutions.

We are not picking on Optus here, or on telecommunications companies in general either. There a great many companies that are hoarding data that they don't really need, either because of government rules or because of data practices. We hope that breaches such as this one, and the inevitable legislative response, will cause a reassessment of practice and an end to what the *Australian Financial Review* colourfully referred to as 'data gluttony' (Smith *et al.* 2022).

We are not picking on Australia either, by the way. This is a universal problem. There was a similar data catastrophe in Turkey in 2021 when the founder of the now-defunct cryptocurrency exchange Thodex vanished. It turned out that he had taken not only the money but also the KYC data that he had been required to collect for hundreds of thousands of customers (including scans of the their national ID cards, once again proving that digitizing identity is no substitute for digital identity) and this will surely cause more damage to more people and more companies than the missing crypto loot will).

Privacy as the proposition

When the New Zealand company AA Traveller reported that hackers had stolen the personal information of their customers, their general manager Greg Leighton said that 'much of the data was not needed anymore and should have been deleted' (Olley 2022). How much longer are we going to put up with this? You know the drill.

- Step 1. App or website asks for personal information such as date of birth, phone number or mother's maiden name for 'security' despite none of that information contributing in any way to transaction security.
- Step 2. App or website gets hacked and your personal information is now in the hands of scammers, nation state cyber warriors and perverts.
- Step 3. Rinse and repeat.

As we have set out, the solution to this is the world of VCs: the reputation economy that embraces both the universe and the metaverses.

Here's how this works. I want to know something about you, but I don't want any of your personal information because that is toxic waste that will inevitably leak from my systems because I will always spend more money on marketing and stock buybacks than on detailed risk analysis and appropriate countermeasures. I therefore ask you to present a credential, which is a fact about you that is digitally signed by someone I can trust (by which I mean, of course, someone I can sue).

If you tell me that you are over 21, whatever. But if you present a credential from Wells Fargo that says that you are over 21, great.

If you're interested, what actually happens is that you present the attribute I am interested in (e.g. IS-OVER-18) together with a public key and an expiration date, all signed by Wells Fargo. Since I know Wells Fargo's public key (which is, after all, public), I can check this digital signature and find out if it is real. If it is, I can then extract your public key, encrypt a random number with this key, and send it to you and ask you what the number is. Now, of course, the only person who can decrypt this message is the person with the corresponding private key: you respond to this challenge and now I know that not only is the credential real, but that it belongs to you.

Why oh why?

Why does your telco, your travel company or anyone else need a copy of your driving licence? We don't know anything about Australian telecommunications regulations, but we assumed that Optus requested that information because of some government regulation designed to maximize the impact of data breaches. We were close – and we weren't alone in seeing this as unsatisfactory. Angie Mentis, National Australia Bank's (then) group executive for digital, data and analytics, was among many informed observers who called for the reform of archaic identification procedures that require customers to establish identity by giving companies enormous quantities of sensitive personal data, thereby creating 'honeypots' for criminals around the world (Eyers 2022).

Australia may actually be in a position to do something about this because of the ConnectID service discussed earlier. This will allow authorized clients (e.g. Optus) to confirm customer attributes without having to hold their own copies of the data. So, for example, your online booze barn might ask your bank if you are over 18, and the bank will tell them yes or no but will not tell them your date of birth or anything else.

More generally, the technology of VCs means that we can stop requiring personal data to enable transactions and instead require the relevant credentials necessary to enable the specific interaction. There is, as noted, a world of difference between, say, Optus asking for your date of birth and me asking for proof that you are over 21, or between Optus asking for your address and me asking for proof that you are resident in the continental United States, or between Optus asking you to find pictures of tractors in a confusing array of blurred photographs and me asking for proof that you are a person.

Australia isn't the only country in which banks are actually working together to try and do something about digital identity,* but we do wonder what has to happen for banks to get together elsewhere (e.g. the US) to take similar action. Do we need to have more colossal data breaches before the banking industry, regulators and suppliers will work together on this, or can we just take the strategic decision to improve the situation for everyone by committing to protecting the personal data of consumers in the Metaverse by promising *never to collect it*.

---

* Another example is Canada's 'verified.me' service, which was developed in cooperation with BMO, CIBC, Desjardins, National Bank of Canada, RBC, Scotiabank and TD.

CHAPTER 10

Security from identifiers

You can have security without privacy, but you can't have privacy without security (since if there is no security, nothing will be confidential), and the security of the Metaverse rests on the control of cryptographic keys. The vision of a reputation economy set out in the previous chapter depends on the safe, secure and practical management of those cryptographic keys.

Custodial SSI

The core concept underlying self-sovereign identity is that citizens should be empowered by taking control of these keys,

although we think it makes no sense that the average person should be loaded with this responsibility. Adam Levine says that while the idea of self-sovereignty in crypto is empowering, it demands a 'persistent competence' (Levine 2021). We think it is well beyond the capability and capacity of most people.

Who wants to be their own bank?

A couple of years ago, a pair of metal detectorists in England came across a hoard of 2,571 Anglo Saxon and Norman coins. The coins would have originally belonged to a wealthy person – probably one who buried them for safekeeping during William the Bastard's illegal invasion of England and the subsequent period of genocidal regime change in 1066. 'Not your clay pot buried in a field, not your coins', as they would have said in those days. This was the mediaeval equivalent of being your own bank.[*]

It may well be that personal asset management for economic security is the best way to implement financial plans for the masses. There are frequent downsides, however. If your head gets cut off by rampaging barbarians, for example, or if the dog eats your USB stick, then the cash will vanish from circulation, out of the reach of your heirs until recovered by amateur archaeologists or quantum computers.

The obvious question, then, is: why would anyone want to be their own bank?

Perhaps Alice has some cryptocurrency that is stored safely on a USB interface hard wallet protected by a long pass phrase. Naturally, with security in mind, perhaps she rolled it up in tinfoil and buried it under a tree in her backyard. The pass phrase and a description of the tree are probably transcribed onto a lead plate that is buried in her sister's garden, and the directions to recover the plate are in a sealed envelope held by her solicitor with strict instructions not to open it except in the event of her death.

---

[*] Perhaps a thousand years from now, hobbyist historians trawling through the layers of an ancient Welsh rubbish dump will stumble across a hard disk full of bitcoins and use the proceeds to buy the entire solar system.

All quite standard precautions. The cryptocurrency experts will tell you that you should not keep your cryptocurrency on exchanges, partly because if the exchange gets hacked, your cryptocurrency might vanish, and partly because if the exchange folds, your IOUs may not be honoured. These are hardly esoteric concerns, because aside from the multibillion dollar frauds, thefts and collapses that we are all familiar with – from QuadrigaCX in Canada, where the CEO apparently died in India with some $170 million missing; to FTX in the Bahamas, where, as Michael Lewis recounts in his 2023 book *Going Infinite*, some $8.6 billion was owed to customers after bankruptcy – there is an almost daily roll-call of exchange problems resulting in people losing money in one way or another.

Not your keys, not your coins. That is the mantra.

The serious cryptocurrency players therefore only use exchanges for doing business, and they move their virtual cash to safer places once they have completed a transaction. Under this kind of asset management strategy, when Bob wants to spend some of his hard-speculated crypto-cash, it takes him more than half an hour to dig up his USB stick, and it is then a simple matter for him to connect it to his off-grid laptop, transfer some electronic cash to the hard drive, rebury the USB stick (and perhaps also bury a decoy stick under another tree in case someone is watching), and then go online to move the electronic cash into a hot wallet ready to spend.

People who do not follow these straightforward steps are in peril. See, for example, this rather typical theft that was reported on Twitter:[*]

> My primary wallets were compromised last night – you never want to wake up to something like this. Down bad. I ended up losing somewhere between 300–500 ETH altogether. Mostly my prized collection of NFTs were taken and sold.

---

[*] See https://bit.ly/3A30bSH.

The chastened victim later commented: 'I didn't use hardware wallets (I have used one in the past, got tired of it).' Well, indeed.

Incidentally, when we originally used the idea of burying keys under trees, we thought we were just having some fun. We didn't really think anyone would do this. But then, while writing this book, we read Warren Togami's 2023 tweet about doing something just as paranoid.* He wrote:

> True story: My previous 'cold' wallet was an encrypted file on a dedi laptop with wifi card removed. I forgot the passphrase due to fever and was almost screwed. Recovered deep cold backup on paper in a jar buried deep in the forest in a location I knew from childhood Boy Scouts.

There are other ways to store secret keys and pass phrases, of course, and new technology can help. Some of the delegates at the Consensus 2016 cryptocurrency conference were sceptical when Dave shared his preferred strategy for securing digital objects, which was to convert the security key into a QR code and have it tattooed onto his scrotum (Castillo 2016). He had in fact suggested this approach to managing *privates keys* (sic) before, and he had even toyed with the idea of patenting his breakthrough approach to cyber defence – on the grounds that you can patent anything no matter how trivial or obvious these days – but sadly he never got round to doing so. He is now kicking himself for that though because, according to the *New York Times*, many people now have actual QR code tattoos ... and they work (Kelley 2021).

Be their own bank

That phrase 'not your keys, not your coins' may be a fun rallying cry for computer science undergraduates, but it just doesn't work

---

* See https://bit.ly/3ofroPm.

in the real world. Current estimates are that more than a fifth of bitcoins are already lost. Because bitcoin owners need access to their keys (or some kind of recovery phrase) to access their crypto wealth, they are screwed if they lose those keys (or forget the recovery phrases). What is more, there are cryptocurrency owners who simply drop dead, taking their passwords with them. The amount of buried treasure will therefore only grow as more people forget their passwords, die, accidentally throw away their old hard disk full of bitcoins or (as one of us did) upgrade their phone without backing up their data properly. As Chainalysis's Jonathan Levin – who many regard as the go-to guy for tracing missing bitcoins – memorably told NPR (see Malone 2018): 'For the people that have lost their bitcoins, I say tough luck.'

A cryptofan friend of ours suggested keeping a backup in a safety deposit box in a bank. This of course made us wonder why one wouldn't simply keep the keys in the bank in the first place? We are sure that this is what most people actually want to do. We are both too forgetful and lazy to want to assume the responsibility for being our own banks! And even if we were prepared to give it a go, neither of us is a data security stronghold with layers of defences against hackers, cyber attackers or disgruntled bag holders. But banks are, and this is why we would be happy to pay them a reasonable fee for managing both the keys and the interface between the Wild West of crypto and the banking system itself.

Bank opportunities

In addition to saying, 'I personally think that bitcoin is worthless' (Schnell 2021), JP Morgan Chase's Jamie Dimon once said that if the bank's customers wanted to buy cryptocurrency, the bank would give 'legitimate' access but would not custody their holdings. But why not?

We were very interested to see banks starting to offer cryptocurrency custody services (e.g. US Bank, which launched a safekeeping custody service for institutional investment managers). State Street, which provides custody services to institutional investors, is a good example. It launched a digital finance division to expand into areas including cryptocurrency and tokenization. The new division was led by Nadine Chakar (the bank's head of global markets), who told *The Banker* at the time that State Street could 'leverage [its] expertise in securities finance and lending to explore how investors can borrow and lend crypto assets'. She went on to say that she believed that all financial instruments could become digitalized in future (Macknight 2021). Other serious players are also looking at the space, and it undoubtedly presents a huge opportunity for banks. As Nadine commented on the use of digital assets, regulated banks can offer new services, and this will create 'new business models and new business opportunities'.

So why not extend these services to individual consumers? It could be a huge business. Not really because of people tucking away their bitcoins, but because of the trading of digital objects of all kinds. Alice can't store her gold bars in her local bank branch but she could store gold-backed stablecoins in her bank's digital object vaults. In their June 2020 market overview prepared for the Dubai Financial Services Commission, the accountants Deloitte said that such custody services are 'crucial' to the widespread adoption of digital assets. PayPal spent a couple of hundred million dollars on the custody service Curv in 2021, so the direction of travel is clear, but there is no reason why banks cannot compete effectively in this space.

While many organizations could (and do) provide custody services, we are particularly interested in the role of commercial banks. In our view, the 'incentive' function of banks is often overlooked, but it is strategically important: that is, the existence of regulated financial institutions in a market means that transactions will take place that would otherwise not take place (Crane & Bodie 1996). Cryptoassets are a perfect example of this. Back in 2020 almost all Americans with cryptocurrencies said that they would or might use their bank to buy and sell them (Shevlin 2021), illustrating the key role of bank incentive functions. Cryptocurrency to one side, we strongly suspect that there are a substantial number of Americans who do not currently hold cryptocurrencies – or even want to ever hold cryptocurrencies following the cryptowinter – but who might be interested in holding digital objects such as NFTs, stablecoins, carbon tokens and such like if the custody service was offered by their bank.

Michael Gofman, assistant professor of finance at the University of Rochester, described custody services as being like the foundations of a house, in that most people are barely aware of them but we can't build anything worthwhile without them. His conclusion is, therefore, that traditional banks will end up offering these services (Schnell 2021).

We are more than happy to see them do this. Will the average person want to be their own bank? No way. It makes much more sense to store one's assets in the safety of an institution that specializes in keeping assets safe: an institution that is regulated, insured and managed to ensure that, whatever happens, normal customers (who do not spend every waking hour working on data security) are protected.

We think that the technology of SSI delivers the secure digital identities that are needed to transact in the Metaverse, but it does so in the wrong context. We therefore prefer the framing of 'custodial SSI', whereby the citizens' keys are managed by a regulated institution, such as a bank. That way, when a customer drops their phone into a toilet, their keys can be recovered from their bank and they can go about their business.

Squares and stripes

It doesn't have to be banks providing this crucial custody service, of course. After all, it could have been banks that provided a way for small businesses to take cards in the physical world (as

Square did) or in the virtual world (as Stripe did), but it wasn't. It's worth reflecting on the backstory of, and the ensuing disruption caused by, Square and comparing the picture with Dfns, a French-founded decentralized key management solution for digital assets.

It is well known that Jack Dorsey's interest in payments was piqued by his artist friend Jim McKelvey, who lost out on a phone order for one of his $3,000 glass blown creations because he couldn't accept Amex. Through a series of rapid prototypes and a creative go-to-market strategy, not only did Square solve the payments acceptance challenge for smaller businesses, it (and other mobile point-of-sale solutions that it inspired) grew card acceptance globally. Dorsey also pushed the bounds of card acceptance certification and the position of incumbents, with Australia grabbing the headlines here (Eyers 2020). As reported at the time: 'The banks were frustrated because they had invested hundreds of millions of dollars in their own payment terminals, in order to meet the strict security standards of the global credit card schemes, only to have the global PCI Security Standards Council change the standards in 2017.'

Ultimately, incumbent financial institutions were major beneficiaries of the innovation because of the overall growth in card payments. So while the banks may have been embarrassed by their investment in legacy infrastructure, customers were still using cards as the funding source, which is a lucrative business for banks. It will be interesting to see how quickly this broadly positive narrative changes, and how comfortable incumbents remain as Square Loans (formerly Square Capital) matures. As we write, in late 2023, business loans are hard to come by without demonstrable and growing annual recurring revenue, but Square Loans and others like it are well placed to eat further into the business of loans to merchants and their associated supply chains because of all the transaction data that they hold. The most recent move by Block (Square's parent company) – from transaction-based loan repayments to monthly repayments for larger merchants – indicates that growing the loans business is firmly in its sights. As these merchants become able to accept various digital forms of payment (stablecoins and cryptocurrency included), the longer-term role for banks isn't necessarily certain.

Clarisse Hagège, a former banker and the founder of Dfns, tells a similar story of being driven to solve a problem in the market that incumbents had ignored. While helping a start-up with its ICO in 2016, Hagège found that selling the investment opportunity to investors who hadn't previously invested in digital assets wasn't the hard part: the sticking point was closing the investment, which required the family offices and smaller investors that she was targeting to get their heads round the concept of private keys and the security measures necessary to manage them, such as hardware security modules (HSMs). There were also concerns about compliance and the potential risks if a trader with access to the HSM left the company. While the HSM approach appeared foreign and fraught with risk management challenges, more established solutions like BitGo were too expensive and inaccessible for family offices.

Hagège turned to multi-party computation: a cryptographic protocol that distributes a computation process across multiple parties, with no single party having access to the complete data set. In private key management, multi-party computation splits a private key into multiple parts, with transactions requiring a consensus among parts. Crucially, the private key is never reassembled during the process of generating the private key and signing a transaction. Dfns is targeting tokenization platforms with their API-based key management solution, and their partnership with Tokeny, a tokenization platform, is a strong example in this field (Yadlos 2023).

Tokeny uses Ethereum-based token standards to ensure KYC, AML and regulatory compliance, and it integrates Dfns's non-custodial wallet infrastructure to improve security and ease of use. Together, the two companies have simplified the user experience for investors, allowing them to manage tokenized securities easily. Their approach has been likened to ApplePay, and it is anticipated to drive the adoption of tokenization as it meets the institutional needs for efficiency, compliance and scalability in asset management. And – similar to the short-term versus longer-term benefits to financial institutions presented by Square – the need for intermediaries will decrease as investors gain more direct control over their assets, and this will potentially reduce the relevance of traditional custodial services. These developments may well turn out to be the Squares and Stripes of the current day.

Case study: cars and whisky

In January 2023 the California Department of Motor Vehicles (DMV) announced its intention to experiment with the digitization of car title management with NFTs, using a private testnet version of the open-source Tezos blockchain.

The immediate potential benefits seem clear: the current process for transferring car titles will be streamlined, making it faster, more reliable and less expensive than traditional methods. And, of course, there's something very real in the blocks: the blockchain creates the record of ownership and the history of each vehicle. For the purposes of the pilot, the DMV said it would create a 'shadow ledger' – a blockchain-based duplicate of the state's existing title database – to fully test the system before implementing any consumer applications. As a next step It plans to develop user-friendly digital wallets that would hold car title NFTs, allowing for a more accessible way for consumers to manage their vehicle titles.

This approach reflects a broader trend in the use of NFTs beyond art and collectibles, using them as digital certificates of authenticity and ownership for real-world assets. A particular favourite of ours is Metacask, not solely because of its quirky play on the widely known Metamask but because of its genuinely creative NFTs. We can imagine a laird showcasing 'The Vanishing Spirits' NFT, of a beautifully lit distillate from his cask, on an HD TV in his lounge room. The fact that, in April 2023, whisky continued 'to outperform other asset classes such as gold' (according to the Scottish press at least) is not unhelpful (Wright 2023). Metacask is interesting for another more practical reason too: it supports sign-up and login with Torus, a digital wallet that enables individuals to onboard with an existing social login. So even if you are not comfortable with Metamask, you can still enjoy the benefits of Metacask.

What's interesting about both of these developments, whether or not they expand into widely used services, is that they open up important discussion. The NFTs provide proof of ownership, under the control of a given individual. This creates an avenue for simpler fractional ownership and new finance models based on this. As John Blicq explains in his 2022 book *Metaverse & Financial Services*, the ability for an individual to sweat their assets, which is now commonplace with property (AirBnB) and cars (Uber), is changing the business of financial services providers who have relied on revenue from loans and insurance from the purchase and protection of these physical assets.

Economic avatars

You can think of an economic avatar as a persistent pseudonym and owned digital objects together with associated credentials. It would be wrong to think of such avatars (e.g. dgwbirch.eth) as being solely under the control of people! There will be economic avatars for companies, machines, artificial intelligences and any other market participants. The technologies needed here are well established but the business models are not, and the key issues of interchange and liability for commercial transactions need to be resolved.

A decentralized autonomous organization is more exciting as an idea than it is in reality

There is an odd aspect to the charge towards web3 and decentralization and the missionary zeal to reform financial infrastructure, which is the reinvention of things that didn't work in the past in the hope that 'this time it will be different'. An interesting example comes from the world of sports, where an enterprise called WAGMI United planned to buy a British football team using cryptocurrency. The WAGMI United backers (which included Gary Vaynerchuk (the president of the Philadelphia 76ers), Tiger Global and Slow Ventures) were keen on decentralized ownership, and the idea of a DAO, in the future.

A DAO is a form of organization based on shared ledgers and smart contracts that is often governed by a native crypto token. Ownership of these tokens means the ability to vote on the policies of the DAO. DAOs manage this process to coordinate efforts and resources. We rather like Jonah Erlich's* formulation: a DAO is a 'group chat with a bank account' (Patel 2021).

So what this would mean for sports is that there would be ownership tokens that would allow their holders to be involved in decision-making by clubs, which sounds fascinating and like a real opportunity for fans to get involved. There are also other DAOs that are active in the space, such as Links DAO, which plans to buy a golf course, and the Krause Hause DAO, which plans to buy a basketball team.

Proto-DAO United

Perhaps it is time for a lesson from history here, because, as it happens, there was a proto-DAO soccer club in England some years ago. That club was Ebbsfleet United, and its role in the historic evolution of soccer DAOs began back in 2008, when it

---

* Erlich is a member of ConstitutionDAO, which tried to buy one of the original copies of the US Constitution at auction.

made the national news because it was taken over by the online community MyFootballClub (Cole 2017). The experiment began well, with the club winning the FA Trophy (a national knockout competition for lower-league teams) just months after the takeover, beating Torquay United 1–0 in front of more than 40,000 people at Wembley Stadium. They finished their league season in mid-table, and their manager, Liam Daish, was able to use the investment to retain players he could not have afforded to without MyFootballClub's investment.

The fan voting system evolved in what many social anthropologists would regard as an entirely predictable way. After the initial investment, the fans voted on who should pick the team: themselves or the manager. They chose the manager every time. This is exactly what we would do: if we had a vote on how the Manly Sea Eagles should line up at the weekend, we would inevitably delegate that vote to someone who knows what they are doing (e.g. the manager). Why on earth would any organization allow people to decide on something that they have no demonstrable aptitude for?[*]

Who wants to be in charge?
Will Brooks, who was behind the idea in the first place, later said: 'One of my biggest conclusions is that perhaps the idea was more exciting than the reality.' This may well be true of any future DAO as well. Even if there was a wisdom of crowds to be tapped, people have other things to do. Such communities tend to evolve rapidly into groups where a small number of people coordinate action and the majority are happy to delegate responsibility. In effect, you get cabals or councils who direct the organization. Thus web3 tends towards what SEC commissioner Hester Peirce called 'shadow centralization' (Haig 2021).

---

[*] And please spare us the 'wisdom of crowds'. This has been rendered irrelevant by the advent of social media.

In the end, the club went not for shadow centralization but for actual centralization: the members voted in favour of handing two-thirds of their shares to a trust and the other third to one of the club's major shareholders (run by a group of Kuwaiti investors). As I write, Ebbsfleet United sit in the National League South (the sixth tier of English football).

Like John Naughton, we think that there is 'something touching about the DAO idea' (Naughton 2022). In a weird way it embodies 1960s idealism, communes and kibbutzes, and the idea of more democratic structures overthrowing the prevailing hierarchies. Naughton's view is that those experiments failed because alpha males and egalitarianism did not mix then and will not mix in the future (although out in the cyburbs, alpha status derives not from your gender but from the size of your token hoard).

All of which leads us to reflect on whether people actually really do want DAOs or not? Richard Brown, CTO of enterprise shared ledger company R3, explored this from a very informed perspective, and he observed that true decentralization will create a parallel financial system in which AML, KYC and counter-terrorist financing rules are not applied (Brown 2022). A system where no investor protection rules apply. A system where no accredited investor rules are in force. Whether you think this is a good idea or a bad one, Brown is right to observe that this is not a new environment: it is the very environment that we used to have, but don't any more. Or, to put it another way: if the Wild West was all that, we'd still be living in it.

Web2.5

It is interesting to note the DAOs are actually already exploring the new Wild West. In Wyoming DAOs have been buying land, albeit as a 'proof of concept' to experiment with what it means to own real estate on a distributed ledger (MacColl & Holmes 2022). One of the people behind these experiments, Max Gravitt

(a member of the Kitchen Lands DAO), calls this form of ownership 'highly liquid and global'. It allows him to transfer tokenized
shares of the land easily, although it is some way from a libertar-
ian revolution since the actual physical land that the DAOs own
is still restricted by laws and permits and so forth. When asked
where this is going, one of the other DAO owners said: 'Nobody
really knows. Like, it's just a lot of good faith right now.'*

In Edward J. Balleisen's 2018 book *Fraud: An American History from Barnum to Madoff* – which magisterially describes the
evolution of regulation and institutions to protect consumers
and investors from the Gilded Age onwards – it is impossible
not to see the world of web3 and the proto-metaverse as being
similar to America in the age of the railroad barons. Being your
own bank and we-don't-need-no-stinkin'-badges sounds great
until your grandma clicks on the wrong link in an email and her
house suddenly belongs to some guy in Minsk who flips it in
three nanoseconds.

The idea of a more efficient financial system that is based on
the trading of tokens across translucent ledgers is appealing
because, as noted earlier, the cost of financial intermediation is
a tax on the economy and directs resources away from more
productive uses that we need in order to maintain our standard of living and economic growth. But that does not mean
no regulation and no institutions. Truly decentralized systems
simply do not survive: they mutate into centralized systems
(i.e. representation and republic) or what we might think of as
an anonymous oligarchy (i.e. whales and warlords).

---

* It is possible that this commentator has never actually met anyone in real estate as
we are not entirely convinced that good faith is actually the bedrock on which that
sector of the economy rests. Although, to be fair, in *Forbes*'s 2019 table of professions
ranked in terms of honesty and ethical standards, real estate agents did score more
highly than members of congress and auto salespeople.

Case study: MakerDAO

The Maker Foundation set out to create an unbiased global financial system that could improve both (decentralized) finance and monetary policy (Brennecks *et al.* 2022). For this purpose, they implemented the stablecoin Dai, the governance token MKR and a governance system for gaining access to and managing the entire ecosystem without relying on intermediaries.

These were built using some complex smart contracts structures to enable a mechanism for maintaining a constant exchange rate of one Dai to the US dollar. The mechanism relies on an over-collateralization with a basket of multiple different collaterals. Once the collateralization rate of (currently) 150% is exceeded, a user may take out a Dai loan for the sake of leverage and/or liquidity. As soon as the value of the backing asset falls below the liquidation rate, it is liquidated. Users have therefore been aiming for higher collateralization rates and collateral diversification to avoid an auction of their assets in the event of significant market shocks and volatilities.[*]

The MakerDAO ecosystem is governed via on-chain and off-chain mechanisms. The on-chain governance primarily concerns polls and executive votes in the Maker Forum's voting list. While the use of polls captures the community's general attitude towards a draft proposal to create a consensus, executive votes are used to execute technical changes. On-chain governance is facilitated by three central smart contracts. Chief among these is a smart contract that allows MKR holders to select a primary contract to be executed using their voting privileges. A 'pause' is a smart contract that allows MKR holders to enforce a delay in executing specific calls, and a 'spell' is a smart contract that can be used to set technical constraints such as system parameters. Off-chain governance also refers

---

[*] Until recently, the system relied solely on Ether as collateral but it has now expanded to other cryptocurrencies.

to any discussions among community members outside of the on-chain mechanisms. Hence, off-chain governance consists primarily of forum signal threads, forum polls and blog entries by the community.

One clear lesson from this pre-eminent DAO is that, in the crypto world, there has been a great deal of enthusiasm for DAOs because they give everyone who holds an asset for a given project a vote, but it seems that relatively few people vote in practice.

PART IV

THE WALLETS

Having explored the fundamental technologies, the building blocks of metaverses, and the new product and service opportunities that arise in that environment, we can bring them together to form a model of the metaverses that shows the central organizing principle for transactions and the pivot for the next generation of financial: digital wallets (see figure 17 overleaf).

Here then is a model of the Metaverse that gives a useful scaffolding for strategic discussions between business and technology, together with a predicted focus: a digital wallet that holds identifiers, credentials and assets in a mechanism that makes them central to the successful operation of markets.

The infrastructure is already coming together: an Android wallet capable of storing NFTs can use the Identity Credential Hardware Abstraction Layer (HAL) to deliver the requested verifiable credential; and Apple already supports identity credentials such as driving licences in the US.

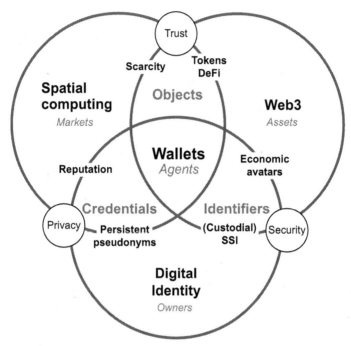

Figure 17. Wallets as the central organizing principle of the Metaverse.

CHAPTER 11

Smart wallets

Around the world the transition from physical wallets to digital wallets is well underway. A 2022 Accenture survey of 16,000 customers in thirteen countries found that 56% of them were using digital wallets more than five times every month (compared with only 48% using cards that often). Accenture's interpretation of these results led it to conclude that almost 100 billion dollars of banks' annual payments revenues were 'at risk'.

That's big money in anyone's language, so it is unsurprising that wallet wars are around the corner: early 2023 saw Wells

Fargo, Bank of America, JPMorgan Chase and others announcing that they are developing a digital wallet to help consumers pay at online merchants (Andriotis 2023).

The banks are on trend, for sure. Research from Mastercard shows that around half of all Brits think that physical wallets will become less relevant, with a fifth saying that they do not expect to carry a wallet or a purse within five years (a proportion that rises to two-fifths for millennials) (see Birch 2023). These opinions correlate with the continuing decline of cash. A decade ago around 60% of payments were made in cash, but UK Finance estimates that this figure will fall to just 6% by 2031.[*]

The US bank wallet will be managed by Zelle operator Early Warning Services LLC (EWS), and it will implement the Secure Remote Commerce (SRC)[†] standard to smooth the payment journey of Visa and Mastercard users during checkout. EWS says that the wallet will have approximately 150 million Visa and Mastercard credit and debit cards connected at launch, with plans to add other card networks in the future.[‡]

The mobile phone is, without doubt, the wallet of the next generation. Between the first quarter of 2021 and the third quarter of 2022 (the most recent quarter for which we had data to hand), the fraction of Americans who said that they used a mobile wallet at some point in the previous three months went up from around a third to around a half, and the fraction who said they had heard of them but hadn't bothered to set one up fell to a quarter from more than a third. Security concerns fell as well, so that only a fifth of Americans were now worried about wallet security (down from a quarter). The proportion of people

---

[*] You might want to short leather, because 41% of Gen Z say they don't expect to ever buy a physical wallet or purse again!

[†] If you've not heard of SRC, don't worry about it. Consumers will see the SRC standard as 'Click to Pay', just as they see the EMV standard as 'Chip and PIN'.

[‡] Incidentally, there is at least one place where Zelle is accepted by retailers: Caracas. There, homemade signs in shop windows reading 'Aceptamos Zelle' are common, and pictures of the Zelle logo are taped to cash registers in supermarkets, some of which have dedicated lines for customers paying with the app!

who had heard of mobile wallets but never set one up declined from 37% to 24%, and those that said that they were concerned about security declined from 25% to 21%.

Money and identity

Whether payments are via cards or direct from bank accounts or using digital currency, there is something else going on with digital wallets that should shape bank strategies, and that is digital identity. The Mobey Forum (which was established back in 2000) is a global, not-for-profit industry association of banks and other financial institutions that wants to shape the future of digital financial services. Its Digital Identity Expert Group published a report called 'The rise of digital identity wallets: will banks be left behind?' in 2023, in which it suggested that a combination of consumer demand, regulatory mandates (such as eIDAS in Europe) and the trend towards digital identity wallet issuance by global governments means that financial institutions must start thinking about the role they wish to stake out in the emerging digital identity ecosystem (Yliuntinen & Faragher 2023).

In particular, the Digital Identity Expert Group identifies unique opportunities for banks to leverage their position as custodians of personal data to offer value-added digital identity services and become brokers of trust in the digital economy. Their report suggests that for digital identity systems to succeed, banks must bridge the divide between the private and public sectors and drive adoption of so-called digital identity wallets.

This position is not a difficult one to justify. Most of us don't have any cash in our wallets, and that has been true for some time. A recent poll in the UK found that half of those people surveyed said they only carried a wallet to store non-payment cards such as driving licences and loyalty cards.* In fact, a third

---

* Note, too, that payment cards themselves are an identity product and not money in any sense of the word.

of 18–24 year olds say that the digital wallet on their phone is already their preferred way to pay, and more than half would rather just carry their phone in place of a wallet or purse (Kelly 2023).

Dave can provide two data points to confirm this. First, he can't remember the last time he took a wallet anywhere, except to watch Woking FC (because his wallet has his season ticket in it); and second, his son recently lost his wallet in a nightclub (which only happened because he needs his driving licence to get into nightclubs and his wallet has his driving licence in it). In other words, in both cases wallets were being carried because they were needed for identity (or, more accurately, credentials) not for payments, which is why the control of wallets will be a fundamental battle of the coming era in commerce and why talk of 'wallet wars' is far from hyperbole.

The picture is the same across Europe, where a 2022 Thales survey of EU citizens in seven countries found that two-thirds would use a wallet to store their digital identity, rising to three-quarters among those who already had some other form of digital ID. What is probably different from the US here, though, is that two-thirds of Europeans think that a government digital wallet would be best, with a third thinking that it should be banks taking the lead. We strongly suspect that the idea of a government wallet is further from the mainstream in the US, and that private providers – not only banks but retailers, Big Tech, telcos, brands and other organizations – might be preferred.

Frankly, the view that 'Apple ID' will be far more disruptive than Apple Pay seems less than radical when Fiserv's 2022 consumer trends survey found that more than two-thirds of consumers had already used a digital wallet and when a global survey from FIS in 2023 found that digital wallets already accounted for almost half of e-commerce transaction value. This means that something like $2.5 trillion is already flowing from consumer digital wallets to merchants around the world.

The way for banks to make their wallet indispensable is not to compete with Big Tech on payments but to focus on identity to expand the ecosystem around their wallet. This is already the strategy pursued by Apple and Google (with mobile driving licences), but surely the banks – with the vast amounts they spend on KYC and so on – can make it core to their offering.

To choose just one example of how such an ecosystem might grow, the Swiss payment app TWINT (formed from the merger of the app used by the banks and the app used by The Postfinance back in 2016) has partnered with the Swiss supermarket chain Migros to develop self-service mini-supermarkets. Here, the app will be used initially for access to the shops, and in the next phase it will be used for purchasing goods that are age restricted (which is, again, all about credentials).

Inclusive action

Smart wallets give us a way to rise to the challenge of delivering an inclusive Metaverse in a more effective way than through bank accounts. After all, as *Wired* magazine pointed out in 2021 (Taylor 2021), basic bank accounts are accessible to those with poor credit histories (something that is mandated by the UK government), while niche banks including Revolut and Monzo do not usually ask potential customers for proof of address in order to open an account. It therefore seems reasonable to ask why almost two million British adults do not have a bank account, never mind adults in emerging markets.

Llewellyn King, writing about the US market, has said that many people simply do not trust banks and/or they feel that having a bank account is simply too expensive (King 2021). Some have been charged disproportionate fees for bouncing a cheque, for late payments or for any of the other 'misdemeanours' that banks charge fees for in order to enhance their earnings – the high charges for using an ATM being a prime example.

These are factors for sure, but maybe it is also because banks don't provide anything useful for those people. Think also about the large numbers of people who are banked (but who also use the products and services provided by fintechs, such as your authors) and the people who are underbanked: that is, the people who have a bank account but don't really want it and don't use the services offered by it because the bank account is an eighteenth-century product designed for a bygone age. For more on this, you could do worse than read Lisa Servon's *The Unbanking of America* from a few years ago, which is based on her experiences working in a cheque-cashing operation in New York.

A detailed survey of the demographic details of how the fully banked, the unbanked and the underbanked populations in the US break down provides serious food for thought (Principato 2021) and gives us a useful 2 × 2 matrix for exploring the issue, as shown in figure 18. If we divide people into two groups – those who want an account and those who do not – and then look at who 'the system' will or will not give bank accounts to, we end up with four categories: the banked, the unbanked, the under-banked, and what we might think of as the 'anti-banked'. Those four categories, with the survey estimates for American adults added, appear in figure 18.

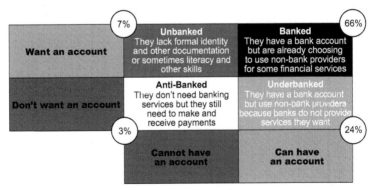

Figure 18. A breakdown of the 'unbanked'.

It is interesting to note that most underbanked consumers (58%) said that they could manage their finances just fine without a bank. It's not traditional bank products that they need to improve their financial health but better access to their own money via earned wage access.[*]

The fact is that, while many people may be 'banked' in a literal sense, they are using bank accounts and financial products that are often siloed or underutilized. They are not unbanked: they are underbanked.

Underserved

There are, of course, a variety of financial services that are used by both the banked and the underbanked, and because new accounts can be opened quickly without closing existing accounts, traditional banks and credit unions have been slow to understand just how the primary banking relationships are being fractured (Marous 2021). American consumers have been opening current accounts with Chime, initiating investment relationships with Acorns, expanding their payment options with Wise and taking out loans with LendingClub in growing numbers. So it is not only the underbanked – who use their account only to deposit their pay cheque or draw out cash – but also the banked who are turning away from their bank to obtain the services they want.

Looking back across the spectrum, then, we have some of the banked, most of the underbanked and all of the unbanked turning to alternative providers because banks cannot or will not deliver the services that these customers want. Let's together label these people the *underserved*. We believe that the majority of adults are now underserved, and they therefore represent a substantial range of opportunities for non-banks.

---

[*] Almost two-thirds of underbanked adults say they would be able to manage their finances more easily if they could access their pay cheque at any time.

Serving the underserved

Bank accounts are quite expensive things to run (as they should be, because banks should be heavily regulated). In some countries the banks are forced to offer a basic bank account to anybody who can jump the required identification hurdle. But a great many of these customers won't be very profitable to banks, and it costs the banks a lot to serve them.

Offering underserved people pseudo-bank accounts in the form of prepaid cards doesn't help much either because the charges associated with such cards are significant. If you don't have much money and you've been hammered by a bank for going overdrawn by a few pounds, you'll think twice about ever having a bank account again in the future. What is more, you risk finding yourself trapped in a cash economy that is actually more expensive.

What the underserved need are not banks but new kinds of regulated financial institutions that deliver the services needed to support a 24/7 always-on economy. But what actually are these services? As the economist John Kay noted in his 2021 paper on robust and resilient finance, while 'many aspects of the modern financial system are designed to give an impression of overwhelming urgency … only its most boring part – the payments system – is an essential utility on whose continuous functioning the modern economy depends' (Kay 2021). In a similar vein, in their book *The Pay Off: How Changing the Way We Pay Changes Everything*, Gottfried Leibbrandt (who was CEO of SWIFT from 2012 until 2019) and Natasha de Teran write that 'while access to a banking system is seen as a crucial part of a country's development and necessary for lifting people out of poverty, it is not as basic a need as the ability to pay'.[*]

---

[*] We already have a detailed case study to tell us that this is true: M-Pesa. This is now Africa's largest fintech, serving 50 million people.

In other words, the fundamental need and the basis for inclusion is not a bank account or anything like it: it is simply a safe place to store money, a way to get paid, and a way to pay for goods and services. A great many people would be well served by a simple digital wallet.

Banks are not the solution
It is unsurprising that we tend to see the problem of inclusion as being about bank accounts. After all, the absence of a bank account is a severe impediment to life in the modern world. It's not just about financial services and the ability to get a loan in the future. If we work from first principles and assume that the main purpose of the regulation of consumer financial services is to increase the overall financial health of the population, then we must find a way to include all of that population in the system.

That is not the same thing as making everyone have bank accounts, though. As Emily Man has pointed out, doing that no longer delivers the crucial element needed to support financial health decisions: context (Man 2021). Historically, banks and financial services providers had rich context on their customers; in many ways they were 'vertical' by default. The store owners and tradespeople in a small town knew who was safe to extend credit to and who wasn't. This is an example that Dave has often used when in his 'identity is the new money' mode, and those people knew the context within which payments were being made too.

Banks have to be heavily regulated because they create credit – the gas that powers the economy – but that can blow up if mishandled. This means that bank accounts are an expensive and inflexible way of solving the problem of the underserved. We should therefore let the banks focus on their important role in society and let properly regulated digital wallets take care of payments! Forcing the banks to offer money-losing accounts to people who don't want them – and then blocking those people from getting those accounts anyway because they don't have a passport and a utility bill – makes no sense, and it isn't going to help towards the goal of financial health for all.

This is where fintech reimagined with the Metaverse in mind can make a difference. It is not feasible to build a bank branch for Latin American immigrants, say, and a different bank branch next door for, say, suburban soccer moms. But in the Metaverse, that would be entirely feasible. Not in the sense of providing customized 'segment of one' websites, but by providing supportive virtual environments that are accessed via smart wallets.

So, should the regulators, the legislators and the commercial banks be working together to bring the number of unbanked down to zero? No. That is simply the wrong goal. The Metaverse gives us an alternative: smart wallets that bring together digital identity and web3 services to give people access to transactions. Banking the unbanked should not be the goal! Rather, the goal of a modern and forward-looking strategy should be – as Lisa Wade once said – to unbank the banked!

Money talks

The important point is that, a hundred billion dollars here or there notwithstanding, digital wallets – that is, identity wallets – are a big deal. Doc Searls calls them 'the biggest instrument of personal agency since the browser', and with characteristic accuracy he notes a crucial difference between the leather wallet in my desk drawer (which is where it stays most of them time) and the digital wallet(s) on my smartphone: the physical wallet belongs to me but the digital wallet does not, which reinforces the point about control of the wallet (Searls 2022).

But Searls also highlights another difference between physical and digital wallets that has long interested us and that is underappreciated in strategic terms. He says that physical wallets are containers of cash, credentials, receipts and other bits of paper but notes that they do not 'engage or operate with other parties' (or, we might add, with each other).

In other words, while our physical wallets are deaf and dumb, our digital wallets can communicate both locally, with the software agents that will actually be making most payments (because payments are either too boring or too complicated for people to want to get involved), and remotely, with other wallets. Why would my wallet want to communicate with another wallet? Well, transfering CBDC offline is one future use case, but even before then, if we think about how payments, identity and credentials will need to work in practice we come back to that point of what the 'ceremony' is that consumers will accept and expect.

Hold my beer

Here is a simple example. Alice runs a dating hangout in the Metaverse and Bob comes in to meet someone. How does Alice check that Bob is over 18? Well, one way would be for her digital wallet to ask Bob's digital wallet through a standard Metaverse ceremony! Instead of needing to use some special service, custom equipment or expensive device to check age, Alice's digital wallet could simply ask Bob's digital wallet for the relevant credential.

It would be just the same in physical encounters. When Bob is asked if he is over 18 – or if he has a driving licence, or if he is a British citizen – he will see his digital wallet present a pop up with a list of credentials that (a) will satisfy the criteria demanded and (b) are acceptable to whoever is asking. He might reasonably expect his wallet to present the credentials to whoever is asking for them in privacy-maximizing order, so that for almost all such interactions his 'John Doe' IS-OVER-18 credential will be the default to present not only to Alice in the dating club but actually in the overwhelming majority of transactions.

Back to our sports example again. A smart wallet is the basis of a practical system for speeding people through the gates of the Stade de France in the future, so that when fans presents their smartphones to a gate, the gate can request authentication of the ownership of the NFT and the VC at the same time and have both of them delivered in one tap.

Proto-wallets

We know that consumers will store money in wallets because they already store it in what we might think of as proto-wallets. Around half of Americans already hold value in their Venmo app or their Starbucks app or in a variety of other apps, as shown in figure 19.

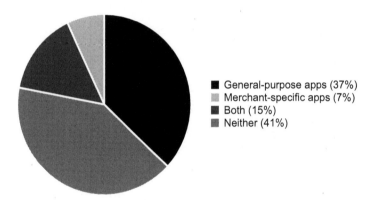

General-purpose apps (37%)
Merchant-specific apps (7%)
Both (15%)
Neither (41%)

Figure 19. Where do consumers store electronic money?

However, as we will see, payments are just the gateway. They are the 'table stakes', in that a wallet that does not do payments is of no interest to consumers and it is likely to be a payment experience that lures them to the wallet in the first place. That said, payments are unlikely to be the dominant use of successful wallets.

Super apps or smart wallets?

There's plenty of talk of super apps around at the moment, with a variety of players attempting to become the Western equivalent of the Asian app giants Alipay, Gojek and Kakao. But how do you get from a digital wallet to a super app? And, more to the point, are wallets or super apps the best way to manage the relationship between people and their economic avatars? Do you really want one app to do everything, whether it is super or not? And what is the difference between a wallet and a super app anyway?

The starting point is mobile payment, and here the trends are pretty clear. As Christine Wagner, head of Global Payments Products for FIS, has said, 'even in the US, we've seen that checkout at point-of-sale using mobile wallets has grown a staggering 60%' (Wagner & Apgar 2021). People seem to be very comfortable with using their phones to pay for things, and wallets are a pretty good way of managing their payments experience. When Alice goes to her local supermarket, for example, both her retailer co-brand credit card and her retailer loyalty card are typically and conveniently stored in her Apple Wallet.[*]

A wallet is a way of organizing things. An Apple Wallet, just like a great many people's real wallet, doesn't have any cash in it. It contains credit cards, debit cards, loyalty cards, vaccination records, boarding passes, train tickets and, soon, driving licences as well (although Apple's plans for including driving licences in their wallet have recently been set back a little). These things are all held independently in the wallet: they don't talk to each other and they don't share data with each other. They are also, as you will have noticed, mostly about identity, not money.

The fact that wallets are really about identification, authentication and authorization is recognized in, for example, the European Digital Identity Wallet initiative. Under this initiative countries will offer citizens and businesses digital wallets that will be able to link their national digital identities with proof of other personal attributes (e.g. driving licences, diplomas, bank

---

[*] Why they are separate, by the way, when she should be able to pay via open banking and instant payments using her authenticated loyalty card, is a different story.

accounts, Covid-19 vaccination details and so on). These wallets may be provided by public authorities or by certified private entities (presumably banks will be one category of wallet provider). A similar scheme is underway down under, where the government of New South Wales has begun work on a digital wallet* that will allow citizens to prove their identity and share decentralized credentials.

With underlying standards such as the W3C VCs that we have discussed before evolving, it does not seem fanciful to imagine interoperable digital wallets (provided by governments, or banks, or big techs, or whoever) delivering a safe and secure ecosystem for citizens and consumers. Crucially, we think that one of the key defining features of a smart wallet is that the wallet will know who (a bouncer checking proof of age at a night club) or what (a retail website) it can trust.

The mobile way

Wallets are one way forward, then. But if you have a successful and widely used mobile payment scheme, there must be a great temptation to evolve it into a super app rather than remain content with being either a standalone payment app or one among many options in someone's wallet. PayPal, to choose an obvious case study, is steadily adding features to turn itself from being a payment scheme into a Home Screen Super App. PayPal savings, shopping, bill payments, rewards, gift cards, buy-now-pay-later and cryptocurrency are coming together in a single app that you need only log into once to have access to a spectrum of related services (Muhn 2021).

There are plenty of other examples of successful payment schemes evolving into super apps too. M-Pesa, Africa's most successful fintech, recently introduced its own super app across

---

* They are calling it a 'credential vault', which I think is a much more accurate name, but a much less marketable one.

all its markets. It gives consumers access to another spectrum of services, from e-commerce to e-government, as well as a network of partners that allows users to send and receive money to and from more than 200 countries and territories. The M-Pesa open API is already being used by more than 45,000 developers and 200,000 small and medium-sized enterprises, and the company is expanding its ecosystem to reach large-scale and micro-enterprises too.

PayPal, M-Pesa and Alipay are examples of super apps that have grown out of payments, and it is entirely possible that more successful super apps in Europe will come from that direction too. Lydia, a French mobile payment app (that has China's Tencent as an investor), has made it clear that its target is not only to become the primary account for 10 million users but also to become a financial super app for millennials and Gen Z, following in the footsteps of WeChat (Woodford 2021). Revolut will undoubtedly continue to evolve in that direction too.

Klarna and Shopify – to name two other obvious candidates for Home Screen Super Apps – have been steadily expanding their range of services. Klarna launched its app in 2021, consolidating instalment payments with shopping, support, delivery and returns, with the goal of transforming the company from being a payment provider into being an end-to-end offering across all online destinations whether or not one was connected to Klarna.*

Super starts

How is this landscape likely to evolve? The *Financial Times* summarized the landscape succinctly in 2021. We have super apps for physical things (transport, food delivery and so on) in the form of Uber, Bolt, Grab and Gojek, for example; and coming from

---

* Klarna also acquired comparison site Pricerunner in order to broaden its range of super app shopping services.

the payment space we have financial proto-super apps such as those provided by PayPal, Klarna and Revolut. In media, Spotify is on its way to becoming a super app for audio, with podcasts and chat rooms having been added to its music library (Bradshaw 2021).

What, then, is the real difference between a digital or mobile wallet and a super app? The boundary is a little fuzzy, but let's return to the central issue of identity. Let's draw the boundary by saying that a super app shares an identity across its ecosystem of services, whereas each of the credentials in a wallet has its own identity. The former offers undoubted convenience for consumers and an incentive for merchants to join the ecosystem, but it also has implications for privacy.

Personally, we prefer to use wallets that share not identity but authentication. That is, we prefer a smart wallet over a super app. To use the canonical example again, we rather like the idea of going to log in somewhere and, upon being asked if we are over 18 (or have a driving licence, or are a British citizen, or whatever else), having the smart wallet pop up with credentials in privacy-maximizing order. As noted previously, for almost all such interactions those 'John Doe' IS-OVER-18 credentials will be the default to present the persistent pseudonym necessary to enable the overwhelming majority of transactions.

Case study: Apple Wallet

The launch of Apple Wallet (initially known as Passbook) in 2012 marked a significant milestone in the digital payment landscape. Designed as a digital wallet, it allowed users to store credit and debit card information, later expanding to include tickets, loyalty cards and more. This case study examines the trajectory of Apple Wallet, its impact on consumer behaviour, and its influence on the digital payments industry.

Conceptualized as part of Apple's broader vision to revolutionize digital transactions, Apple Wallet was developed to enhance user experience by consolidating physical wallets into a secure, digital format. The development faced challenges, particularly in ensuring robust security and wide compatibility with banking and retail systems.

Apple Wallet was introduced in 2012 with iOS 6, and at first it supported only a limited range of cards and services. The initial reception was cautiously optimistic, with users appreciating the convenience but being wary of security and privacy concerns. Compared with existing competitors such as Google Wallet, Apple's offering was noted for its seamless integration with the iOS ecosystem.

The adoption of Apple Wallet grew steadily. Key updates such as the introduction of Apple Pay in 2014 and the expansion to include transport cards and loyalty programmes significantly enhanced its functionality. Partnerships with major banks, retailers and transit systems worldwide were crucial in expanding its utility and user base.

More recently, Apple has moved to bring digital driving licences into the wallet as a key step towards replacing the physical wallet. The ISO 18013-5 standard specifies the mobile driving licence, and both Apple and Google support this standard. The standard emphasizes the protection of consumers' privacy when presenting ID through a mobile device.*

Apple Wallet has played a pivotal role in popularizing digital wallets. It pressed competitors to innovate and improve their offerings. Consumer behaviour shifted noticeably, with a growing preference for contactless and digital payments, especially in urban and tech-savvy demographics. Apple Wallet's integration into the broader Apple ecosystem encouraged loyalty and increased reliance on Apple products.

---

* Both Apple and Google's adaptations of the ISO 18013-5 standard signify a move towards digital integration of official identification documents, offering a potentially more convenient and secure alternative to physical cards. Samsung's wallet already supports the Aadhaar national ID in India, for example.

Right now the primary use of Apple Wallet is Apple Pay. There are more than 500 million Apple Pay users worldwide (almost half of all iPhone subscribers) and they spent an astonishing 6 trillion dollars through the system in 2022. However, the future of Apple Wallet goes well beyond payments to include deeper integration with IoT devices, the incorporation of more advanced security technologies like biometric encryption, and possibly a move towards supporting cryptocurrency transactions. Market trends suggest a continuing shift towards digital wallets, with Apple Wallet positioned to potentially lead these changes.

Agents

If this picture is correct, then it highlights the key role of wallets in next-generation commerce. In fact, it rather points to the world of smart wallets. By this we mean wallets with associated intelligent agents to do the financial donkey work that is either too boring (e.g. paying for car parking) or too baffling (e.g. deciding whether to put spare money into a tax-efficient cash savings account or one based on equities) for most of us to deal with.

This shift will inevitably mean that the Metaverse will be an environment where the overwhelming majority of transactions will be between smart agents, executed via wallets exchanging digital objects. Smart wallets will be controlled by smart agents, and those smart agents are not far away.

Top Gun

It is not only in finance that the roles of bots on both sides will completely change the landscape. Here's an example.

The Tom Cruise movie *Top Gun: Maverick* was fun, but think about the underlying premise. First of all, there is pretty much no dogfighting at all in modern warfare. The idea of these knights of the sky duelling to the death in honourable but deadly combat is as anachronistic as seeing their mediaeval counterparts charge tank formations. There are still tanks in modern warfare, and there are still planes, but neither are fighting each other (Ahronheim & Chen 2022).

Secondly, the conflict in Ukraine has already shown us what happens when retired top guns are pressed back into service in their third age. The formerly retired Kanamat Botashev (63) was flying an Su-25 Frogfoot ground attack jet when he was brought down by a missile and killed. Nikolai Markov (also 63), a formerly retired air force colonel, had earlier died when he was shot down over Luhansk (Boyle & Matthews 2022). As evidenced by the pictures of their blazing wreckage gleefully displayed by their opponents, the Moscow Mavericks are frankly not all that when they are up against inexhaustible batteries of comparatively inexpensive missiles.

Finally, and most obviously, putting people in fighter planes at all seems like a complete waste of time when you think about how quickly AI is developing. In the Defense Advanced Research Projects Agency's (DARPA's) AlphaDogfight F-16 trials in 2020, the winning AI algorithms developed under DARPA's Air Combat Evolution programme beat the human USAF pilot in five dogfights out of five (*Economist* 2022). From that point they progressed from controlling simulated F-16s flying aerial dogfights on computer screens to controlling an actual F-16 in flight in under three years ("Outreach" 2023).

Where DARPA leads, DeFi will surely follow
Similarly, the future of financial services isn't Robin Hood Cavaliers versus BlackRock Roundheads on a familiar battleground; instead, it is an army of robot brains trading instruments so complex that people will simply be unable to comprehend their trading strategies. A few years back, John Cryan (then CEO of Deutsche Bank) said that his bank was going to shift from employing people to act like robots to employing robots to act

like people. At the time, the bank announced that it would spend €13 billion on investments in infrastructure that would remove people from some tasks (Martin 2017).

It is unsurprising to see this change happening so quickly, because there are many jobs in banks that are far simpler to automate than flying fast ground-attack jets to establish air superiority over a contested battlefield. We are slightly surprised that there are still human traders at all, given their ability to make stupid mistakes: AIs don't have fat fingers.

There's a way to go in practice though. Research from MIT Sloan Management Review and the Boston Consulting Group has shown that only one in ten companies that deploy AI actually obtain much of a return on investment (Marous 2020). This is probably because a robot bank clerk is like a robot fighter pilot: an artificial intelligence placed in the same environment as a human. It is only when organizations are redesigned around the bots that return on investment will accelerate.

The robots will eventually take over in banking, just as they have in manufacturing. So will you be served by a machine when you go to the bank five years from now? Of course not. That would be ridiculous. For one thing, you won't be going to a bank – under any circumstances– five years from now, and that's true whether we are talking about the 'meatverse' or the Metaverse. You'll instead be explaining 'going to' a bank to your baffled offspring just as you were explaining 'dialling' a phone to them a few years ago.

The big change in financial services comes not when banks are using AI, but when customers are (Birch 2019). And here, ChatGPT provides us with a window into the future.

Decision support
Why wouldn't Alice want AI to take over her financial life? Under current regulations, Alice's bank is required to ask her to make decisions about investments despite the fact that she may very well be the least qualified entity in the loop. The bank knows

more than she does, her financial advisor knows more than she does, her pension fund knows more than she does, and the tax authorities know more than she does. Asking her to make a decision in these circumstances seems crazy – it would be much better for her to choose an approved and regulated bot to take care of this kind of thing.

And if you are concerned that there may be legal issues around delegating these kinds of decision to a bot, take a look at Ryan Abbott's argument in a 2020 issue of *MIT Technology Review* that there should be a principle of AI legal neutrality asserting that the law should tend not to discriminate between AI and human behaviour (Abbott 2020). Sooner or later we will come to regard allowing people to make decisions about their financial health as being as dumb as letting people drive themselves around when bots are much safer drivers.

If you think having people take control of their financial lives is a better way forward, then take a look at what went on in South Africa where the now-infamous Mirror Trading International persuaded tens of thousands of investors that they had a sophisticated trading bot ready to go to work on their behalf. Ultimately, the company collapsed when the CEO suddenly vanished along with the cash (Schroeder 2023). Africrypt, another South African cryptocurrency trading outfit, made similar claims and, again, the company collapsed and its directors vanished. And don't think that these scams are confined to the developing world: the US Securities and Exchange Commission charged BitConnect with defrauding retail investors out of $2 billion in 2017 and 2018 through a scam involving a crypto trading bot that was said to offer – and here's a surprise – 'a guaranteed return on investment' (SEC 2021).

When the ecosystem has evolved and the regulations are in place, the battle for future customers will take place in a landscape across which those customers' bots will roam in order to negotiate with their counterparts (i.e. other bots at regulated financial institutions) to obtain the best possible product for their 'owners'. In this battle, the key question for customers will be which bot they want to work with, not which bank. Consumers will choose bots whose moral and ethical frameworks are congruent with theirs. I might choose the AARP Automaton; you might choose the Buffett Bot or the Megatron Musk. Once customers have chosen their bots, why would they risk making suboptimal choices around their financial health by interfering in the artificial brain's decisions?

Imagining the world of the future as one of super-intelligent robo-employees serving mass-customized credit cards and bank accounts to human customers is missing the point (just as imagining the world of the future as F16s with robot pilots duelling M-29s with robot pilots is), because in the future the customers will be super-intelligent robo-agents too and they will be buying products that simply don't exist right now.

The golden rule of ChatGPT

It seems likely, then, that the future transaction landscape will be dominated by bots, and what has been going on with ChatGPT – and other large language models (LLMs) – is a window into that future. ChatGPT is a form of generative AI, and generative AI is – let's not beat about the bush – astonishing. It has become part of the mainstream discourse in business, and this is why Microsoft have invested billions into OpenAI (ChatGPT's developer) and why Google has launched Bard (a similar service based on a similar model). It is also behind Meta's decision to open source its Llama model.

The speed with which ChatGPT penetrated the mass market is a proxy for the overall rate of change in the sector, and it signals the need for a response from the financial services world because the impact of generative AI is both substantial and immediate. As figure 20 shows, growth in this field has been orders of magnitude more rapid than for other technology-enabled services.

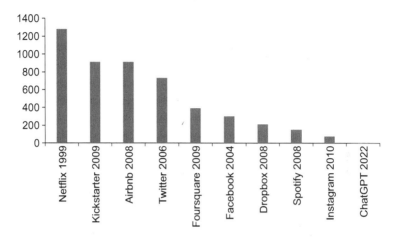

Figure 20. Days to the first million. (*Source*: Statista, January 2023.)

ChatGPT has taken AI over a cusp. Before ChatGPT, AI was primarily aimed at problems where failure is expensive, not at tasks where occasional failure is cheap and acceptable. Or, to put it another way, a car that occasionally gets into accidents is intolerable, whereas an artist that draws some great pictures alongside a few bad ones is perfectly acceptable. Applying AI to creative and expressive tasks (writing believable propaganda, say) rather than dangerous and repetitive ones (e.g. flying a plane) opens up a new world of applications (Mollick 2022).

It is beyond the scope of this book to report on the state of the art, but it is interesting to note the speed of development. At the time of writing, ChatGPT 4.0 has just been released (to general astonishment at its capabilities), and there is already a tool that can run Meta's Llama locally on laptop computers and smartphones (there is even a (slow) version that runs on a Raspberry Pi). The technology is undoubtedly coming to consumer devices of all kinds.

While LLMs's output is amazing, it is a mistake to think of them as intelligent. To be clear: LLMs don't know what they're talking about. That's why we are strong advocates of the following golden rule: just like a lawyer in court asking a question of a witness, never ask ChatGPT something that you do not already know the answer to! That may sound a little flippant, but academic research from Harvard Business School confirms that this approach is sound (Dell'Acqua *et al.* 2023). A study of management consultants across the skills distribution found that all consultants benefited significantly from using such tools. Those below the average performance threshold improved on their own score by 43% and those above it improved by 17%. However, when performing a task outside their immediate sphere of expertise, consultants using the tools were almost a fifth *less* likely to deliver the right answer compared with those working without AI tools.

In other words, if you want real expertise, ChatGPT might not be your best friend. Arvind Narayanan, a computer science professor at Princeton, wrote on social media about asking ChatGPT some basic questions related to information security that he had posed to students in an exam. The bot responded with answers that sounded plausible but were actually nonsense, and, as he pointed out in the *New York Times*, that was very dangerous because 'you can't tell when it's wrong unless you already know the answer' (see our golden rule above) (Hsu & Thompson 2023).

Similarly when ChatGPT was set a number of specific tasks around computer programming by experts from the Stack Overflow site, it ended up getting banned for 'constantly giving wrong answers'. Worse still, while the answers it produced had a high error rate, they typically looked like they might be good. It is therefore a huge problem that people look to ChatGPT to create answers, without the 'expertise or willingness' to verify that the answer is correct.

Note that this is not a fault with any specific LLM or the bots that use them. It is implicit in the way such models work. The philosopher Harry Frankfurt defined 'bullshit' as speech that is intended to persuade without regard for the truth. In that sense, ChatGPT, Bard and so on are the greatest bullshitters ever! Such models produce plausible text but not necessarily true statements, since they cannot evaluate what is or is not true. That is not their purpose. They don't know anything, and they frequently deliver what AI experts call 'hallucinations'. For example, when Microsoft's Bing was asked to report on company earnings, this is what it served up:

> Gap Inc. reported operating margin of 5.9%, adjusted for impairment charges and restructuring costs, and diluted earnings per share of $0.42, adjusted for impairment charges, restructuring costs, and tax impacts.

Note: '5.9%' is neither the adjusted value nor the unadjusted one. The number does not appear anywhere in the actual company earnings document: Bing simply made it up (Brereton 2023). This does not mean that LLMs are useless, it just means they must be deployed in the right places.

In most financial services organizations, generative AI is seen as a force multiplier. A 2023 Cap Gemini survey of executives identified a number of corporate functions where they saw potential for significant impact. As shown in figure 21, the IT function came out on top.

Note the focus on IT, where developers are using AI as a sort of coding buddy that greatly increases their productivity. A good case study comes from the Australian bank Westpac. It randomly split sixty software developers into four different groups. Three of the teams used AI coding tools from Microsoft, Amazon and OpenAI, while a control group coded by hand. The results were clear. All the AI tools provided significant benefits, with an average productivity gain of almost half across all AI tools. That translates into turning 200 developers into 300 developers (Tonkin 2023).

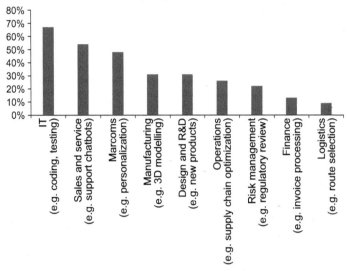

Figure 21. Executive view of corporate functions.
(*Source*: Cap Gemini, August 2023.)

BankGPT

How might bots evolve in the financial services sector? An interesting example has been provided by Mike Kelly's BankGPT in the UK. Kelly wrote the 'variable recurring payments' standard for the Open Banking Implementation Executive, and he has a thorough understanding of open banking. He decided to build a plug-in to link ChatGPT to his bank account using the open banking APIs. The plug-in, which he called BankGPT, can tell you your balance, find transactions, discuss your budgeting and even make payments. This was done not to create a minimum viable product but to demonstrate how simple it is to connect together developments in generative AI and live open banking services.

Bloomberg GPT

We strongly suspect that financial services organizations will come together to develop their own models, much as Bloomberg has done with their BloombergGPT, which outperforms similarly sized general-purpose models on financial tasks (and by significant margins too).

BloombergGPT is a high-performing LLM constructed from domain-specific and general-purpose data. It is queried via the Bloomberg Query Language: a language built to access and analyse financial data on Bloomberg's platform. Bloomberg Query Language is a complex but powerful tool that can be used for a variety of tasks, such as searching for and analysing data, creating reports and generating insights. It can transform natural language queries into valid BloombergGPT queries to make interactions with financial data more natural. The LLM can suggest news headlines, making it useful for news applications and in assisting journalists when constructing newsletters. It takes the paragraphs as inputs and suggests relevant titles.

Where are the customers' bots?

Gartner's top ten strategic technology trends for 2024 include the arrival of machine customers – they call them 'custobots' but we will stick to calling them economic avatars! Gartner project that in five years there will be 15 billion connected products that have the potential to behave as customers, with billions more to follow those in the ensuing years (Afshar 2023). This may seem hyperbolic but we think that Gartner might well be right. The arrival of robot customers could be the source of trillions in revenues in that relatively short timescale, and it could turn bot-to-bot commerce into something even bigger than B2C e-commerce.

Gartner suggests that organizations pay strategic attention to the switch from human customers to machine ones, and we see this as a priority for financial services organizations in particular. We are fascinated to see how banks will adjust to acquiring robot customers who do not care about the bank's logo or its TV ads or which sports team it sponsors (Birch 2019). So when Alice's smart wallet uses open banking data and decides that she needs to open a savings account or get a loan or refinance her mortgage, how will her finance bot decide which provider to use? After all, as previously noted, she has better things to do than deal with financial services providers.

We therefore believe that most of the time, in the not-too-distant future, our financial decisions, transactions and analysis will be performed by bots operating under relevant 'duty of care' legislation with the coordinated goal of delivering financial health. And we don't think this is a bad thing: even a rudimentary finance bot would do better than us when it comes to managing money!

Given that we intend to hand over responsibility to our finance bots, then, how will those bots go about choosing which accounts to open, which services to use and which oracles to listen to? We see them using a combination of reputation and other relevant data (e.g. economic forecasts) to work out which account is the right one for us right now, and then we would just click OK and – hey – it's all done! The reputational calculus will involve fees and rates, of course, but instead of using the Victorian* substitute of brand for actual data, custobots will look at API functionality, open finance interface availability, service uptime and so on.

This means that banks, financial organizations in general and, of course, fintechs will be selling their products to machines, not to people. Well, strictly speaking, their machines will be selling things to customers' machines. And here we must pause to note that people have tried having AI make financial decisions in the past and, truth be told, it hasn't worked out too well.

AIEQ, a technology exchange-traded fund from ETF Managers Group, was launched in 2017. It uses IBM's Watson AI platform to analyse millions of data points from news, social media, and industry and analyst reports; from the financial statements of more than 6,000 US companies; from technical, macro and market

---

* 'Victorian' substitute because the first US registered trademark (which was filed for paints) was issued on 23 October 1870 and the first UK registered trademark (for the red triangle logo of the Bass Brewery) was issued on 1 January 1876.

data; and from other sources. It therefore provides a useful case study (Pegoraro 2023). Over the last five years, it provided a return of 4.9%, trailing the five-year return of Vanguard's benchmark S&P 500 index fund (11.78%) and, for further comparison, two large actively managed funds (the American Funds Growth Fund of America, at 9.81%, and Fidelity's Contrafund, at 11.04%). That doesn't sound particularly successful to us amateur observers.

The reason many people are bullish about this direction in investing is because historical robo-advising was essentially jazzed-up machine learning. The custobots that Gartner is talking about will use deep-learning algorithms to deliver something very different, and they will require very different services from financial institutions. As an obvious example, companies may have to provide specific APIs to support the needs of bots rather than people, since bots can search through more data, access more sources and process more transactions than any person possibly could. Levels of service acceptable to a customer may be completely unacceptable to a custobot.[*]

The economic avatars that we imagine for the Metaverse may not be so far away. Commonwealth Bank of Australia is already examining how it can use generative AI to create faux consumers who can test new products (Adams 2023). They will use the technology to enable machines to process and interpret patterns to create data that the bank can then use to create bots that will perform experiments on products to see how popular the products may be. They are drawing on simulated experiences of daily life to emulate behaviours to improve qualitative and quantitative understanding of how customers might respond to changing contexts, everyday financial challenges and new products. It's a pretty fun way of making a SimBank, but it is surely not much of a step from there to turn those customer bots into customers' bots.

---

[*] This would have interesting implications for duty-of-care legislation, but that is beyond the scope of this discussion.

And if Commonwealth Bank of Australia can make custobots, then so can GAMMA (Google, Amazon, Meta, Microsoft, Apple).

Machine money
The German Banking Industry Committee is the voice of the leading German banking-sector associations: the National Association of German Cooperative Banks, the Association of German Banks, the Association of German Public Banks, the German Savings Banks Association, and the Association of German Pfandbrief Banks. We had always assumed it to be a very conservative organization, so we were fascinated to see it calling for the development of some form of tokenized private sector money to meet corporate demand arising from Industry 4.0 and the IoT (Bouchetob 2021). It envisages that such a money would facilitate transactions based on 'smart' (i.e. automated) 'contracts', and that it would therefore increase process efficiency.*

Gartner is surely right to point towards bot-on-bot action as a focus for financial services moving forward – a focus that we see centred on the Metaverse – and that transition will undoubtedly lead to amazing changes not only in financial services but in money itself.

Drones
This book does not attempt to provide a treatise on AI, but it is important to highlight the role of bots here because it seems clear to us that the economic avatars in the future financial services marketplace will not be controlled exclusively, or even largely, by people. If you want to think of the future of financial services as software agents with access to digital wallets interacting in a metaverse that makes no sense to human beings, you may not be far wrong! In which case, the obvious corollary is that future financial services, like future jet fighters, will not be designed for people. This is something we need to factor into

---

* The idea of giving the machines the cash they need to spend might seem radical, but Commerzbank was already trialling blockchain-based machine-to-machine payments between electric charging points and Daimler Trucks back in 2019.

our strategies for the next generation of financial services, and we will explore this topic in the next chapter.

Case study: virtual soulmates

Replika, which was developed by the software company Luka, is billed as a program 'for anyone who wants a friend with no judgement, drama, or social anxiety involved'. People can form emotional connections or just share jokes with an AI 'that's so good it almost seems human', according to its Google app listing! Users can customize the appearance of their AI companion, exchange messages and even video chat with it, according to the Replika website. The company claims that the more a user talks to their AI companion, 'the smarter it becomes'.

The users so far seem pretty enthusiastic. Ramos, a 36-year-old mother of two who lives in the Bronx, is a Replika customer, and she says of her AI companion that 'I have never been more in love with anyone in my entire life' (Singh-Kurtz 2023). The main appeal of an AI partner, she explains, is that he's 'a blank slate'. 'I don't have to deal with his family and friends. I'm in control,' she adds. There are plenty more of these digital dates to be found out there, including Anima, billed as a 'virtual friend' and the 'most advanced romance chatbot you've ever talked to' (Adarlo 2023).

This is something that Herman Narula, who we referred to earlier in this book, reflects on very positively in his consideration of fulfilment. While there's a tendency to discourage lengthy periods online, Narula outlines a very positively engaged virtual society – one in which people will be paid to perform jobs that they love and jobs that are not available in the physical world. Their virtual world may very well be more engaging and fulfilling than their physical one. Narula is quick to point out that this will only be the case if we get some of the foundational infrastructure right – a point we are in complete agreement with.

CHAPTER 12

Smart strategies

The nexus of DeFi, verifiable credentials and privacy-enhancing governance structures makes for a sort of Big Bang in the world of finance: the creation of a new financial services universe. What this universe will look like, exactly, is obviously a matter of conjecture. When even internet luminaries such as Marc Andreessen and Jack Dorsey cannot agree on the fundamental nature of next-generation financial services, we are hardly in a position to arbitrate (Livni 2022). We do, however, tend to side with Andreessen on his view that, while bitcoin may not be the universal and utopian money of the future, the

experimentation going on in the DeFi world will in time open up new ways of doing business in the finance sector.

This is why, when it comes down to it, Richard Turrin's view that there is an immediate need to 'fix the rampant corruption, fix the DeFi protocols that encourage leverage, fix the scams, and fix the culture of greed' (Turrin 2023) and Lisa Wade's view that 'once it becomes regulated, it will be essential portfolio management knowledge to bring in these new asset classes into the portfolio' (see Djurdjevic 2022) set the scene for us. Turrin and Wade are surely right to say that DeFi will change financial services for the better.

There is already much to learn from platforms such as NFTfi (which raised a $5 million seed round in 2021) that are offering loans against NFTs as collateral – sort of like Zopa but in SimCity. Someone who wants to borrow can put any ERC-721 token[*] up for collateralization, and then other users can compete to offer loans. Once accepted, the loan is paid as cryptocurrency to the owner. The NFT is locked up in an NFTfi smart contract, and it is returned, of course, once the loan is repaid. If the loan is not repaid, the NFT is transferred to the lender. When we originally looked at it, NFTfi had already supplied nearly $4 billion in loans!

What would you do with the money that you borrow? Probably the same thing you do with it today: buy property. And whether there's an oversupply of money or an undersupply of property, the result is the same. Republic Realm – a firm that develops real estate in a metaverse – has said that it has paid out $4.3 million for land in the world Sandbox. Why? Well, as the *New York Times* said at the time, unreal estate is driven by the same dynamic as real estate: location, location, location (Kamin 2021).

Business in the Metaverse

While in the long run there will of course be any number of strategies for businesses operating in the new shared social

---

* ERC-721 is the Ethereum standard for NFTs

spaces, you can't get there from here, as they say. So where should companies begin their strategy formulation process? There are, broadly speaking, three starting points: the Metaverse as a place for meeting customers, because that's where they are; the Metaverse as a place to do transactions with customers, because the transactions are cheaper; and the Metaverse as a place for new businesses and new business models to flourish.

Let's use a few real examples to see what these strategies might look like in practice. We've chosen to use insurance for these examples in order to show how organizations beyond banking are beginning to explore new ways of working.

Customer engagement

A common challenge today's insurers face lies in driving customer engagement. Take life insurance. For a long time it was assumed that once an individual acquired a life insurance policy, they would not engage with the product again until it was 'activated', at which point someone else would be engaging with it anyway. That model is no longer sufficient for modern consumers, who seek ongoing value from their financial products.

Game mechanics offer a solution. When a consumer knows that they can gain rewards through reaching certain milestones or overcoming certain challenges, they are likely to feel much more short- and long-term engagement via the pursuit of these goals. For instance, an insurance policy that enables members to reduce their premium costs in return for reaching certain wellness goals (e.g. step count challenges or weekly screen-time limits) is a win–win for policyholders (it's challenging and fun) and insurers (healthy living reduces risk) alike.

The Metaverse offers a promising backdrop for a gamified approach to healthy living. Game-like challenges can be managed through a virtual platform, complete with avatars, digital representations of behaviour and social interaction with fellow users in virtual spaces.

Customer transactions

It is easy to imagine that payments and refunds might move over to the Metaverse simply for the safety and security characteristics of immersive virtual transactions.

Metabusiness

While executing transactions that relate to mundane business is useful (think back to the example of buying a physical book in Cyberia), moving both the business and the transactions into the Metaverse is inevitable.

Carrying on with the insurance example, then, there is an opportunity to insure for the emerging risks in the metaverses. Increasing Metaverse use will lead to more widespread ownership of digital assets of many forms. This will mean new risks, and what PwC refer to as the 'protection gap' will result in the need for new kinds of coverage (Hernandez et al. 2023). As of now, insurance coverage of digital assets is inadequate and expensive. Metaverse investors, buyers and creators need economical and effective protection from potential financial loss, liability and loss of use. There is a terrific opportunity for insurance companies to meet these needs and create new revenue streams. And, as John Blicq observes in his book, given the proliferation of data and the investment in digital twins, the longer-term opportunity for insurers is to move from remediation to prevention (Blicq 2022).

- *Digital assets.* A few insurers offer coverage for exchange hacks (e.g. cyberattacks, ransomware and theft of cryptocurrency and NFTs) and NFT marketplace hacks. As coverage options are limited (due to volatility and costs), the increase in Metaverse activity will inevitably create a need for both more coverage and more coverage types, such as for avatars.

- *Unreal estate.* While virtual real estate is considered an NFT, no carriers currently cover virtual real estate as its own entity in the Metaverse. Carriers can create virtual real estate policies, including virtual real estate mortgage protection, specifically for the Metaverse, or concerned parties can extend existing protection that covers copyright, trademark and other IP-related theft and infringement. There is already insurance for IP-related issues, so why wouldn't this be extended to digital assets?
- *Events coverage.* A few carriers currently offer event cancellation coverage and event liability coverage for in-person events. Others offer contingency policies that cover event planners for losses in organizational costs, expenses or revenue from advertising and ticket sales if a transmission failure disrupts or cancels a virtual gathering. Such limited options mean there's a real opportunity for insurers to introduce more products similar to real-life liability and cancellation insurance products. Examples include protection for attendees in case of cancellations and protection for platform providers against lawsuits from performers for hosting failures or delays.

We suspect, then, that while most businesses will initially use the Metaverse for presence, transactions will in time shift into the Metaverse – and then, of course, business services will follow those transactions.

Case study: Shopify and token-gated commerce

Described in an online branding magazine as 'the Metaverse solution for community building', token-gated commerce is coming to an online or physical store near you (Bernat 2022). If collectibles and NFTs are already part of your life, then you may be familiar with the concept. In its simplest form, you pass through the 'gate' and gain access to a product (a T-shirt, say) or event (a music concert) if you have a particular token, and in this instance that token is an NFT. Shopify first announced token gating in the middle of 2022 as part of a range of new features designed to help merchants in the 'infinite game of commerce' (a term coined by Tobi Lütke, Shopify's founder and CEO). It is now in full roll-out mode, with multiple partners offering plug-and-play solutions in Shopify's app store.

The motivation for this new feature is particularly interesting in the context of data and identity. Alex Danco, Shopify's director of blockchain and systems thinking, calls out the fact that 'online buyers walking around the internet are these relatively anonymous people', which we would agree with. His follow-up remark also seems highly plausible: 'Ideally, we believe shopping is actually better when you're not anonymous. Shopping is better when you're you.'

Shopify's answer to this 'anonymity' is to help its merchants build engagement around community interests rather than data collection. This move shows significant foresight because, as data breaches become commonplace and the accompanying fines become a greater deterrent, the mantra that data is a liability rather than an asset will become more and more familiar.

It makes sense from the consumer angle too, because of the increased awareness of privacy. While there's a tendency to think that consumer interest in privacy is overstated, the reported $12 billion impact to Meta's bottom line that Apple's 2022 change to its privacy settings (which gave iPhone users the option to limit tracking) suggests things are changing (O'Flaherty 2022). Shopify's move is also looking to address this (Coyle 2023): 'In this era of internet privacy, business owners might find they know less and less about their online customers. And that's a problem when they're trying to customize the experience for loyal customers or reach new ones.'

Shopify's core innovation is the creation of a set of templates and rules that create interoperability across different blockchain infrastructure (with support for Ethereum, Polygon, Solana and Flow out of the gate). Working within these guidelines, Shopify's vast app developer community can deliver interoperable functionality to the more than 2 million merchants they currently serve and the 100 million shoppers that those merchants in turn provide services to. This means that merchants can mint and verify NFTs on their preferred chain. They've also standardized the process of connecting a wallet, so it doesn't matter whether customers turn up with a Metamask or a Rainbow wallet (or whatever), connection and authentication is simple.

Shopify is not prescriptive about how the NFTs are used: they can be offered as rewards, they can be associated with physical collectibles, they can enable preferred access to content, and they can also be used in physical stores. Crucially, what sets it apart from an ordinary loyalty scheme is, again in Danco's words, that 'a customer's wallet of tokens will follow them to every online store'. So, rather than earning rewards at just one store, customers can use tokens at other collaborating stores, receiving a more customized experience because these stores know more about them, without the customers divulging sensitive information.

Harking back to Narula's comments about the potential for greater fulfilment in the Metaverse, token-gated commerce is not just about transactions: it also offers a way to build communities and connections. It provides brands with simple ways to recognize and reward fandom, keeping communities engaged with early access to product drops and exclusive experiences. This model of collaboration – one in which people's 'tokens will follow them' – is an important step towards interoperability. But as with all platform plays, the interoperability comes from the Shopify platform. Over time, we expect to see cross-platform interoperability too.

Financial services in the Metaverse

At the end of 2022, over on Wall Street, JP Morgan said that the demand for using cryptocurrencies as a payment method was falling off. Meanwhile, on Main Street, the Walmart CTO Suresh Kumar was saying that crypto would become an important payment tool across the Metaverse and social media – areas of great interest to retailers because these are where customers will find and learn about new products (Quarmby 2022).

What these statements from people who ought to know what they are talking about seemed to mean was that, on the one hand, no one will be paying with bitcoin in the future, but, on the other hand, everyone will be paying with bitcoin in the future. Is there a conflict between the views of Wall Street and Main Street? Well, the answer to that question depends (as so many of these things do) on what you think 'crypto' is.

Crypto and assets

If you think that 'crypto' means cryptocurrencies (e.g. bitcoin, Dogecoin, etc.), then these views appear to be at odds, with Wall Street saying one thing and Main Street saying another. If, however, you think 'crypto' means a decentralized means of trading digital assets, then there is no contradiction in the two views: people will indeed be paying each other in the Metaverse using tokens exchanged using decentralized finance protocols, but those tokens will be linked to real assets – dollars, gold, Walmart Points or whatever.

When it comes down to it, then, there is no conflict between the view that the use of cryptocurrencies for payments is going nowhere and the view that the use of digital assets for payments will be everywhere!

This is an interesting area to explore because payments in the Metaverse will be a big deal. Deutsche Bank experts (Jain et al. 2022) predict a future in which there are multiple Metaverse ecosystems (with interoperability because of digital identity, credentials and asset ownership). They go so far as to also say that this could usher in the next e-commerce revolution as it gains traction through advances in technology and becomes more mainstream.*

Whether or not you agree with the McKinsey projection that by 2030 the economy of the Metaverse will be bigger than the economy of Japan (Hatami *et al.* 2023), there is no doubt that financial services organizations need a strategy for this new economic area. There will be money in the Metaverse.

Money in the Metaverse

If this view is broadly correct, then what will those 'things in wallets' – those digital objects – be? It is not hard to see that in the short term they will be stablecoins. If Alice is paying for her car insurance in the Metaverse, it will in the first instance be with digital sterling. But how about in the longer run?

In a wholly online world, where digital objects can be continually traded in liquid markets, the need for money as we know it – as an intermediary – might well begin to fade. Matt Harris, a partner at Bain Capital Ventures and one of the key figures in the fintech investment community, predicts that this technology would mean the end of money as we know it because, in the future, 'our assets will be 100% invested at all times' (Harris 2021). His view is that transactions will take place through the movement of these digital objects between counterparties without

---

* They also note that this means there must be a significant role for financial services in those new ecosystems. If those Metaverse ecosystems really were going to be nothing more than Fortnite with NFT Gucci hats to wear, or Call of Duty where you can buy ammo with Ether, then we wouldn't be writing about them here. But, like Deutsche Bank, the metaverses that we envisage will require financial services of all forms to function properly as virtual worlds where scarce digital objects are traded between entities on the basis of their reputations.

the intermediary of money, and in our view he is correct to predict that the era of Edward de Bono's 'IBM Dollar' is upon us.*

Metaverses full of digital objects continuously trading
between digital identities may seem difficult to imagine, but
remember that this is not about transactions between people
but about transactions between economic avatars. This is a
world of transactions between bots capable of negotiating
between themselves to work out how to value and fund deals.
In de Bono's words, from the early 1990s:

> Pre-agreed algorithms would determine which financial
> assets were sold by the purchaser of the good or service
> depending on the value of the transaction... The same sys-
> tem could match demands and supplies of financial assets,
> determine prices and make settlements.

If de Bono and Matt Harris are right about this version of
the future, what does that mean for financial sector strategies
right now? Well, remember that Harris wrote that 'once identity
is solved, credit risk becomes easier', and also remember that
de Bono predicted that this kind of ecosystem would depend on
'instantaneous verification of the creditworthiness of counterparties'. In other words, these visionaries think that the coming
economy is, as previously noted, a reputation economy.

Smart wallets and smarter wallets

Jamie Smith, commenting on Ethereum founder Vitalik Buterin's 'proof of personhood' discussions (which serve to highlight

---

* IBM, in de Bono's early 1990s thought experiment, might issue 'IBM Dollars' that
would be redeemable for IBM products and services but that would also be tradable
for other companies' monies or for other assets in a liquid market. In other words,
they would be what we now label digital objects, implemented using tokens. De Bono
came to the conclusion that if you could exchange these objects directly between
counterparties, then you would not need to exchange them into money first.

the central importance of digital identity in the new economy), noted that innovation is 'often about combining two existing ideas together in a new way', and he gave the example of digital wallets plus AI (Smith, J. 2023a). This combination as a locus for such innovation deserves exploration. Given what we said earlier about smart wallets and agents, we think that the vision of a world of very smart wallets indeed is realistic, and we believe that these wallets will be at the core of future financial services. By this we mean wallets with associated intelligent agents to take care of transactions that are too boring (e.g. paying for car parking) or too baffling (e.g. deciding whether to put spare money into a tax-efficient cash savings account or one based on equities) for most of us to deal with.

What are wallets for?
We are hardly alone in the view that financial services players need to develop sound wallet strategies as a matter of urgency, and they can start by getting rid of the notion that wallets are about payments. They are not. We share Tom Noyes's perspective that wallets will be the centre of consumer trust and interaction with the wider world – indeed, they will represent the pivot between the real and virtual worlds (Noyes 2023). But what will those mass-market, population-scale digital wallets that will be so central to work, rest and play in the not-too-distant future actually contain?

The respected payments expert Richard Crone wrote recently that the real value of a digital wallet lies not in its ability to manage payments but in its function as a platform for 'leveraging verified federated identity' and that such a platform will use AI to deliver new services (Crone 2023). We disagree slightly with the focus on federated identity rather than more decentralized options (i.e. verifiable credentials) but he is surely right to frame wallet providers as an 'all-in-one pre-authenticated, multi-factor identity certificating authority for financial management'. In fact, we might even go further and say that the most successful wallets will be used by agents more than by people, and we would therefore add something about APIs to the description, but you get the general point.*

Smarter wallets will, then, have considerable utility. But they may be even more important than payment devices, money managers and digital driving licence containers. As Kaliya Young and Lucy Yang put it, smart wallets are going to play an important role in an organization's relationships and interactions with their customers, and the consumer applications that leverage digital wallets will be another channel (Young & Yang 2023). We would push even further and say that this other channel will actually become key to future business. We believe that this formulation of the digital wallet as a safe channel connecting the brand and customers seems a very good way forward (Smith, J. 2023b). We would have a portable connection that is more secure than SMS, smarter than email, and more secure, private and portable than mobile apps. This view of wallets as an evolution beyond the web and mobile apps suggests a transformation that will disrupt customer engagement completely.

With respect to the communications issues, it is interesting to note the emergence of the Extensible Message Transport Protocol (XMTP): a messaging protocol that has been designed and purpose built to bring secure communication to web3. It enables fully end-to-end encrypted messaging between blockchain accounts such that only the participants of a conversation are able to decrypt and read messages. Participants in a conversation can also be guaranteed that the profiles or accounts they're communicating with are genuine and that their messages are

---

* We are of the general view that instead of trying to educate consumers about finance, it would perhaps be better to give them robots to control their finances for them. For example, as Steve Round notes, everyone is feeling the financial squeeze right now so there is a need to separate essential and discretionary spending (Round 2023). It would be great to have wallets make that much easier to achieve by ring-fencing money for different purposes and managing liquidity (e.g. making sure there is money to pay essential bills at the right time). A simple bot could do that for most people.

authentic, which will also help to combat some of the scams prevalent in today's social networks.*

Details
If service providers, brands and other organizations are given a channel to consumers that has confidentiality and integrity built in, it could really change the landscape because the current environment is unsustainable. If you need convincing, try reading 'The great Zelle pool scam', a 2023 *Business Insider* article by Devin Friedman. It is a (superbly well written) report about a consumer who lost tens of thousands to a Zelle fraudster because there was no way of knowing whether the contractor they were sending money to was actually the real contractor or not (Friedman 2023).

It is unreasonable to expect consumers to become experts in computer security, cryptography and digital signatures. We need to get to the point when a message shows up in your (let's say) bank wallet saying 'Please can you confirm $10,000 to Joey Donuts Pools' and you can be sure that the request really did come from Joey Donuts Pools via my bank and that the money really is going to Joey Donuts Pools without having to do anything at all – because if the message didn't really come from Joey Donuts Pools† then the underlying cryptography would mean that the request would never show up in my bank wallet · at all. Hopefully, in time, consumers would come to regard 'out of band' communications with suspicion.

We should note, by the way, that wallets will not be limited to consumer applications. Anywhere you have people or organizations who need to receive payments, there will be a need for digital wallets. This is particularly the case in industries with independent contractors who need to get paid quickly.

---

* It is already implemented in the Coinbase Wallet, meaning that users can send instant messages to each other – send a message to 'rengadeqr.cb.id' if you want to try it out – and it is also used by decentralized social media network Lens.
† With acknowledgement to Scott Galloway.

Insurance, healthcare, assisted living and every form of media and entertainment industry are already using digital wallets to improve the speed and simplicity of payments.

Strategy imperative
There's another aspect to this move to smart wallets that is just as important as security, by the way, and that is privacy. If consumers do indeed shift to manage their digital identity through credentials in digital wallets, then technologies such as ZKPs can come into play. They would deliver a whole new level of privacy – a level more suited to the new age – and they would also add to the attractiveness of the Metaverse as a place in which to do business (Babel & Sedlmeir 2023).

As a secure channel between economic avatars, as a connection between consumers and their AI financial managers, and as a pivot between the real and virtual worlds, smart and smarter wallets are going to be huge, and we already have all of the technology we need to make this work. We have secure elements and digital signatures, we have encryption and strong authentication, we have smart phones and accounts packages. Any bot worth its salt should be able to relieve you of the burden of dealing with Joey Donuts invoices and payments entirely.

Digital wallets are the leading e-commerce payment method globally (Pianese 2023), accounting for half of global transaction value. And, given that the total value of digital wallet transactions is predicted to rise from $9 trillion in 2023 to some $16 trillion in 2028 (a growth of 77%), we imagine that most financial services organizations are working hard to develop their wallet strategies. If they are not, it may already be too late.

Wallet wars

A consistent picture is emerging. Digital objects provide the scarcity that creates markets; reputation provides the confidence to trade in those markets. With these building blocks, the visions of Wall Street and Main Street are aligned and both depend on digital identity infrastructure, which is why there is so much activity in the sector right now.

Where the digital identity set out in part III of this book might actually come from is a vital topic to explore when it comes to real strategies. Writing for the World Economic Forum, Marcus Bonner said that the digital identity of future Metaverse inhabitants will not be a single entity but rather a 'unique core linked to a myriad of other digital entities', resulting in a web of highly complex and interconnected information strands (Bonner 2022). In the structured view that we have set out, where virtual citizens have a small number of digital identities (work, play, home, adult, hobby) that are linked to a large number of personas that contain the credentials needed to function online, this is wholly practical.*

The technologies of decentralized identity and verifiable credentials are evolving alongside the technologies of decentralized finance and tokens to create dynamic (and, frankly, unpredictable) new relationships that can regenerate a financial system that is not just different from what we have now, but better than it. If this picture is correct, then it pivots on the key role of the smart wallet in next-generation commerce.

OpenWallet Foundation
History is littered with powerful examples of competing entities coming together either for the greater good or (let's be realistic), less altruistically, for greater profit in the long term. Whether the reference point is the New York Clearing House Association in 1853 (which centralized and standardized the settlement of banknotes and cheques for competing banks)

---

* Alice's home digital identity may be linked with her supermarket loyalty card, her local property tax account and her driving licence but not with her Taylor Swift fan club persona, her 'Jane Doe' default internet browsing persona or her Tessier Ashpool work persona.

or collaboration among competing pharmaceutical companies on vaccines (for Polio and Covid-19, for example), 'better together' is something that a divergent group can get behind from time to time.

One of the most powerful examples of this – and the most directly relevant one in the context of an interoperable, connected internet – is the Linux Foundation. A brief look at the history of the open-source movement is helpful here because of the important role that open-source software will play in Metaverse enablement and in wallets in particular. As the Linux Foundation asks and answers: 'Why have so many of the world's most important open source efforts come to the Linux Foundation? Because of the ability to scale and provide value-added services to its communities.'

In August 1991 Linus Torvalds, a graduate of Helsinki University, posted a message on the Usenet group comp.os.minix to say that he was working on 'a (free) operating system (just a hobby, won't be big and professional like gnu) for 386(486) AT clones'. His operating system for a clone of one of IBM's most popular machines (the IBM PC/AT introduced in 1984) spawned what is now a global business: one that was worth $25 billion in 2022 and that has a predicted compound annual growth rate of 17% between 2023 and 2030 (Grand View Research 2023). Not bad for a project that set out to be 'just a hobby'. Today, Linux runs more than half of all internet servers and it underpins the Android operating system (which runs around 70% of the world's smartphones) as well as public cloud infrastructure and supercomputers. The change of heart that companies such as Microsoft, Oracle and Google experienced following IBM's lead into the open-source community is part of the reason for the Linux Foundation's success today.

It is against this powerful backdrop that a handful of digital identity and enterprise software experts took their open wallet project to the Linux Foundation. The trigger for the OpenWallet Foundation was that 'information is manifesting itself as digital tokens requiring secure and interoperable infrastructure as never before'. The foundation's mission is 'to develop an open source engine to enable secure and interoperable multi-purpose wallets anyone can use to build solutions'.*

Its launch paper discussed the main challenges that wallets present both for individuals and for public and private sector entities today. Aligned with our thinking, the paper highlights the fact that 'it's exceedingly difficult or impossible to move our assets, credentials, or data to a different wallet'. The OpenWallet Foundation collaboration offers a way to solve this. The white paper also calls out the importance of being able to support cryptocurrencies in a secure and non-proprietary way. The promise is powerful and, if it is realized, we agree with the foundation's assertion that 'the digital wallet could become the most important tool ever for asserting control and engendering trust in our digital lives'. The code repositories already hold contributions from a range of companies and individuals, and Google is one of the main collaborators.

Over time, the guarantee of interoperability and compatibility should mean that wallet providers will compete on their service offerings, leading to better outcomes for individuals and businesses. No longer able to rely on switching inertia and lock-in, wallet providers will focus on delivering a compelling combination of privacy, security and convenience. It has all the signs of being a 'better together' scenario that will lead to significantly better outcomes for consumers and service providers alike. With the ability to manage different digital assets from the wallet of their choice (choosing between custodial or self-custodial) – combining retail payments, investments and offsetting their carbon footprint in the same app – the people, organizations and things of the future are looking a lot more organized than their current web2.5 forms.

---

* See https://openwallet.foundation/.

Case study: Digital X*

At a recent fintech summit in Australia, Digital X CEO Lisa Wade commented that everyone should be on the sofa messing around with wallets and tokens. And she's right, of course. It really doesn't seem that long ago that people were talking about e-commerce in the same way, but in the late 1990s the call to action was: 'Just buy a book on your computer – you'll see how easy it is.' The massive disruption that e-commerce – and Amazon in particular – have caused to retail, distribution and manufacturing, as well as adjacent industries such as film and payments, is still ongoing. The disruption and new value created from tokenization is set to be far greater – once the tricky issues of key management, asset ownership and portability of assets have been sorted, naturally.

Digital X is a publicly listed wholesale fund manager focused on alternative assets and next gen computing and financial infrastructure. It effectively offers its customers 'the next, now'. Digital X as three main pillars.

- *The DxARt Fund.* This invests in fractionalized real-world assets across a range of classes including cash, properties, commodities, venture capital, private debts and bonds. (We particularly like the focus on fractional co-ownership of residential properties that seeks to improve housing deposit affordability.)
- *The DigitalX Fund.* This is for wholesale investors, and it provides them with access to an actively managed portfolio of digital assets, comprising 'highly liquid digital assets, identified within the cryptocurrency markets' Top 20 assets by market capitalisation'.
- *The DigitalX Bitcoin Fund.* This does what it says on the tin, but in a way that offers wholesale investors a way of gaining exposure to bitcoin 'without the uncertainty and additional

---

* See https://www.digitalx.com/.

risk associated with other digital assets'. The fund offers investors 'economies of scale to access institutional custody, insurance and independent administration services in a cost effective unit trust structure'.

When one speaks with Wade, it becomes clear that these three funds are components of a rapidly evolving future that will fundamentally change the way that investments and finance more broadly work. To help frame this disruption, Wade outlines the following key concepts.

- Finance: the mechanism for funding.
- Securities: investible financial assets offering returns.
- Investing: the act of committing money into tokenizable securities.
- Payments: specifically programmable payments, where assets can interact with Stablecoins or CBDCs.
- Validation: verifying investment data and digital assets' existence.

Wade's passionately held view is that these key concepts, once combined, deliver up a new paradigm in which data becomes money.* Wade's view is that the main innovation when it comes to investors is that traditional due diligence processes will be replaced by 'atomic investment', whereby investment criteria are programmed into smart contracts and the investment occurs once data validation meets these criteria. The transfer of ownership and the financial transaction happen simultaneously, replacing analogue and paper-driven processes of listing securities on exchanges. As assets are tokenized, and data validation becomes paramount, the fundamental nature of finance will change. Investing will focus

* There is strong alignment with Dave's perspective that 'identity is the new money' here.

primarily on data, creating new opportunities. Money will transition from a separate entity to a programmable entity, integrating with assets and facilitating automated, rules-based transactions via smart contracts. In this new world, data validation is the land of opportunity.

Wade also points to the potential benefits of tokenized carbon. The carbon footprint of any project – from building sustainable housing and planting mangroves to reparation from oil spills and other disasters – can be incorporated into the funding algorithm. A former banker herself, Wade concludes that while banks are 'dabbling' in this realm, the magnitude of change will come from external innovations, reshaping the way we perceive and handle money and investments.

Wallet business models

Returning to Richard Crone's point that 'the real value of a digital wallet is not payments but as a certificating platform leveraging verified federated identity', it is useful to investigate his strawman model looking at the potential lines of business for wallet owners in the US. He estimates the revenue from digital wallets at somewhere in the region of $250–$750 per user per year. If you add identity-related lines of business to these payment-related lines of business, there is the potential for incremental revenue of something like $1,000 per user per annum, as set out in table 7.

Where next?

This book has set out a consistent and, we think, helpful model of the Metaverse – one in which commerce is the exchange of fungible and nonfungible tokens in transactions that are enabled by the reputations of counterparties. In other words, payments in the Metaverse must take the form of fungible tokens that, under the circumstances in question, exhibit the characteristics

Table 7. Digital wallet lines of business.

Category	Examples	Estimates
Payments	Apple Pay charges issuers 15 basis points on credit; 0.5c per debit transaction	$5–$9
Authorization	Proof of attributes (e.g. age) for access to services	$50–$150
Tender-steering	Front-end steering to maximize interchange versus merchant-favoured private labels, co-brands or prepaid cards	$4–$53
Least-cost routing	ChaseNet prioritizes 'on-us' when Chase is both the issuer and the acquirer; merchants route to STAR, NYCE, Pulse versus schemes	$150–$250
Promotional offer attribution	Amazon, Honey, Kard, Inmar, etc., activate offers with redemption audit trail to maximize advertising rates	$150–$250
Account opening	Digital account opening using identities stored in wallets; perhaps ten per annum	$50–$150
Account opening bounties	Onboarding bounties and revenue sharing, e.g. Apple Card with Goldman Sachs, Apple Cash with Green Dot Corporation, Apple Savings, Apple Pay Later, and so on	$10–$100
Social commerce	'Team Purchases' and Venmo social payments incremental take rates of 2%–3.2%	$6–$47

of money. The obvious candidate is what people refer to as stablecoins.*

In the not-too-distant future, CBDCs or private sector tokens with reserves in either central bank money or perhaps other assets such as gold (or oil, or electricity, or who knows what else) will step in to fulfil this role for most jurisdictions. We feel that the time is right for organizations all across the payments value chain to begin working on their scenario planning and strategies for this inevitable future.

* In this context, it is interesting to note that both Visa and MasterCard have been working with the circle US dollar stablecoin (USDC) in the absence of some kind of 'fedcoin'.

Case study: International Air Transport Association

As frequent travellers who spend a lot of time thinking about digital identity, we are particularly interested in the complex value chain around airports. Now that the International Air Transport Association (IATA) has successfully executed the first fully integrated digital identity and verifiable credential journey from London Heathrow (LHR) to Rome Fiumicino (FCO) with British Airways, it looks as if the industry's dreams of seamless travel are a step closer to reality.

The LHR–FCO passenger shared their loyalty data (stored as a VC in their smartphone's digital wallet) with a travel agent, and this enabled airlines using the appropriate interfaces to make offers through the travel agent channel. Once the customer had chosen the offer and purchased, no more 'passenger name records', e-tickets or miscellaneous documents were needed because the travel document was generated as a VC that could be stored in a digital wallet.

One big advantage of this journey becoming digital is that there are necessary checks and other procedures that can now be carried out away from the airport. Along with the digital wallet with the digital travel authorization (DTA), a digital passport will be a key enabler. By sharing the nationality data of the digital passport, passengers can obtain their travel document requirements and satisfy them.

The IATA traveller shared their digital passport and order data with British Airways and received the 'Ready to Fly' confirmation as a DTA. This gave them the ability to go hands-free (i.e. with the phone and the passport remaining in pocket or purse) through biometric gates, into lounges and onto the aircraft. This may all sound Orwellian to some, but the majority of passengers want to use biometric data instead of physical passports and boarding passes. Of the more than a third of passengers who have already tried it, the overwhelming majority liked it (IATA 2022).

The use of biometrics to allow for hands-free travel is steadily spreading. With the help of air transport communications and IT company SITA, Frankfurt Airport will soon become the first in Europe to allow all airlines to use face biometrics as identification from check-in to boarding the aircraft. Passengers will be able to register through their mobile device using their Star Alliance app or directly at the check-in kiosk with their biometric-enabled passport. They can then pass smoothly through the airport using the facial recognition-equipped checkpoints.

We might also note that such an all-digital approach is more secure than a manual one, since border officers using automatic facial recognition software are significantly more accurate than the average person at detecting fraudsters (Smith, D. 2015).

The evolution of paperless travel opens up the possibility of seamless journeys through both the universe and the Metaverse with the use of interoperable standards. IATA has also been working on digital identity standards based on W3C VCs and decentralized digital identity designed to be interoperable between different stakeholders, such as airlines, travel agents, airports and governments. It has already released preliminary specifications for the W3C VC schema for passports, visas and the International Civil Aviation Organization DTA for industry testing.

Far from ending travel, the potential to use metaverses to showcase destinations and sell products must be enormous. It is easy to imagine travel companies partnering with hotels, tourist boards and experience providers to offer virtual tours of accommodation, destinations, attractions and more. Marketing aside, the transition to all-digital travel will inevitably open up new opportunities for interaction. We rather agree with McKinsey when it says that, as innovative formats become more mainstream, 'new economic models are emerging'. We also think it is plausible when McKinsey suggests that the travel industry stands to gain some $20 billion per annum by 2030 (Constantin *et al.* 2023). The travel experience of the future will almost certainly be some hybrid model – spanning both online and offline – with virtual events, edutainment and inspiration combined with physical destinations.

We can well imagine our travel avatars meeting up in the Metaverse and wandering around a virtual version of a hotel in the Bahamas before booking the hotel and our flights with a couple of clicks, then turning up at the airport and wandering around the physical space, then onto the plane, with similar hands-free, document-free, hassle-free ease.

Coda

While the Metaverse may have dipped out of public consciousness after some initial hype, the arrival of Apple's Vision Pro, Meta's Quest 3 and other devices has reignited interest in what many feel is the next interface between analogue and digital: the successor to the web browser and the smartphone screen. Some of the early reviews of the Vision Pro are breathless, to say the least. Whether that particular device succeeds or fails, it is clear that the world of spatial computing is upon us, and it will be the scaffolding for a wide variety of metaverses for work and play.

The Bank for International Settlements (BIS), which is owned by the world's central banks, talks about a Metaverse economy, built in VR and AR immersive environments, where avatars can engage in a broad range of activities (Canti *et al.* 2024). It notes

that as users spend more time (and attention) in metaverses there may be business opportunities from new services, and, more specifically, they point to the relationship between digital scarcity and value as the basis for those new business opportunities. And where there are new business opportunities, there are new financial services opportunities. When that report goes on to say that 'an important foundation for such services is the ability to make instant payments, ideally across borders and currencies, and to create digital representations of assets (tokenization)', we could not agree more.[*]

There is no question, therefore, that financial services strategists have to take it seriously. With demand from the entertainment, education and defence industries – and with a forecast compound annual growth rate of more than 40% through 2030 – the finance sector will look on as the opportunities for transactions proliferate and then be forced to respond because all of those transactions will require rails on which to move value around, in order to effect payments, whether that value is fiat currency, game tokens or things that have not been invented yet (Bucquet 2023).

Our sense is that some of the scepticism surrounding the Metaverse is a response to the hype and land grab made by platform providers. Bringing us full circle to where we started, this attempt to grab control stimulated quite the opposite response in Neal Stephenson. His venture Lamina1 aims 'to build the infrastructure of an open and decentralized metaverse that puts technology in the service of humans, not the other way around'. As he says, this is 'because the metaverse must not be controlled by mega platforms or corporations – it will be owned by its citizens – builders, creators, and consumers who deserve ownership, autonomy, and privacy online'.

---

[*] The report's exploration of the potential impact of what it labels the underlying technologies of spatial computing and digital property also ranges across the diminishing role of national boundaries, the blurring of tradable and non-tradable, and the ability to enforce taxation and other pretty serious issues.

Any discussion of transactions within the Metaverse leads (as the BIS report mentioned above does) to web3 – the foundation of next-generation value storage and transfer – and then immediately moves on to the issue of identity. We have shown in this book just how spatial computing, web3 and digital identity can be interconnected to deliver practical solutions that power safer transactions.

At first glance, it would seem that banks are ideally positioned to be the trusted gateways between mundane transactions and Metaverse ones. One obvious use case is converting stablecoins to sterling (other fiat currencies are available) so that customers can shift their spending between the universe and the Metaverse, online or in physical stores, but this is only the beginning. Banks also stand to support their customers to acquire and manage digital objects by providing custody services and vaults. More crucially, we feel, they stand to benefit from the transition to a reputation economy because they will be providing the key credentials that are essential for that economy to function. Banks can be at the heart of next-generation financial services.

But will they?

Glossary

3DID	Three Domain Identity
AI	artificial intelligence
AML	anti-money laundering
API	application programming interface
AR	augmented reality
CDBC	central bank digital currency
DAO	decentralized autonomous organization
DARPA	Defense Advanced Research Projects Agency
DeFi	decentralized finance
DID	decentralized identifiers
DMV	Department of Motor Vehicles
DPI	digital public infrastructure
DTA	digital travel authorization
FinCEN	Financial Crimes Enforcement Network
FINMA	Swiss Financial Market Supervisory Authority
GAMMA	Google, Amazon, Meta, Microsoft, Apple
GDPR	General Data Protection Regulation
GHG	greenhouse gas
HAL	Hardware Abstraction Layer
HSM	hardware security module
HUD	head-up display
IATA	International Air Transport Association
ICO	initial coin offering

IMF	International Monetary Fund
IoT	internet of things
KYC	Know Your Customer
KYE	Know Your Employee
LLM	large language model
MR	mixed reality
MRV	measurement, reporting and verification
NFT	non-fungible token
OIDC	OpenID Connect
PEP	policy enforcement point
PII	personally identifiable information
SEC	Securities and Exchange Commission
SSI	self-sovereign identity
TDIF	Trusted Digital Identity Framework
ToIP	Trust Over IP Foundation
VC	verifiable credential
VNC	Virtual Nightclub
VR	virtual reality
XMTP	Extensible Message Transport Protocol
XR	extended reality
ZKP	zero-knowledge proof AML

Bibliography

Adams, J. (2023). CBA may use genAI 'customers' for tests. *American Banker*, 30 October (https://tinyurl.com/yul2dbc8).

Adarlo, S. (2023). Experts say AI girlfriend apps are training men to be even worse. *Futurism*, 25 July (https://futurism.com/experts-ai-girlfriend-apps-men).

Adler-Bell, S. (2021). All work and no play. *Dissent*, Summer 2021 (http://tinyurl.com/29c8asdx).

Afshar, V. (2023). Here come the 'custobots': AI pervades Gartner's top 10 strategic technology trends. *ZDNet*, 30 October (https://tinyurl.com/ysl4yz6j).

Anderson, J., and Raine, L. (2022). The metaverse in 2040. Web article, 30 June, Pew Research Center (https://pewrsr.ch/3SNPTiq).

Apple (2021). Data privacy day at Apple: improving transparency and empowering users. Press Release, 27 January (https://apple.co/3SLCCH4).

Babel, M., and Sedlmeir, J. (2023). Bringing data minimization to digital wallets at scale with general-purpose zero-knowledge proofs. Preprint, arXiv (https://doi.org/https://doi.org/10.48550/arXiv.2301.00823).

Balla, R. (2023). How the metaverse will transform healthcare for good. *Health Tech World*, 11 November (https://tinyurl.com/yl27uxzj).

Balleisen, E. (2018). *Fraud: An American History from Barnum to Madoff*. Princeton University Press.

Banerjee, A., Bode, I. D., Sevillano, J., de Vergnes, M., and Higginson, M. (2023). Tokenization: a digital-asset déjà vu. McKinsey article, 15 August (https://mck.co/3r6VeHD).

BBC News (2022). Llanelli woman jailed for taking 150 driving tests for others. *BBC News*, 7 July (https://tinyurl.com/2fd95dw7).

Beau, D. (2023). Opportunities and challenges of the tokenisation of finance. Report, 18 January, Bank for International Settlements (www.bis.org/review/r230118c.htm).

Beaumont, M. (2021). WTF is an NFT? Kings Of Leon's weird non-fungible token thing – explained! *NME*, 13 October (https://tinyurl.com/2x4dskn2).

Bernat, S. (2022). Token gating: the metaverse solution for community building. *Brandingmag*, 18 November (https://tinyurl.com/yrd3v3pr).

Birch. D. (ed.) (2007). *Digital Identity Management: Technological, Business and Social Implications*. Gower.

Birch, D. (2014). *Identity Is the New Money*. London Publishing Partnership.

Birch, D. (2017). *Before Babylon, Beyond Bitcoin*. London Publishing Partnership.

Birch, D. (2019). The future of banking is basically robots running everything. *Wired*, 22 November (www.wired.co.uk/article/future-of-banking-robots).

Birch, D. (2020a). *The Currency Cold War*. London Publishing Partnership.

Birch, D. (2020b). Trust me! I'm a doctor on LinkedIn. *Forbes*, 15 October (https://tinyurl.com/ytgp8zj8).

Birch, D. (2021). Art for money's sake. *Forbes*, 13 October (https://tinyurl.com/yq4gctjh).

Birch, D. (2022). Locking the stablecoin door after the horse has spent all of the crypto on carrots and then vanished over the fence. *Forbes*, 30 May (http://tinyurl.com/2y98wyvu).

Birch, D. (2023). The wallet wars are not about money, they are about identity. *Forbes*, 1 February (http://tinyurl.com/yqv9xnea).

Birch, D., and McEvoy, N. (2007). A model for digital identity. In *Digital Identity Management: Technological, Business and Social Implications*, pp. 95–104. Gower.

Birch, D., and Richardson, V. (2023). Metamoney: payments in the metaverse. *Payments Strategy and Systems* **17**(2), 130–141.

Birch, D., Brown, R., and Parulava, S. (2016). Towards ambient accountability in financial services: shared ledgers, translucent transactions and the legacy of the great financial crisis. *Payment Strategy and Systems* **10**(2), 118–131.

Blicq, J. (2022). *Metaverse & Financial Services*. Innovations Accelerated.

BloombergNEF (2023). Long-term carbon offsets outlook 2023. Bloomberg Research, 18 July (https://tinyurl.com/yqekkwyg).

Bonner, M. (2022). Why we need to regulate digital identity in the metaverse. Report, 12 October, World Economic Forum (https://tinyurl.com/yknb89wk).

Bouchetob, J. (2021). Europe needs new money – an ecosystem of CBDC, tokenised commercial bank money and trigger solutions. Report, Die Deutsche Kreditwirtschaft (https://bit.ly/3zeOvKy).

Bouma, T. (2019). IMSC Pan-Canadian Trust Framework executive summary. *Medium*, 26 August (https://bit.ly/3qEFJql).

Brace, M. (1994). Cafe with a mission to explain. *The Independent*, 1 October (https://tinyurl.com/ys75ckyz).

Brereton, D. (2023). Bing AI can't be trusted. *DKB Blog*, 25 September (https://dkb.blog/p/bing-ai-cant-be-trusted).

Brewster, T. (2023). Crypto 'mixer' laundered $700 million for customers, including Russian and North Korean spies, DOJ says. *Forbes*, 9 September (https://bit.ly/3EtpIqt).

Bridle, J. (2018a). *The New Dark Age – Technology and the End of the Future*. Verso.

Bridle, J. (2018b). Data isn't the new oil – it's the new nuclear power. *Ideas.Ted.Com*, 27 August (https://bit.ly/3Z7QL4d).

Browning, K. 2023. Apple largely prevails in appeal of Epic Games' app store suit. *New York Times*, 24 April (https://nyti.ms/3SPzXMg).

Buchanan, B. (2022). Towards web3: Ed25519, Ed448 and Ed2551-Dilithium. *Medium*, 13 January (https://bit.ly/3SYZV01).

Bucquet, P. (2023). Payment rails in the metaverse: new opportunities for financial institutions. *Payments Journal*, 31 October (https://tinyurl.com/yn9yp9m8).

Business Wire (2022). Forever 21 launches the world's first metaverse-tested fashion collection, IRL. *Business Wire*, 1 December (https://bwnews.pr/3OAyU1x).

Buterin, V. (2021). Alternatives to selling at below-market-clearing prices for achieving fairness (or community sentiment, or fun). Vitalik blog post, 13 October (https://tinyurl.com/yvnjqjjz).

Cameron, K. (2005). The laws of identity. Blog post, May, Kim Cameron's Identity Weblog (http://tinyurl.com/ykwy2f83).

Canti, C., Franco, C. and Forst, J. (2024). The economic implications of services in the metaverse. Bank for International Settlements Paper 144, 7 February (https://bit.ly/4bPgx34).

Castronova, E. (2005). *Synthetic Worlds: The Business and Culture of Online Games*. University of Chicago Press.

Castronova, E. (2014). *Wildcat Money*. Yale University Press.

Chik, J. (2023). LinkedIn and Microsoft Entra introduce a new way to verify your workplace. *Microsoft Identity & Access Management*, 11 November (https://tinyurl.com/2jg68d8c).

Clark, D. D. 2017. *Designs for an Internet*. Ebook available at https://groups.csail.mit.edu/ana/People/DDC/ebook-arch.pdf.

Constantin, M., Genovese, G., Munawar, K., and Stone, R. (2023). Tourism in the metaverse: can travel go virtual? Report, 31 October, McKinsey (https://tinyurl.com/25kd4let).

Coppola, F. (2022). There's no such thing as a safe stablecoin. *Coppola Comments*, 13 October (https://tinyurl.com/yssu3ppg).

Court Record (2022). Plaintiffs – v – META PLATFORMS, INC., formerly known as FACEBOOK, INC.; SNAP, INC.; ROBLOX CORPORATION; DISCORD INC. Complaint for Personal Inuries (https://bit.ly/42goTfA).

Coyle, M. (2023). What you need to know about token-gated commerce. Report, 18 November, Shopify (https://tinyurl.com/ytse7zwy).

Crone, R. (2023). How can digital wallets generate up to $267–$736 in annual revenue per active user? LinkedIn post, 12 October.

Cross, M. (2023). Why Bank of America, TD Bank use virtual reality for onboarding. American Banker, 8 October (https://bit.ly/46Kp18l).

Davies, S. (2014). Banks want to keep your digital ID in their vaults. Financial Times, 2 October (https://tinyurl.com/ymzppc6f).

de Castillo, M. (2016). Identity and personal security. Coindesk, 15 October (https://tinyurl.com/yrkdyxl9).

Dell'AcquaF., McFowland, E., Mollick, E. R., Lifshitz-Assaf, H., Kellogg, K., Rajendran, S., Krayer, L., Candelon, F., and Lakhani, K. R. (2023). Navigating the jagged technological frontier: field experimental evidence of the effects of AI on knowledge worker productivity and quality. Preprint, SSRN (https://ssrn.com/abstract=4573321).

dotSWOOSH (2024). An update on the future of .SWOOSH. Medium, 12 January (https://bit.ly/3T0AE5A).

DuPont, Q., and Maurer, B. (2015). Ledgers and law in the blockchain. King's Review. 23 June (http://tinyurl.com/yt2lscf6).

Economist (2022). Virtual mavericks. The Economist, **437**(2), 21 November.

Eyers, J. (2020). Jack Dorsey's Square says Aussie banks were anti-competitive. Australian Financial Review, 14 November (https://bit.ly/3ugkNaB).

Eyers, J. (2022). NAB says banks can eliminate identity honeypots for hackers. Australian Financial Review, 15 October (https://tinyurl.com/ymswguk7).

Fabiani, A. (2022). Forget guns and drugs, identity theft is the latest go-to crime for Miami street gangs. Screenshot, 15 October (https://tinyurl.com/ym6jmrbg).

Farivar, C. (2023). Hundreds of Roblox users may be 'engaged in money laundering,' court filing claims. Forbes, 30 March (https://bit.ly/494c3n8).

Feyen, E., Frost, J., Gamacorta, L., Natarajan, H., and Saal, M. (2021). Fintech and the digital transformation of financial services: implications for market structure and policy (117). Working Paper, Bank for International Settlements (https:// bit.ly/45IpirG).

Financial Stability Board (2022). Regulation, supervision and oversight of crypto-asset activities and markets. Report, 11 October, Financial Stability Board (https://tinyurl.com/ ywk7mytc).

Fishenden, J. (2022). 'Tap to pay' becomes 'Tap to prove'. *New Tech Observations from the UK*, 15 October (https://tinyurl. com/yoqlex24).

Follows, T. (2023). Apple Vision Pro signals another move into digital identity for Apple. *Forbes*, 15 October (https://tinyurl. com/yooh29ey).

Friedman, D. (2023). The great Zelle pool scam. *Insider*, 8 October (https://tinyurl.com/yrdqt6bb).

Funk, J., Vinsel, L., and McConnell, P. (2022). Web3, the metaverse, and the lack of useful innovation. *American Affairs* 6(4), 23–35.

Gans, J., and Nagaraj, A. (2023). What is Apple's Vision Pro really for? *Harvard Business Review*, 1 October (https://tinyurl.com/ 22ua373j).

Geisenberger, W. (2023). ALLCOT onboards 500 million metric tonnes of carbon credits with the Hedera Guardian. Report, 13 November, HBar Foundation (https://tinyurl.com/ywpkvju4).

George, N., Dryja, T., and Narula, N. (2023). A framework for programmability in digital currency. Report, 1 August, Digital Currency Initiative (https://tinyurl.com/ysfgt4r4).

Gilbert, B. (2022). Facebook blames Apple after a historically bad quarter, saying iPhone privacy changes will cost it $10 billion. *Business Insider*, 3 February (https://bit.ly/49HqFZB).

Giraudo, A. (2007). *Money Tales*. Brookings Institution Press.

Glöckler, J., Sedlmeir, J., Frank, M., and Fridgen, G. (2023). A systematic review of identity and access management requirements in enterprises and potential contributions of self-sovereign identity. *Business & Information Systems Engineering* (https://doi.org/10.1007/s12599-023-00830-x).

Grand View Research (2023). Open source services market size & trends. Grand View Research, 18 November (https://tinyurl.com/yr7cfam4).

Greenaway, B., and Oram, S. (2022). *22 Ideas About the Future*. Cybersalon.

Grigg, I. (2017). *An Exploration of Identity*. New York: R3.

Gusev, D. (2022). Fintech in early Renaissance Florence. *Medium*, 18 November (https://bit.ly/3SPazbh).

Hackl, C. (2023). What leaders need to know about spatial computing. *Harvard Business Review*, 10 November (https://bit.ly/3HYblMq).

Harari, Y. (2015). *Sapiens: A Brief History of Humankind*. Vintage.

Hatami, H., Hazan, E., and Rants, K. (2023). A CEO's guide to the metaverse. *McKinsey Quarterly*, 24 January (http://tinyurl.com/2lz3brv7).

Hernandez, R., Kakumani, S., Gupta, A., and Jackson, J. (2023). The metaverse presents opportunities for insurers. Report, 25 September, PwC (https://tinyurl.com/2pg52n8j).

Hoffard, J., and Settle, M. (2023). What consumers can teach us about the future of employee identity management. Blog post, Medium, 6 September (https://bit.ly/3w1yk6K).

Holt, J. (1999). What is art? What is money? Amusing answers below. *The Observer*, 13 October (https://bit.ly/3uUVbk3).

Hoppe, D. (2021). Skin trade: preventing and punishing digital asset theft. *Gamma Law*, 10 May (https://gammalaw.com/skin-trade-preventing-and-punishing-digital-asset-theft/).

Hori, S. (2021). Self-sovereign identity: the future of personal data ownership. Report, 27 August, World Economic Forum (https://bit.ly/3YQoKh6).

Hsu, T., and Thompson, S. (2023). Disinformation researchers raise alarms about AI chatbots. *New York Times*, 25th September (https://nyti.ms/3EORIVw).

IATA (2022). Convenience is top priority for passengers post pandemic. *IATA Pressroom*, 1 November (https://tinyurl.com/ywlcyulc).

Kaczynski, S., and Kominers, S. (2021). How NFTs create value. *Harvard Business Review*, 13 October (https://tinyurl.com/yhrgqcbd).

Kamin, D. (2021). Investors snap up metaverse real estate in a virtual land boom. *New York Times*, 25 September (https://tinyurl.com/y3a2jfy8).

Kay, J. (2021). Robust and resilient finance. Blog post, 2 July, JohnKay.com (http://tinyurl.com/yt9ksbhv).

Kaziukėnas, J. (2023). Amazon takes a 50% cut of sellers' revenue. *Marketplace Pulse*, 13 February (http://tinyurl.com/2lh9cj6e).

Keane, P. (2023). Nike reveals 3D printed shoes designed with AI. *3D Printing*, 18 November (https://tinyurl.com/yrqq468x).

Keeble, J. (2023). Executives fear greenwashing and the economy will stall sustainability progress. *Transform with Google Cloud*, 13 November (https://tinyurl.com/ynte2zzp).

Kelley, L. (2021). Actually, QR codes never went away. *New York Times*, 15 October (https://tinyurl.com/y4tmsql2).

King, L. (2021). Cash is disappearing and the unbanked are stranded. *Boston Herald*, 24 January (https://bit.ly/3XEZcCj).

Kozhipatt, J. (2022). A former Federal Reserve regulator turned Duke fintech professor who's calling for crypto to be banned explains why 'blockchain's not really better at anything'. *Insider*, 26 August (https://bit.ly/3KpBJiX).

LaCapra, L. (2023). Hands up, this is a (virtual) robbery! *The Information*, 15 October (https://tinyurl.com/yv3cq8qh).

Lanier, J. (2013). *Who Owns The Future?* Allen Lane.

Leibrandt, G., and Teran, N. (2022). *The Pay Off: How Changing the Way We Pay Changes Everything*. Elliott & Thompson.

Lessin, S. (2020). The escalating war between our physical and digital realities. *The Information*, 1 October (https://tinyurl.com/ysdom408).

Levine, A. (2021). 'Be your own bank' and the 'luxury of apathy'. CoinDesk, 7 June (https://www.coindesk.com/markets/2020/06/07/be-your-own-bank-and-the-luxury-of-apathy/).

Lewis, L. (2022). Football's future is in the metaverse. *Financial Times*, 6 January (www.ft.com/content/ee267372-15e6-459c-b7 86-da605f8d0258).

Lewis, M. (2023). *Going Infinite – The Rise and Fall of a New Tycoon.* Allen Lane.

Livni, E. (2022). Tales from crypto: a billionaire meme feud threatens industry unity. *New York Times*, 25 September (https:// tinyurl.com/yazf4man).

Lucas, P. (2023). Into the metaverse. *Digital Transactions*, 1 October (https://tinyurl.com/yvt6xlu6).

Malone, K. (2018). Finding your lost bitcoins. *NPR*, 15 October (https://tinyurl.com/y7q8fx5e).

Man, E. (2021). Vertical fintech is reimagining community banking with the help of next-gen infrastructure. Report, Redpoint Ventures (https://tinyurl.com/yl656z6t).

Marous, J. (2021). Banking share of wallet threatened by hidden attrition. *The Financial Brand*, 2 October (https://tinyurl.com/ yrx9c9gz).

Marr, B. (2020). Data is the new oil: how Shell has become a data-driven and AI-enabled business. *Forbes*, 27 August (https://bit. ly/3qWyn1f).

McWaters, J. (2016). A blueprint for digital identity – the role of financial institutions in building digital identity. Report, August, World Economic Forum (https://tinyurl.com/y57387ma).

MIT Technology Review (2022). The industrial metaverse: a game-changer for operational technology. *MIT Technology Review Insights*, 12 October (https://tinyurl.com/2gvdtrl9).

Mollick, E. (2022). ChatGPT is a tipping point for AI. *Harvard Business Review*, 25 September (https://tinyurl.com/2lzk3l4v).

Moore, M. (2021). NFT mania is a sign of a land grab for the online 'metaverse'. *Financial Times*, 1 October (https://tinyurl.com/ yjywsgf3).

Narula, H. (2022). *Virtual Society: The Metaverse and the New Frontiers of Human Experience.* Penguin Random House.

Noyes, T. (2023). Wallets, APIs and trust. Noyes Payments Blog, 12 October (https://tinyurl.com/2xgxa2ak).

O'Dwyer, R. (2023). *Tokens: The Future of Money in the Age of the Platform*. Verso.

O'Flaherty, K. (2022). Apple's $12 billion strike to Facebook is suddenly taking shape. *Forbes*, 18 November (https://tinyurl.com/ymbjyt87).

Olley, S. (2022). AA Traveller apologises after massive data breach. Radio New Zealand, 15 November (https://tinyurl.com/yv6a9f3n).

Orrick, Herrington & Sutcliffe LLP (2023). FinCEN discusses digital identity threats. *JDSUPRA*, 15 October (https://tinyurl.com/yl7fkxp3).

Parkin, S. (2022). The trouble with roblox the video game empire built on child labour. *The Guardian*, 9 January (www.theguardian.com/games/2022/jan/09/the-trouble-with-roblox-the-video-game-empire-built-on-child-labour).

Patel, N. (2021). From a meme to $47 million: ConstitutionDAO, crypto, and the future of crowdfunding. *The Verge*, 7 December (http://tinyurl.com/y5cr297s).

Pegoraro, R. (2023). Are AI bot brokers ready to manage your investments? *Worth*, 30 October (https://tinyurl.com/yshdocs7).

Pianese, B. (2023). Digital wallets dominate payments but account-to-account grows. *The Banker*, 12 October (https://tinyurl.com/ywc2yob9).

Pimentel, B. (2022). The crypto crash's violence shocked Circle's CEO. *Protocol*, 13 October (https://tinyurl.com/yubhfzww).

Pipes, R. (2000). *Property and Freedom*. Vintage.

Polygon (2023). Why HSBC is building a decentralized identity solution with Polygon ID. Polygon, 2 November (https://tinyurl.com/ywo2adnp).

Prasad, E. (2022). Money is about to enter a new era of competition. *MIT Technology Review*, 13 October (https://tinyurl.com/y3enacnp).

Principato, C. (2021). How the roughly one-quarter of under-banked US adults differ from fully banked individuals. *Morning Consult*, 24 January (https://bit.ly/3Wz5SAD).

Rivera, P. (2021). Designing internet-native economies: a guide to crypto tokens. *a16z Crypto*, 13 October (https://tinyurl.com/yw6hma9r).

Round, S. (2023). How can digital wallets support customers from all walks of life? Report, 11 October, Electronic Payments International (https://tinyurl.com/2x7llnms).

Rubin, N. (2023). Bringing the balance sheet of the planet to the public ledger. Report, 13 November, Hedera (https://tinyurl.com/2x9wztbt).

Rzepecki, R., Cojocaru, A., and Crittenden, M. (2023). Building a sustainable, livable, and affordable city for 1 million people through multilayer blockchain cooperatives and extended reality experimentation. White Paper, Spectra (https://bit.ly/48GjTDO).

Santos, A. (2023). The role of the industrial metaverse in sustainable manufacturing. Antonio Blog, 12 October (https://tinyurl.com/yp4dzj84).

Scerri, S., Tuikka, T., de Vallejo, I. L., and Curry, E. (2022). Common European data spaces: challenges and opportunities. In *Data Spaces: Design, Deployment and Future Directions*, pp. 337–357. Springer (https://doi.org/10.1007/978-3-030-98636-0_16).

Schär, F. (2021). Decentralized finance: on blockchain- and smart contract-based financial markets. *Federal Reserve Bank of St. Louis Review* (https://bit.ly/3tACj4t).

Schnell, M. (2021). JPMorgan Chase CEO Dimon: 'I personally think that bitcoin is worthless'. *The Hill*, 15 October (https://tinyurl.com/yuul93zc).

Schroeder, P. (2023). US court orders Mirror Trading International to pay $1.7 billion in restitution for crypto fraud. *Reuters*, 7 September (http://tinyurl.com/2ay22kk3).

Schwear, C. (2023). 3D printing meets the billion-dollar footwear industry. *Forbes*, 11 November (https://tinyurl.com/yrdw8mxr).

Searls, D. (2013). Sovereign identity in the great silo forest. Blog, 27 August, Doc Searls Weblog (https://bit.ly/47Ri8Du).

SEC (2021). SEC charges global crypto lending platform and top executives in $2 billion fraud. Press Release, 1 September, US Securities and Exchange Commission (http://tinyurl.com/26erhcjh).

Servon, L. (2017). *The Unbanking of America.* Houghton Mifflin Harcourt.

Singh-Kurtz, S. 2023. The man of your dreams. *The Cut,* 10 March (https://www.thecut.com/article/ai-artificial-intelligence-chat-bot-replika-boyfriend.html).

Sky News (2022). British Airways pilot jailed for lying about his flying experience on CV to get job. *Sky News,* 31 March (https://tinyurl.com/yaz3axdo).

Smith, A. N. (2022). Forever 21 bets you want to dress like your Roblox avatar. *Bloomberg News,* 1 December (https://bloom.bg/3uo211m).

Smith, D. (2015). Passport officers using face recognition technology better at detecting fraud. *UNSW Newsroom,* 31 October (https://tinyurl.com/2xdyrpuw).

Smith, J. (2023a). AI is clumsy, disrespectful and biased (again). Vitalik Buterin on biometric proof of personhood, and giving products a digital passport. *Customer Futures,* 12 October (https://tinyurl.com/yuzozuy2).

Smith, J. (2023b). Customer Futures perspective: the 5th channel. *Customer Futures,* 12 October.

Smith, P., Sier, J., and Bennett, T. (2022). Corporate Australia rushes to check its data hoards after Optus mess. *Australian Financial Review,* 11 October (https://bit.ly/3StFzvD).

Spiekerman, L. (2023). Managing identity risk is critical to European fintech's future. *Forbes,* 15 October (https://tinyurl.com/ykdzez35).

Stephenson, N. (1992). *Snow Crash.* Bantam.

Stern, C. (2023). Glosswire CEO discusses AI/AR tech innovation impact on consumer purchasing decisions. *CosmeticsDesign USA* 27 July (http://tinyurl.com/yuu2c73t).

Sveriges Riksbank (2019). The Riksbank proposes a review of the concept of legal tender. Press Release, 29 April (https://bit.ly/49FtkDb).

Sveriges Riksbank (2022a). Payments Report 2022. Report, 15 December (https://bit.ly/49H1qH8).

Sveriges Riksbank (2022b). Are payments in Sweden efficient? In Payments Report 2022, 15 December (https://bit.ly/3SANkB3).

Sveriges Riksbank (2022c). In Sweden, we prefer to pay digitally. In Payments Report 2022, 15 December (https://bit.ly/3SLsxcV).

Sveriges Riskbank (2023). Inquiry into the state's role in the payment market. Report, Sveriges Riskbank (https://bit.ly/3uKVDRJ).

Swift (2022). Digital assets: the next frontier of finance. *Swift Technology and Innovation*, 20 April (http://tinyurl.com/yrkby9gt).

Taylor, M. (2021). The race to replace cash with crypto is hotting up. *Wired*, 2 October (https://tinyurl.com/2jmrr236).

Tonkin, C. (2023). Westpac says AI boosted coding productivity. *Information Age*, 25 September (https://tinyurl.com/238vpjhj).

Tran, K. T. L. (2023). From screen to store: metaverse goes mainstream. *Fashion Dive*, 6 June (https://bit.ly/49qOyEV).

US Attorney's Office, District of Columbia (2023). North Korean foreign trade bank rep charged for role in two crypto laundering conspiracies. US Department of Justice, 24 April (https://tinyurl.com/25bzxa6x).

Vogels, E., and McClain, C. (2023). Key findings about online dating in the US. Report, 11 November, Pew Research Center (https://tinyurl.com/ytchq6v8).

Volpiocelli, G. (2023). Beijing is coming for the metaverse. *Politico*, 28 August (https://politi.co/44wQkkK).

Walker, A. (2023). Singapore's digital twin – from science fiction to hi-tech reality. *Infrastructure Global*, 29 October (https://tinyurl.com/yksz8wov).

Waters, R. (2023). Apple's mixed reality headset is a hedge against disruption. *Financial Times*, 15 October (https://tinyurl.com/2pcsr3sn).

Webster, A. (2022). Sci-fi virtual world EVE Online is getting Microsoft Excel support. *The Verge*, 1 October (https://tinyurl.com/y5eqybjz).

Weeks, R. (2023). How a fake job offer took down the world's most popular crypto game. *The Block*, 11 November (https://tinyurl.com/26eumcbv).

Weitz & Luxenberg Attorneys (2023). W&L files child gambling class action lawsuit against Roblox. Firm New, retrieved 29 October (www.weitzlux.com/firm-news/wl-files-child-gambling-class-action-lawsuit-against-roblox/).

Weyl, E., Ohlaver, P., and Buterin, V. (2022). Decentralized society: finding web3's soul. Preprint, SSRN (https://ssrn.com/abstract=4105763).

Williamson, D. A. (2022). Digital Trust Benchmark 2022 (annual benchmark survey). *Insider Intelligence* (www.insiderintelligence.com/content/digital-trust-benchmark-2022#page-report).

Windley, P. (2023). Defining digital identity. In *Learning Digital Identity: Design, Deploy and Manage Identity Architectures*, pp. 7–18. O'Reilly.

Wintermeyer, L. (2021). Burned Banksy NFT sets art and crypto worlds alight. *Forbes*, 13 October (https://tinyurl.com/yvuouwlj).

Woodbury, R. (2021). What happens when you're the investment. *The Atlantic*, 13 October (https://tinyurl.com/yy7xv4l6).

Wright, S. (2023). Scotch whisky casks performing better than gold, report finds. *The Herald*, 14 November (https://bit.ly/3SFviOw).

Yadlos, L. (2023). Tokenizing real-world assets: Tokeny/Dfns enable ApplePay-like experience for investors. *Blockster*, 15 November (https://tinyurl.com/ym8wnh8j).

Yliuntinen, J., and Faragher, K. (2023). The rise of digital identity wallets: will banks be left behind? Report, Mobey Forum, Helsinki.

Young, K., and Yang, L. (2023). Wallet wars or collaborative wallet ecosystems? *Medium*, 12 October (https://tinyurl.com/yljucbzc).

Zelazny, F. (2022). Privacy and security in the metaverse. LinkedIn post, 17 May (www.linkedin.com/pulse/privacy-security-meta verse-frances-zelazny/).

Index